DATE DUE

Race for Theory and the Biophobia Hypothesis

Race for Theory and the Biophobia Hypothesis

Humanics, Humanimals, and Macroanthropology

MELVIN D. WILLIAMS

Westport, Connecticut
London

Library of Congress Cataloging-in-Publication Data

Williams, Melvin D. 1933–
    Race for theory and the biophobia hypothesis : humanics,
humanimals, and macroanthropology / Melvin D. Williams.
      p.   cm.
    Includes bibliographical references and index.
    ISBN 0–275–96076–5 (alk. paper)
    1. Race.   2. Race awareness.   3. Human behavior.   4. Phobias.
5. Behavior evolution.   I. Title.
GN269.W56   1998
305.8—dc21   97–18063

British Library Cataloguing in Publication Data is available.

Library of Congress Catalog Card Number: 97–18063
ISBN: 0–275–96076–5

First published in 1998

Praeger Publishers, 88 Post Road West, Westport, CT 06881
An imprint of Greenwood Publishing Group, Inc.

Printed in the United States of America

The paper used in this book complies with the
Permanent Paper Standard issued by the National
Information Standards Organization (Z39.48–1984).

10 9 8 7 6 5 4 3 2 1

*To my grandchildren
Christopher, Calvin, Melvin, and Mikhail,
who can conquer their biophobias and be prepared
for life during the Ecological Revolution*

Contents

Preface

In approaching this task, it seems wise, if only to head off needless argument, to deny any intention of supplying a single master key to a lock that has defied the efforts of great talents from the time of the classical civilizations to the present. It seems obvious that sequences of events other than those sketched here could, in the proper circumstances, have had similar results. Indeed, I am eager to entertain other possibilities and hope hereby to stimulate others to offer countersuggestions. It will also be obvious to the reader that substantial trains of thought herein stated are merely borrowed and not created by me. (Fried 1968:251)

This volume continues the development of the themes introduced in my previous books: *Community in a Black Pentecostal Church*, Williams (1974), *The Human Dilemma* (1992), *The Black Middle Class* (1992), and *The Academic Village* (1993). We have arrived at a time in human history when the problems of human identity—classism, racism, ethnocentrism, sexism, sectarianism, ageism, nationalism, and speciesism (CRESSANS)—threaten the survival of the human species. For more than a million years, humans have adaptively interpreted birth, struggle, and death—or sex, death, and digestion—be denying, defying, and defiling these "lower" animal characteristics in themselves. Because of the resulting human divisiveness and destruction (of Earth), humans must now learn to celebrate their animal kinship and their magnificent bodies if they would live in peace with "races," classes, and genders and even with Earth itself. Humans can no longer deny and domesticate their own insecurities by means of denying, defying, and defiling their animal kinship (DDDAK). That state of denial undermines the lives, health, and planet of human beings.

In this book I continue the evolutionary analysis of the origin, development, and demise of human denial. I offer an evolutionary alternative (the Ecological Revolution) to human divisiveness and extinction. That alternative will eliminate all the artificial and contrived categories of human inferiority, denigration, and degradation. Humans will finally discover the pervasive influence of DDDAK in the creation of those categories: the poor, homeless wretched, unhappy, criminals, delinquents, convicts, illiterates, uneducated, addicted, and CRESSANS. My overarching theory suggests that human divisiveness has been an adaptive strategy but that in the twenty-first century humans must establish their security and survival by means of a new and different human nature. Humans are components of Earth, and they cannot continue to "conquer" it and its people and avoid human extinction.

This book is a new evolutionary approach to comprehending race, class, and gender. As the subtitle suggests, this approach sets the problems within a global context. The central argument is that race, class, and gender are the culmination of human biophobia (i.e., the fear of sex, death, and digestion). That adaptive phobia has resulted in a human inferiority complex that dominates human behavior. I describe some of that behavior and the hopelessness of treating the symptoms of this global malady. I also suggest some solutions—the end of biophobia, the creation of biocentrism—that will culminate in the Ecological Revolution.

In the process of presenting the argument, I take a different and critical look at the pain and suffering generated by race, class, and gender in America. Race remains a second-class concept in the quest for social theory. Like poverty, African Americans, and class, race has been overstudied in this century with few significant results. Americans and others seem obsessed with race; it helps to define their own identity. Like the "lower" animals, race has become a major symbol of human identity. As with pornography, victimography, and ethnography, raceography seems to satisfy a primal scholarly urge to study the "inferior." But the study and practice of pornography contributes little to understanding the marginality of women in the social world. Feminist theorists had to hake the helm of that theoretical ship to put wind into its sails. Today there is a whole new breed of neoconservatives who are establishing their careers and fortunes as "intellectual" hustlers and pimps of race, but there is little theory.

The epistemological, methodological, and substantive issues being negotiated by feminist theorists around gender make race pale into conceptual inferiority, notwithstanding its longer history among sociological theorists. Feminist theory is a result of political movements responding to changing situations and experiences of women (Alway 1995). Where is the corresponding race theory?

Race theory does not have to be race-centered or seek to end racial subordination. It can be formalized, public explanations (hypotheses) of the social world that produces and reproduces subordinate races. Race need not be the central analytical category of race theory; there can be a variety of such categories (e.g., biophobia). But the location, voice, and experience of race theory can revolutionize sociological theory. Much of feminist theory is being ignored (Alway 1995); race theory remains largely invisible. The Afrocentric marginality and exclusion, inside and outside the academy, has left it theoretically sterile. Race is ripe for a major contribution, not from its pimps and hustlers, but from its scholars and from sufferers who are committed to comprehending the humanics that keep them subordinated in the social world.

Race is a reflection of a social life that is hierarchical. Race is a phenomenon not only of individuals and their behaviors, but also of social structures and conceptual systems. If race can be understood, those structures and systems become accessible to our analytical tools. The species becomes comprehended in its origin, development, and future. This can lead to a general theory of social life, or a coherent theoretical framework. My complex theory attempts to begin this trek. It proceeds not by presenting race as a central problematic but by using it as one component of human divisiveness. It embodies social actors. Like feminist theory, it forces the biological—the body, the natural—into the social domain (Alway 1995). "It upsets a very basic opposition—that of nature and culture" (ibid.: 217), which fundamentally brings biological and cultural anthropology together.

African Americans are called roving packs, monkeys, coons, water buffalo, gorillas in the mist, and other "lower" animals. Black Americans are believed to be and treated by many as "uncivilized," hot-blooded, wilding, oversexed, large-penised (accompanied by a cruel history of mob castration), and promiscuous. Much of this is a part of the enterprise of producing and reproducing social inferiority. But neither the lower" animal referents nor the other characteristics are inherently inferior. What kind of "humanimal" behaves this way? A different look at race and human divisiveness will help provide some answers. Race theory neglects the emphasis on signs, symbols, symptoms, and circumstances. It deconstructs the quest of arbitrarily oppressed populations for power, position, and prestige under the guise of the demand for equality. Race theory focuses on what has become the human pathology—the inferiority complex.

Acknowledgments

There is no health in a society afflicted by Racism and Discrimination.
—Justice Thurgood Marshall, Foreword to *Racism and Mental Health,* 1973 (see Willie 1973)

As most readers know, authors are supported and facilitated by many people and agencies. Listing them usually entails omitting some. This volume is the result of a long career and much support; most of it has been acknowledged in my other books.

One important aspect of my experience is that of an African American working and living among predominantly white populations. That exposure and a lifelong interest in race have provided long and critical observations of race as "THE HUMAN DILEMMA." In this book I attempt to give the reader the benefit of those observations. I have some ambivalence about acknowledging that strange and lifelong journey.

I have never been inferior, but I have always been socialized so and treated as such. It is a great personal comfort to understand this human pathology called race that E. Franklin Frazier (1927) began to explain to us seventy years ago. But he, too, was an African American, and the power elite in scholarship rarely accepts such white-focused hypotheses from "inferior" Black scholars. So in 1997 we continue to "learn" and experience what African-American scholars had already taught us many years ago. I thank them again. My family remains intact and continues to support and enable me. I do have three more grandsons to acknowledge—Melvin, Calvin, and Mikhail.

Part I

Sex, Death, and Digestion

Chapter 1

Introduction

This book argues that the origin and development of human nature are rooted and fixated in hierarchical values and attitudes. It focuses on classism, racism, ethnocentrism, sectarianism, sexism, ageism, nationalism, and speciesism (CRESSANS), as well as the denial, defiance, and defilement of our animal kinship (DDDAK), as two dimensions for understanding those values and attitudes. I suggest that a holistic approach to examining the human *idée fixe* on hierarchy will open a new chapter in solving the old social problems of humans in the twenty-first century. Such a chapter requires a new vision for anthropology specifically and for the social sciences generally.

Today's irrational emotions and behaviors about race (see Frazier 1927) are but examples of the hierarchical essence of human nature that is fixed in the human past and in fear (biophobia) of the animal limitations of human existence. Those emotions and behaviors are learned, social, and inculcated; they can be transformed. Humans are able to have and to hold a new and different human nature that will transcend many of our old and persistent social problems.

This book is about an old human nature (inferiority complexes) that is inadequate and obsolete for a new human century. I look at race not just to describe again humans' inhumanity to humans, but to find a final answer (see Weinberg 1992a, esp. chap. 3) to that perennial human dilemma. I even suspect that the age-old habit of describing racism and its companions (CRESSANS) creates a sense of superiority among writers and readers alike and is thus itself a component of the hierarchical process and system. There is more written and read on race, class, and gender than can be explained without invoking a human obsession. The cultural critiques continue, "and we are not saved."

Tomorrow our terrorists may have weapon-grade plutonium. Humans may destroy their nest trying to prove their superiority. Scientists may create supergerms or human monsters. If we continue to tinker with peace and international coop-

eration without a transformation in those values, we will remain at risk to a tin-
derbox someplace in the world that will destroy us all.

This book argues that the old values of "progress, success, and superiority"
enabled some primates to become human and dominate Earth. But dominion has
lost its essence in the twenty-first century; we now need peace and international
cooperation. The book thus demonstrates the relationships between old values
and the need for power and between new values and the inherent flow of peace
and international cooperation. It compares, contrasts, and differentiates the old
values of the past and the new ones of the future. The new values are not alien to
us; they have been among our ideals for centuries. We need only to realize that
humans have few alternatives and very little time to transform the ways we live. A
popular article, "Human Nature, Culture and the Holocaust" (Browning 1996),
shows the relationships between violence, culture, and human nature, as I do in
my course "Culture, Racism, and Human Nature." In this book I focus on peace
and international cooperation in those relationships.

Narratives allow humans to provide structure to their worlds and discover meanings in their lives. All religions have sacred stories and narratives. These narratives establish important components of human identity. For almost a million years,
some of our major narratives have been about heroes and supremacy (Campbell
1968). These have served us well in dominating Earth and "inferior" populations.
We now need new narratives about peace and international cooperation, or we
will face the serious threat of extinction. This book grapples with these issues.

THE DECONSTRUCTION OF BIOPHOBIA AND
PEACE WITHIN OUR SPECIES

A crucial part of my thesis is that the human body must be reconceptualized
in order to respect and appreciate our own biology and that of the globe (Williams
1996a, 1996b, 1997). Our present view of our bodies is symptomatic of a
supremacy of obsession that is attempting to tolerate the human gross disrespect
for the human body. Today we may be able to stop the evolution of human insecurity that drives us to our own destruction. We may examine holoculture.

Supremacy narratives and performances are the evolution of human insecurity.
Humans create and perpetuate conflict and violence as well as seek power to
secure and enhance their fragile identities. I argue that a firm establishment of
human identity will create a global community based on embodied respect for all
living species. Evolutionary psychology and cognitive anthropology (Barkow
1989:179, Barkow et al. 1992, Buss 1995, Walters 1994, Wright 1995) are examining the nature of prestige in human affairs but are not placing the obsession for
supremacy at the center of the human behavioral paradigm.

Humans are miraculous animals and one component of a magnificent web-of-
life. If we learn to value and respect our bodies, our Earth, and the wonderful
nature of life itself, we can begin to establish a peaceful global community with
international cooperation. We can inculcate these values into our children and
revolutionize panhuman relationships. Much of sociocultural interests today con-

cern "inferior" people and power relationships. I am arguing for the expansion of those interests to the entire human species, human nature, and macroanthropology. Then we will understand and be able to explain the human obsession with supremacy. This is an exciting period in the social sciences. Discourses about globalization and transnationalism are being overtaken by the processes themselves. Our institutions—family, church, economy, and education—are being transformed even while we sleep (both literally and figuratively). We are being challenged to see, explain, and participate in these great transformations just as the changes of the eighteenth and nineteenth centuries created the social scholarship of its day. Peace and international cooperation are absolute necessities in the twenty-first century. This book explores why.

Global social divisiveness, pollution, overpopulation, deforestation, and human obsession with technology, information, and supremacy are all related to some peculiar adaptive human values. If we alter those values, we can alter the course of human monsters. This view enables us to understand the origins of the supremacy obsession that today sprays the globe with classism, racism, ethnocentrism, sexism, sectarianism, ageism, nationalism, and speciesism (CRESSANS).

Humans have never been secure with their bodies. Those bodies look and perform similar to the bodies of the "lower" animals. Thus humans stood erect, acquired language, made tools, and engaged in myriad body-modification activities: corporeal art, circumcision, clitoridectomy, cutting, piercing, tatooing, adorning, footbinding, body building, head shaping, hairstyling, body painting, implants, body disguising, and body hiding to enhance and extend the natural body. Humans are animals that perspire, and perspiration has its odor. We secrete from the eyes, ears, lungs, skin, bronchial tubes, sinuses, nose, sexual organs, and colon. We salivate, masticate, expectorate, regurgitate, urinate, defecate, masturbate, fornicate, gestate, exudate, suppurate, lacrimate, fight, kill, sleep, hemorrhage, die, and decay. Yet we reject our animal kinship and even subordinate other humans arbitrarily defined as inferior to prove our own superiority. Of course, I am not referring to the body only literally but also to the perspectives, values, attitudes, and behaviors that surround the human body. These have destroyed mountains of human bodies in war, sacrifice, genocide, disease, violence, and CRESSANS.

Why does so-called intelligent life treat our most valuable possession so ruthlessly? Humans have a peculiar relationship with their bodies, and that relationship, I argue, has significant clues for understanding human nature. I refer to that peculiar relationship by means of the biophobia hypothesis.

I argue that humans conceptualized and created humanness out of a peculiar identification of "lower" or other animals (see Shepard 1995). In that process we established a duality, social distance, and denial with our own bodies. That duality, social distance, and denial is, in part, feeding many of the social problems around the globe. If my argument has some validity, then, we can create a new basis for humanness in the future and transform the world's social problems. The privileged primates (humans) will deconstruct their delusions of superiority, understand the biophobia hypothesis, and transform the supremacy narratives and the supremacy performances.

SUPREMACY AND THE INFERIORITY OF PLACES

Human history is replete with identifiable levels of quality in arbitrary human hierarchies. This book demonstrates that this is the soil from which human violence grows. "Elite" people produce and reproduce social inferiority to sustain human hierarchies, and that production process will deny us local and global peace. This archetype pervades human perceptions of places as well as of people. I suggest that place and identity are components of historical, geopolitical, and psychogeographical perspectives (see Rifkin 1992).

Human behavior is influenced by people's efforts to assuage their feelings of social inferiority. The production and reproduction of social inferiority thus dominates human perceptions of locality, space, and identity. This book discusses one example of how violence is exploited to create social inferiority and dominate human behavior.

In the continuing quest for interdisciplinary efforts to understand human divisiveness, geography can be a salient example. Humans attach themselves to social and material objects for social meanings and for security. Geographical places are important human attachments (Altman and Low 1992). This book describes how identity by geographical location is not the source but the result of human divisiveness. Certain human characteristics result in social and psychological attachments that culminate in the utilization of hearth, home, university, city, country, and continent for human divisiveness.

Place and identity are especially problematic today with: (1) the greed-driven fragmentation of global economies; (2) the resurgence of nationalism; (3) the reemergence of "ethnic cleansing"; (4) the ghettoization of third world economies in the world market; (5) the growing antagonisms toward "foreign" workers in a shrinking world economy; (6) the polarization of cities and countries into racial, class, and ethnic enclaves; (7) and the emergence of transnational literatures, criticism, and theory. Place politics are increasingly a basis of interpretation in history, geography, and literature.

The ideal of universalism—often associated with modernism—has diminished with an increased emphasis on social and cultural diversity rather than on what unifies the contemporary human experience. With that focus on diversity, a broadly spatial language has permeated literary and social discourses: subject position, sites, mapping, grounding, location, and locality. Efforts to establish identity politics or new social movements adopt the local rather than the global as source and target of political action.

The local is becoming the "real" and the authentic in contrast to the abstractions of the global and the universal. The local is the mythology of the tangible, the identifiable, the solid, and the nature of boundaries. Humans must recapture the ideals of universalism. This can begin with *the study of locality myths and their artificial boundaries in body as well as in place.*

Humans are a very insecure species. Evolution involved traumatic psychological experiences as the great perceptual powers of humans emerged within common animal bodies and with common animal needs. Those perceptual powers enabled humans to contrive the image of themselves as "superior" animals within the animal kingdom. That contrivance, and the human hegemony developed to validate it, were a successful adaptive mechanism to survive, persist, develop, and evolve, as well as tolerate, the ambiguities of their very existence. That contrivance also carries the cognitive baggage of inferior feelings among humans because humans must live with animal bodies and animal needs notwithstanding cultural evolution and revolutions. These inferiority complexes (after Alfred Adler) endow humans with the obsessions of producing and reproducing social inferiority among themselves including the obsession of creating "inferior" geographical areas. Geographical space is pressed into service to collaborate in the polarization of people, both local and global. A sociobiological origin of inferior feelings is assuaged by geopolitical power and control, both economic and political.

Former president Jimmy Carter spoke in Dayton, Ohio, in September 1992 and told the audience that there were 132 wars in the world. He asked them why they could name only two or three. He then answered that it was because the great majority of the wars did not involve white people or oil ("I am the only United States President who has ever visited [sub-saharan] Africa," he noted). (This statement was prior to President George Bush's troop visit to Somalia in December 1992.) But the rapid spread of "smart weapons" will soon make even small wars obsolete.

In the last two centuries the Eurocentric perception of the Earth has been as a series of concentric circles radiating from a sacred inner (or ethnic) circle (Europe). Geographic areas extending further from that inner circle were more and more "inferior," unless they were conquered lands and the victors had a direct mythical connection to Europe. Even within the inner circle itself, North has been "superior" to South and Baltic (Nordic) Europe has been "superior" to Mediterranean Europe. The inferiority of Eastern Europe as a "vast slave-breeding [i.e., Slavic] ranch" was invested by the kings of Germany (the Holy Roman emperors). The Germans dominated the urban affairs of Poland, Bohemia, and Hungary. From the cities the Germans controlled navigation and transportation. In the Balkans the South Slavs were usually under foreign rule (e.g., Croatia from 1102) or were considered barbarians menacing Byzantine civilization or as heretics or Christians under the Turkish yoke.

In the "Long Sixteenth Century," Poland ("a Tartar state") was peripheralized into agrarian backwardness as whiteness was developed in the West (Foss, personal communication, 1992). "The same attitude was to persist among sophisticated Germans, such as Max Weber, the patriarch of 'value-neutral sociology,' who said, upon hearing of Polish independence, 'Why, it is only thanks to us that the Poles are human beings'" (ibid.). Subsequently "scientific racism," disguised as physical anthropology, emerged as a replacement for the earlier ideological/geographical division between Western Europeans with historic nations and Slavs without them. Then cranial measurements and angles were used to divide even "white" humans of Europe into Teutonic, Alpine, Mediterranean, and Slavic races.

Today the world is divided into first, second, and third world nations. There are seven GATT (General Agreement on Tariffs and Trade) industrial nations. There are countries behind the erstwhile Iron Curtain and in front of it. There are banana republics that require gunboat diplomacy and "backward" nations that demand complete domination. There are "dark continents" and enlightened ones. There are imperial powers with their trusts, territories, and possessions. There are "barbarians," "savages," and aborigines without western civilization. The United States is described as the leader of the West and the "free world." There are the teeming populations of the Orient that were once described by a distinguished social scientist as "the Yellow Peril" threatening California by their immigration.

Canada, "Czechoslovakia," Somalia, the former Soviet Union, and Yugoslavia threaten to disintegrate with a geographical identity rationale, among other divisive ones. Within the national borders of the United States there are distinct qualitative geographical identities: rural America, Appalachia, the Deep South, Yankee country, suburbs, and inner cities. Cities are divided into tenderloin districts, downtown, uptown, across-the-tracks, slums, and "cultural" districts.

In the inner cities there are gang neighborhoods with crack houses, schools that require combat pay, and graffiti cleanup squads and storefront churches with "gut music" and pie-in-the-sky messages. As St. Clair Drake (1965:777) describes it:

The bedlam of an occasional brawl, the shouted obscenities of street corner "foul mouths," and the whine of police sirens break the monotony of waiting for the number that never "falls," the horses that neither win, place, nor show, and the "good job" that never materializes. The insouciant swagger of teen-age drop-outs (the "cats") masks the hurt of their aimless existence and contrasts sharply with the ragged clothing and dejected demeanor of "skid-row" types who have long since stopped trying to keep up appearances and who escape it all by becoming "winoes" (and drug addicts).

This is a world whose urban "folkways" the upwardly mobile Negro middle class deplores as a "drag" on "The Race," that the upper classes wince at as an embarrassment, and that race leaders point to as proof that Negroes have been victimized.

These are brief illustrations of humans creating "inferior" and "superior" geographic areas and the "inferior" and "superior" peoples who inhabit them. Such psychogeography of inferiority/superiority is only one of the many techniques of human divisiveness: classism, racism, sexism, sectarianism, ageism, nationalism, and speciesism. Such human divisiveness has become obsolete in the twentieth century. Racism and sexism are not local. Localities are metaphors as well as places (see Anderson 1978 and 1990, Gans 1962, Hunter 1974, Jargowsky 1996, Jencks 1988, Kornblum 1974, Liebow 1967, Milgram 1976, Rainwater 1974, Smith and Williams 1986, Suttles 1972, Whyte 1943, and Zorbaugh 1929). Humans can cease to countenance the localization of human divisiveness. In the next century, humans can appreciate the diversity among people and other life forms, among human cultures, the Earth's topography, the world's climates, and the varied natural resources of ecosystems. This cannot occur until geographical attachments are purged of ranked and "inferior" identities and human bondings are ripe with embodied respect. The Earth is too small, too populated, and too threatened for the geographical xenophobia of the past. Humans must identify with their planet and their species; they must destigmatize identity by geographical location and rationally reconstruct human societies. I describe and analyze these behavioral dynamics in this book.

The final section documents how human divisiveness helped to create, manipulate, perpetuate, and control global geopolitical and psychogeographical exploitation of human insecurity. I do this by placing human insecurity into its historical, developmental, political, global, and panhuman contexts. I refute the mythological inferiority of people and places. All people are heroes and heroines; they are born that way. I expose locality myths and the artificial perimeters of our bodies and our places. I provide some ethnographic documentation and some theoretical linkage between personal security, the exploitation of local metaphors, and global human divisiveness. I analyze the security-driven geographical identity of the past two hundred years to document the relationships between human divisiveness and human conceptions of territory. The Greeks had their games; the Romans had their wars. The global village will have its emotional security for peace on Earth. We can end international violence and social divisiveness. In this book I document how.

Xenophobia, biophobia, and "inferior" people and places are products of the production and reproduction of social inferiority that permeate most human activities. Those same activities are rapidly destroying the human nest. Humans can change. We can create various maps for such transformations. I propose my cartography in this volume. Humans will continue to develop models, myths, movements, and magic for themselves, but those developments will cease to be divisive within and without our species and destructive to the ecosystems of Earth.

THE ECOLOGICAL REVOLUTION AND
PEACE AMONG ALL SPECIES

We will become global citizens in a global village. In our interdependent world, relationships with "others" pose urgent social problems as long as we participate in supremacy narratives and performances. We live on a poisoned and overpopulated planet where the respect for the web-of-life and ecosystems cannot compete with an emerging pathological human insecurity. An alternate human value system of embodied and ecosystem respect can set the human stage for peace on Earth.

The origin and evolution of human culture appear to be accompanied by some persistent values and attitudes that have eventually allowed humans to dominate and endanger Earth. Thus these once adaptive propensities have become maladaptive in the global village. I argue that these same propensities create social conflict and divisiveness. Humans can transform the human values and attitudes that are the basis for these behaviors; they can begin with the children. My volume describes new values that will position humans within the web-of-life, make them components of Earth, allow them to perceive all forms of life as vital parts

of the living community, and permit them to eradicate the production and reproduction of social inferiority. Humans eat Earth and deposit their waste there as all
other forms of life. We can respect life to the extent of banishing the myths of
inequality.

I revisit Erving Goffman to appreciate the nature of supremacy performances
in human behavior. Both Freud and Alfred Adler will reinforce that appreciation.
If a million years of adaptable human behavior is to be altered, there must be a
suitable costume, stage, and script for the future human performers. If the anthropologist Leslie White is accurate, and human culture is significantly autonomous,
then there needs to be a description of the global conditions that will precede the
cultural explosion—the Ecological Revolution. That description will be facilitated by the historical records of the cultural revolutions, both the agricultural and
the industrial. Darwin provides the raw material to launch our discussions, and
cognitive anthropologists will guide our efforts in the socialization of children for
a new world order—the rational reconstruction of society.

Ecosystems, education, and human culture are examined together to socialize
and educate humans for the next century, for the next stage in social development
in the global village. Humans will begin to perceive themselves as being part of
Earth rather than living on it. During this period, "ecosophy" may become one of
our most important disciplines.

Human efforts to control their environments (including arbitrarily identified
populations), and to control most forms of life within those environments, have
allowed humans to adapt, multiply, and spread over Earth. Now our efforts will
be to understand our impact and to transform those outdated values and attitudes.
We have devoted many of our resources to attempt to change human habits that
are harmful to our ecosystems, but I argue that we will also transform the nature
of human culture itself. That culture that has allowed us to master our environments will be altered to protect them.

This book presents a social science approach that creates an understanding of
the social dimension of renewable natural resource management problems and of
the dissemination of research findings, and that creates efforts for the promotion
of a conservation ethic and the idea of sustainable development at global, regional, national, and local levels. I develop a vision of human attitudes and values
that sustain those ecosystems—a new moral order. A major component of that
vision is to identify attitudes and values that enable people to comprehend and
accept the necessity for conserving and protecting the world's biological diversity and to create technology and public policy that will support these efforts.

Policy studies, conservation ethics, human rights, and new technology for effective biological diversity and conservation require a new human culture. That
culture will eliminate social identity dependency on class, race, ethnicity, gender,
religion, age, nation, and species. These new global citizens will be committed to
the protection of our ecosystems, including our children, our aged, our poor, and
our ill. The social commitment will be one that combines the education of parents, educators, policymakers, and industrial and military managers with the so-

cialization of children to view the world's ecosystems and its biological diversity as crucial parts of human life and health itself.

Adaptive cultural evolution now emerges with a dangerous cultural lag—attitudes and values that are not compatible with present levels of science, weaponry, and technology. This book examines value and attitude transformations and determines how new worldviews about ecology and human populations can be formulated and channeled into action: global change, curriculum development, interdisciplinary courses, and state, local, regional, national, and global leadership training. This effort presents a new balance to the positivistic-deconstructionist antagonisms. It creates some common research interests and new working relationships among the humanities and the social and natural sciences. We may finally be able to understand race and CRESSANS as supremacy narratives and performances.

MACROANTHROPOLOGY: DISCOVERING UNITY IN THE SEARCH FOR OURSELVES

The greater our knowledge of how man arose and how he functions, how he has developed and is developing the culture which makes him human, the greater our chance of using such knowledge in the culture process of which it becomes a part. With every increase in awareness and in our ability to articulate new social concepts which the scientific study of man makes possible, we become different human beings because our stature is enhanced by the culture we share. (Mead 1960b:341)

Cultural anthropology can be dynamic and effective in its postcentennial period in America and in the twenty-first century in the world. The discipline can utilize all of its fields—practice, ethnology, archaeology, biology, and linguistics—to help make the world safe for humanity. If we continue to search for human nature, focus on the panhuman dilemmas of our times (see Williams 1992b), and help to sustain the ecosystems of the global village, we will learn to comprehend the human search for security. The privileged primates (humans) will deconstruct their delusions of superiority, determine the biophobia hypothesis (Williams 1992b:192), and welcome an Ecological Revolution. I call this approach macroanthropology in order to recognize our kinship with the other social sciences that have used similar terms.

Within the context of a macrotheoretical approach to humans and to ecosystems, this book explores the social and environmental violence of humans by means of the biophobia hypothesis. The intractable destruction of Earth, including human communities, can be explored in terms of the origin, nature, and development of the human species itself. I discuss some aspects of that destruction (e.g., classism, racism, ethnocentrism, sexism, sectarianism, ageism, nationalism, and speciesism—CRESSANS) and locate the ultimate course of that destruction (human extinction) and its diversion (the Ecological Revolution) in a rational reconstruction of human societies. That reconstruction is commenced by a new and different perception of the human body and of Earth.

The postmodern era, with its global economic, ecological, ethnic, and military threats of human disaster, can benefit from macroanthropological explanations and analyses. Contemporary times suggest that the social sciences might concentrate on the behaviors of the species. The biophobia hypothesis permits that concentration.

For almost twenty years, cultural anthropology has been drifting around and among other social sciences and humanities for the structures of its own identity. Reflexivity and self-examination have created no clear trajectory for cultural anthropology. Today history, cultural studies, literary criticism, development studies, and the continuous reformulations of colonial power dominate cultural anthropology. None of them shows us the future of cultural anthropology. At many universities the four-field approach has been almost abandoned, and where it does exist, the fields do not communicate well with one another. Cultural anthropology textbooks introduce students to very little that will be their course work in undergraduate and graduate curricula and even to less that will encumber their lives in the global village. I assume that undergraduate and graduate courses will change in the immediate future to reflect postcolonial cultural anthropology.

If the present situation in cultural anthropology continues, it, as a major field in anthropology, may cease to exist in the academy. But it need not continue. Macroanthropology waits in the wings. Macroanthropology asserts that the exploration of diversity is not an anthropological end but merely a means to search for ourselves as a species. One goal of cultural anthropology is to understand and explain the species. The history and development of the discipline document that. The exploration of diversity is useful only as long as it helps along that way. In fact, that exploration taken too far becomes exploitive for the human propensity to produce and reproduce social inferiority. Macroanthropology is designed to understand and explain the species as well as to be contemporary and future oriented. It recognizes that the human species has no future unless it solves some of its major problems on Earth, and macroanthropology can help by exposing the human dimensions of those problems. It is no longer enough to describe and explain the wide array of human behaviors. We must learn why humans are threatened with global suicide. Such knowledge may allow some social transformations that alter the courses that humans now steer.

Anthropology began as a search for *Homo sapiens* and human nature. Such a broad quest has taken its practitioners in many directions. Some of those directions have been found faulty, but we continue the search.

Macroanthropology proposes to return to the roots, to recapture the vision of our ancestors. It proposes to ask research questions about the species, about human nature, about "THE HUMAN DILEMMA" (e.g., population, poverty, and pollution). Macroanthropology will design its questions such that each of the five fields of anthropolgy can make a contribution. I provide an example below when I ask, what about the body?

In my example I suggest that many of the problems of the species are a result of our conceptions of our bodies, but each of the five fields of anthropology can easily grapple with the question. In a research team, each of the participants can decide its own focus. The objectives of all of the perspectives are to determine where anthropologists can work to contribute to the question.

Biological anthropology has been working with the body since it began, but I propose a broader perspective for it and "scientific" anthropology. What I envision is a perspective that tackles human insecurity about the body and its functions; a perspective that examines health, well-being, and longevity; a perspective that might transform all previous perspectives.

Humanistic approaches to the body are popular and are reflected in the literature, but I would nudge them to include some attention to the body's relation to self-esteem; on language and the failure of communication; on language and human divisiveness; and on language and a support system for the animal functions of humans.

Scientific anthropology can explain why and how humans abuse their bodies. How did such devaluation begin and why does it continue? How are such devaluations distributed in the world's populations and how do they vary among them? These concerns about the body will translate into concerns about Earth (practice), violence, and human divisiveness.

There are many ways to approach this task. The present suggestions are but examples. The human quest (often appearing irrational) for power, and the exploitation and misappropriation of natural and human resources in that quest, are beacons for us to search for human nature. Power seems a pervasive human addiction, and the exploitation of resources support the habit. Power has always required the exploitation and often misappropriation of Earth's resources and still does. The global transformations in technology, communications, transportation, weapon systems, and commerce are all being diverted to the quest for power in a world in which natural resources are limited. The global waste of those resources for power is symptomatic of a species gone amuck.

Humans have always had each other to exploit and abuse for power and comparisons; we continue today (e.g., CRESSANS). But the postmodern demand for natural resources has reached an apex. This book discusses that demand as a pervasive symbol and substance that has an eternal impact on human affairs. I examine the human quest for power and comparison that appears to be a crucial component of human history and human nature. The human drive to be superior can be humbling in its display of a lack of self-respect and self-control. Materials for an economy and polity, the means and structure for earning a livelihood, and culture-nature relations, all have implications for power. Material and charismatic bases for power are mutually reinforcing.

The Gouro elders' power, for example, rests on the control of objects, people, and the symbolically separate market and prestige spheres of exchange. Power is, therefore, encoded in symbols, enacted in relationships, and grounded in things. (Dimen-Schein 1977:211)

The relationships in production, distribution, and consumption reveal some basic power relationships in a culture. Contrary to Marx, the means of production is only one conduit to power. There are others: types of games, social relations, marriage, and natural resources.

Power, then, exists in different domains within each culture. It has material, psychological, and social dimensions, and its constitution varies accordingly: strength in rape, tools in production, "pull" in getting a job, charisma in group leadership, decision making in politics, or the manipulation myth in propaganda. Its psychosocial dimensions include awe and noblesse oblige, respect and contempt, sadomasochistic relationships, among others. Its behavioral expressions vary. (Dimen-Schein 1977:211)

Together natural resources and power constitute here the deep ecological discussions that describe a course for humankind. Much of the discussion focuses on how natural resources and power produce and reproduce social inferiority in "others," and how that production and reproduction are driven by an abiding inferiority complex in humans. The biophobia hypothesis attempts to explain this phenomenon. Most scholarship has been prey to it. Decades of research on social stratification, race and ethnicity, gender, sectarianism, age discrimination, nationalism, and speciesism do not address the human vulnerability to the eternal social divisiveness that threatens to destroy our Earth or at least our species. I postulate that it is the character of becoming and being human that has prevented humans from discovering the fundamental basis for this abiding social divisiveness. On the contrary, scholars have taken a perverted kind of pleasure, like the "dirty old man" who spends a lifetime of well-funded research on pornography, lecherously studying "classography, raceography, ethnography, feminography, sectography, gerontography, poverography, poorography, victimography," inferior nations and species. This book is not about blame. It asks why humans must produce and reproduce social inferiority in order to exploit it, even by perennially studying it. The biophobia hypothesis says that it is because humans have a phobia about their animal biology that creates an inferiority complex in them.

In this book I begin to develop a macrotheory to introduce the student to theory as a working component of reading ethnography. Macroanthropology is an approach of cultural anthropology that focuses on the species and relies on a certain theoretical framework—complex theory. This theoretical framework is in its early stages of development. The approach is to take "small" and "identifiable" populations and study them by means of ethnography but to add the impacts and impingements of global forces on them. Most textbooks drown students in ethnography and concepts. Theory is assumed to be above them. This is a hybrid book that accommodates both theory and ethnography; they are not the traditional pedagogic isolates but are woven together. Theory in anthropology does not have to be a mountain that only the superior can climb. It does not have to be literary jargon that disguises the dearth of theory in cultural anthropology. Theory can be as simple as ethnography and just as much fun. But it can also be wrong. That is why we call it theory. Until proven wrong, it enlivens and often gives universal

meaning to ethnography. So ethnography fits into the students' own lives, and theory is just an abstract rope to attempt to tie it all together until the bundle no longer makes sense in the light of new discoveries and requires new rope. Learning becomes self-discoveries and is exciting. The material is about people we know and can now understand because it includes our own behavior.

Macroanthropology creates new concepts—biophobia, CRESSANS, DDDAK, PRSI (the production and reproduction of social inferiority), humanics, humanimals, inferiority complexes, and so on—to understand and explain new contexts and uses traditional anthropological concepts where they are effective. Students can study ethnographic material with these new perspectives. The perspectives allow them to examine contemporary life in the global village within anthropological paradigms. Complex theory, unlike world systems theory, incorporates human emotions. I begin this book with some autobiographical material. This helps to explain my own feelings of inferiority and my potential biases.

Chapter 2

Human Inferiority Feelings and Two Anthropologists

Man would necessarily have succumbed before the assault of the powers of nature if he had not employed them to his advantage. . . . Climatic conditions compel him to protect himself from the cold by clothes, which he takes from animals better protected than he is. His organism requires artificial housing and artificial preparation of food. His life is only assured by means of division of labor and by sufficient propagation. His organs and his mind toil continually for conquest and security. To all this have to be added his greater knowledge of life's dangers and his awareness of death. Who can seriously doubt that the human individual treated by nature in such a stepmother fashion has been provided with the blessing of a strong feeling of inferiority that urges him towards a plus situation, towards security and conquest? This tremendous, enforced rebellion against a tenacious feeling of inferiority as the foundation of human development is awakened afresh and repeated in every infant and little child. (Alfred Adler in Becker 1962:35)

Tocqueville, after all, posed the prospect of an America without classes—an "equality of conditions"—yet one where people still remained restless unto death, forever seeking to find some manner of living in which they felt authentic, worthy of being respected, dignified. Equality of conditions, he wrote, does not dampen the evils of individualism; to the contrary, he thought in America equality would lead to an increase in individual anxiety and self-doubt. A modern social commentator, Robert Nisbet, has said that in this, Tocqueville created a picture of status insecurity outside the boundaries of class analysis. (Sennett and Cobb 1973:257)

My own feelings of inferiority (described below) are not unusual, as I have suggested in these pages. As Frazier (1968:178) has stated, most African Americans feel inferior: "Not all middle-class Negroes consciously desire . . . to be white in order to escape from their feeling of inferiority. . . . But when one studies the attitude of this class in regard to the physical traits or the social characteristics of

Negroes, it becomes clear that the Black bourgeoisie do not really wish to be identified with Negroes."

And as his student, Nathan Hare (1979:33), has expanded:

Black Anglo-Saxons are chiefly distinguishable in that, in their struggle to throw off the smoldering blanket of social inferiority, they disown their own history and mores in order to assume those of the biological descendents of the white Anglo-Saxons. They relate to and long to be part of, the elusive and hostile white world, whose norms are taken as models of behavior. White society is to most of them a looking-glass for taking stock of their personal conduct. . . . They must keep on grooming to make what they think white society imagines itself to be, accord with what they themselves would like to be: like whites.

However, the artificial distinctions of race sometimes obscure the fact that whites feel inferior, too. Humans feel inferior, and those feelings and the actions they take to compensate for them or to deny and erase them constitute much of the social life of mankind.

The African-American middle class must understand the American social system. It is not designed to share power with Blacks, only to provide the illusion of power to sustain the African-American quest for power. Any exercise of power must be directed toward other Blacks, and even then, such an exercise cannot succeed if the recipient Black has a powerful white patron.

The middle-class Blacks assuming positions in the wider society will be increasingly called upon to keep the lid on things by whites and at the same time will be under pressure from below to identify with the continuing Black struggle. . . .

The colonial analogy becomes misleading when it is used to suggest the possibility of meaningful Black independence within the context of American Society. As the size of the Black middle-class increases, the cohesiveness of common racial identity may be lessened and a long term sustained effort to achieve independence made even more difficult. At the same time strengthening the Black community's economic and political power increases its bargaining position vis-à-vis the white society. (Tabb 1971:442)

As is often whispered, some psychologists and psychiatrists pursue their careers because of their own emotional dilemmas. For anthropologists, it seems to be a deep sense of personal inferiority that drives some of them to study "inferior" people. That inferiority complex accounts for many of the personal conflicts within academic anthropology departments.

Anthropologists, like all other humans, are products of their cultures. In America, the pressures for upward mobility are severe, and those without exceptional athletic, business, or entertainment acumen and opportunity may choose academia for such mobility.

As I have suggested above, all humans have feelings of inadequacy, but anthropologists seem to exhibit strong ones. Who else would choose careers that obligate them to live for years among "inferior" peoples of the world? For anthropologists, the statement by Thackery is most pertinent: "Birket-Smith said: 'There is no rank or class among the Eskimos, who must therefore renounce that satis-

faction, which Thackery calls the true pleasure of life, of associating with one's inferiors.' The same may be said of other primitive societies" (Sahlins 1960:85).

These feelings of inadequacy help explain why anthropologists who work in academia and have what they consider "the best jobs in the world" create so much stress and anxiety for others and themselves in their workplace. The story of two anthropologists that follows attempts to show the human side of these professionals who, like most humans, feel compelled to prove their superiority.

Children are not born feeling inferior. They learn that they are not beautiful, strong, tall, intelligent, articulate, graceful, agile, talented, rich, clean, righteous, principled, virtuous, W.A.S.P., white, or perfect. In a competitive and materialistic society, they are continually taught these lessons. Regardless of their achievements, they will be surrounded by people and things that remind them that there is "more."

As two examples of middle-class achievements that suggest how notions of inferiority develop, I describe here some of my own life experiences and those of another anthropologist.

MY PURSUIT OF THE MIDDLE CLASS

I was born in Mercy Hospital and reared in the Hill District of Pittsburgh. When I was born, my parents lived in a basement at Mercer Street and Webster Avenue (Lorant 1975:350, "The Sun Shines in the City" and 1975:344, "The Hill in the 30's"). During my childhood we were evicted many times, but I spent most of my early life in a three-story frame apartment complex at Reed and Soho Streets (2303 Reed Street; Lorant 1975:349, "Upper Soho") and in a decaying house at Cassatt (a street named for Mary Cassatt, the American painter, who was born in Pittsburgh and lived there from 1845 to 1926) and Crescent Streets (no. 4 Cassatt Street; Lorant 1975:343, 345, "The Habitat of Humans, Shanties in the Hill District").

My parents reared their six children (one died at age four) by means of welfare and menial jobs. Neither of my parents completed high school, and only one of my siblings did so. Only I attended college. So I am a stranger to the middle class and an alien in the academic village.

The house we occupied at no. 4 Cassatt Street was condemned by the city in 1951, and we moved to other Black ghettos. Later, with a professional degree and occupation, I moved to middle-class neighborhoods. But after I abandoned my native habitat, I discovered that I belonged nowhere. Middle-class values (in movies, books, and mentors) had enticed me out of the ghetto, but they never integrated me into the places where I arrived. With this alien character, I have a proclivity to study those who surround me. This is the tradition of anthropology.

I will describe my life in the third person (using "Donald," as my parents, siblings, and early acquaintances called me) to facilitate the recollection as objectively as possible.

Donald's father came to Pittsburgh from Alabama after the death of Donald's grandfather. The older children of the family (Donald's aunts and uncles) arranged for their entire family (mother, three girls, and three boys) to travel to Pittsburgh. Donald's father often recounted his family's hardships in coming to Pittsburgh when there was neither welfare nor Social Security. The family often slept in one room with the children sleeping in shifts because beds were in short supply. When one of them was fortunate enough to obtain employment, he or she would help support the entire family. This process continued until each member "got on his feet."

Donald's mother and her family were from Virginia. She went to Pittsburgh after her mother's death to live with her oldest sister, who earlier had left home, married, and settled there. She was the third sister to go to Pittsburgh; the others were married homemakers while Donald's mother still attended school. Becoming bored with school and the limited provisions of her oldest sister, she soon found a job in a laundry.

While she was working, attending church, and dating, Donald's mother met her future husband. Donald's father had held various menial jobs; he was unemployed when he met his future wife, however. Still, he was frugal with his money, and his oldest sister, Hannah Williams-Hunter, whose husband was employed, provided his meals, shelter, and "spending change." Donald's mother once described his father as "a good dresser who could fool you to death." Persuading her that he had money, a job, and "came from a good family," he joined her church and cajoled her into marriage.

Only after marriage did she discover their plight—no job, no money, and no home. Her sister, Carrie Barnes-Hill, had warned her not to get married, suspecting that the future husband was a "ne'er-do-well." She insisted that if her sister got married against her will, she could no longer live with her. Nevertheless, the young couple started upon their rugged path of life together. The husband's sister continued to help, and he worked periodically. The nearly constant lack of security for herself and the children was a psychological trauma that Donald's mother would never forget. She was frequently ill and worried.

Donald's mother explained that her "bad nerves" were a result of incidents such as moving into vacant houses before leasing them and moving out before being discovered by the landlord (a homeless family). Many times, Donald's paternal aunt, Hannah, became the family doctor when no physician would come to the house. She also fed them when the cupboards at Donald's house were bare. In fact, for many years, his father ate his meals at her house to keep from using the meager resources at his own home.

Donald's oldest maternal aunt, Carrie, divorced her husband and moved to another city; another older sister (Mattie) of his mother's moved to Pittsburgh and married a man with a secure job. This sister never had any children of her own, so she helped Donald's mother. She continued to help Donald and his siblings even after most of them reached adulthood.

Donald's oldest brother had died at the age of four, so Donald was reared as the eldest for most of his life. His mother believed that poor obstetrical care in the delivery room had injured the brother so that he never fully recovered. His congenital injury was complicated by the lack of adequate health care due to the family's low income.

Donald begins his own story with the statements, "I was born in the Hill. My parents lived in a two-room basement apartment." He continues, informing us that his father had a bad heart due to a case of rheumatic fever and that the heart condition kept the father unemployed for many years. His family moved several times during Donald's early childhood, and Donald recalls his father's many survival techniques during those bleak days. When most of the neighbors' electricity was shut off for nonpayment of a bill, his father secured power for the family "by climbing the tellie pole and putting a jumper on the electric wire." In this way they had a refrigerator when such luxuries in the neighborhood were rare. Occasionally, the children received large expensive toys such as a new fire engine that could seat two children up front and one in the rear. These purchases were made on credit. Once, when confronted with one account in arrears that was not likely to be paid, his father denied the purchase. When asked to sign the paper, he wrote an "X" for his signature; the frustrated creditors dismissed him. These survival tactics continued through Donald's childhood, and he recalls, "How proud we kids were when we went out riding in one of the very few cars around here." Such tactics often required that valuable property, such as automobiles, be legally owned by relatives. It also required that the father learn a trade (paperhanging) so that he could work on those rare occasions when he felt well enough. Frequently, all members of the family were gainfully employed, the children with newspaper and shoeshine routes.

Donald recalls spending much of his childhood with his neighborhood peers. He learned early from them that one's place in the world was ranked according to size and aggressiveness. The larger boys would twist his arms behind his back and force him to call them "Daddy" to amuse the groups and display their rank. Even at this tender age (approximately eight years old), these ghetto boys had learned to value the elusive "Daddy" that several of them lived without. The older girls would often beat him for the same reason—to display rank. One had to be bold and aggressive, albeit somewhat accommodative, to avoid too much bruising. Aloofness and individuality were not tolerated. In fact, Donald explained that his younger brother was accepted by the group before Donald because he conformed and cooperated more than Donald.

By the time Donald was seven years old, the neighborhood girls had already introduced him to sexual petting, and he learned to enjoy the pleasure of these tactile experiences before he was able to have intercourse. He had his first girlfriend at the age of seven and walked her home from school and visited her after school. The girl's mother would often allow him to enter the house to avoid the nuisance of their communicating from opposite sides of the first-floor window. Another girlfriend of Donald's would keep him and his male companion waiting for hours outside just to catch a glimpse of her at her second-floor window or in the corridor. Her parents were not so tolerant, but it was worth every waiting moment just for the rare pleasure of seeing her. "It was just fun to be near her house," Donald remembered.

Donald received no allowance, nor did he have any conception of what it meant. He earned most of his spending money by running errands, selling scrap metal and rags, and establishing a network of adults in the neighborhood who provided money for various reasons. This network became so well organized that many of the homes he visited (scheduling visits so as not to be a "pest") were a source of money with or without any related chores, because of the good will he had established with the residents. Many of these sources were homes of relatives or his parents' friends with whom he made a special effort to become acquainted. In general, at a very early age Donald was spending much of his time in the neighborhood streets—hustling, playing, and courting. He explained that if he or his brothers remained in the house during mild weather, his mother suspected that "something was wrong."

Donald did not know what a library or a museum was. He would not learn about them until years later during the school field trips. He was never taken downtown, and his parents subscribed to no newspapers or magazines. There was no television, and children were not permitted to use the radio. These were his formative years during which he developed alternative values.

Throughout Donald's recollections weaves a thread of violence—among his peers, his teachers, and in the streets. One of his early experiences with violence in the streets was when he was about five years old and witnessed a woman being beaten near his house. According to Donald, "She kept crying and he kept hitting her and hollering at her. She looked white and seemed so pretty and helpless. I was high yellow or 'shit-color' and I knew how many times I got beat just for that so I felt sorry for her. She was out of place in that neighborhood just like I was out of place everywhere." In addition, certain neighborhood parents "went for bad," welcoming any excuse for an altercation to display their prowess for aggression. Disputes among their children were frequent sources of these excuses.

One of the family's heroes during these early years of Donald's life was his maternal uncle, Thurman Barnes ("Big Man"). "He was a good-looking man, a gambler and a braggart. The women liked him and gave him money, while the men liked to hear him talk. It didn't matter that he was separated from his wife and two children, without a job, frequently in jail and had had several children out of wedlock. Still, he would maintain: 'They ain't no kids of mine.'"

When Donald was eight years old, his family moved again. He enjoyed recalling the small details of this house where he spent many years. He remembered the several months of labor that his father, his brothers, and he had put into the five-room brick house before it was fit for human habitation. Even with these efforts, it was still a modest house with two bedrooms on the second floor and a frame kitchen set off from the house. Without a basement under it or a room over it, the kitchen was the coldest room during the winter. The only heat came from the range. Often, the water was left running to keep it from freezing and bursting the pipes. Initially, the house was heated by a large coal burner in the dining room and a living-room fireplace that also burned coal. Later, the fireplace was abandoned for a small gas space heater and the coal burner was moved to the basement with a large opening in the dining-room floor directly above it. The arrangement allowed better use of the precious space and made the only bath, located in the basement, more tolerable.

The house sat on the side of a precipitous hill that overlooked the Allegheny River, Bigelow Boulevard, and the Pennsylvania Railroad Station. Donald discovered many riches here in this poor, predominantly Black neighborhood. The geographical location was a treasure for boyhood play and imagination. Thirty feet away, at the edge of the hillside, he could clearly see the boats guiding their freight up and down the river. He could watch the trains moving in and out of the station. He could watch the vehicles racing up and down the boulevard. Donald saw his first seaplanes in action along the river; a river terminal was used for excursion flights. He could fly his kites up and over the hillside, free from the usual obstacles of the urban streets. Donald spent many hours playing in the streams that ran over the hillside. Part of the hillside was covered with trees and brush, so he and his peers had their own urban forest. They would roam or camp there for hours, often with food, only a hundred yards from home.

Donald remembers with great pleasure the "bull rope" swings that the larger boys would mount. On another portion of this hillside, these swings extended from the upper reaches of a telephone pole. The boys would swing in Tarzan fashion from one side of the hill, around the pole and out over the precipice, to the other side of the hill. The ride was dangerous but thrilling. The younger boys had few opportunities to swing while the larger boys were on the rope, but it was a pleasure just to watch the excitement. Then, at the end of the day, the big boys would abandon the swing, and Donald and his peers could ride until dark. When there was no school, they would rise early in the morning and race to the swing to occupy it for several hours before the older boys arrived.

Donald seems especially appreciative of living in this small ecological niche. From large cardboard boxes, he and the boys would make sleds to ride the loosely packed dirt down the steep hillsides. They had rock wars with the boys who lived much higher on the hillside, boys with whom they did not associate in other ways. They sat upon favorite stoops and porches and through interaction established cohesive peer groups that endured until they moved away or became adults. These stoops were usually located on a corner so that they could see neighborhood activities in four directions. They observed, talked, told stories, sang, joked, and humiliated one another. They teased the girls, the neighborhood drunk, and the local imbecile. The drunk had been gassed in World War I, and he walked on his heels. They called him "Staglee," and he answered to the name. They would call to him, "Why do you walk on your heels?" He would answer, "To save my sole." He would often threaten them when they were disrespectful, and they enjoyed the threat of danger. The imbecile was about nineteen years old, and his energy never seemed to wane; he chased the boys for hours. Their fear of him made the play more exciting.

During the winter, they made tracks for running and sliding on the sidewalk, battled with snowballs, and sledded down their steep streets. When the weather was warmer, they played football and baseball in the streets. Their form of baseball was one in which they bounced the ball off a wall into the playing field instead of hitting the ball with a bat. They went swimming in the recreation center pool and often took the time to play in the center's ball field or the schoolyards as well.

During these years, school was an extension of the street. One was forced to abide by certain rules that seemed to have little meaning. For example, one was encouraged to be "bad" by peer-group pressure. Often, this merely meant that one behaved in school as disruptively as one did outside of school. Teachers put the "agitator" in a corner or under the desk. Sometimes they would beat his knuckles with a ruler or lead him by his earlobe to the principal's office, where he spent the rest of the school day waiting for a paddling, all the while displaying his bravado to his peers. As one peer expressed it:

My teachers were white and they seemed so clean that they made me feel dirty. And when I was bad that's when their true colors would show. Starting in the first grade you could sense that when their own children were bad they didn't treat them like they treated you when you were bad. They could look at you like you were an animal and if they had to touch you it was with the tips of their fingers or a mean kind of grab. They never really touched you like they did the one or two white kids in the class. They never got close to you, hugged you, or put their arms around you so you could feel a part of the school. They talked at me, taught at me; they were teaching in the room and I could catch it or not. The school belonged to them and I could stay in the building as long as I watched myself, stayed in my place. Once in that building, you were out of the ghetto and you better act like it. The school was not part of the ghetto, which was part of me.

In the ghetto, Donald not only had to contend with the ethos of teachers and their mainstream institutional control and restrictions, but he also had to fight or avoid altercations resulting in physical injuries or humiliation. The pecking order in his school was determined not by grade averages but by aggression, as was status in the neighborhood. Aggression as a major source of excitement and entertainment was almost impossible to avoid. Even when there were no fights, the threat still hung over one like the fabled sword of Damocles on its slender thread: "I'm gon' beat your butt after school," or "I better not see you outside," or "You gon' get your butt kicked." Then, there were the bullies who, upon passing a smaller guy in the hall, would grab him by the collar and demand money or sweets or just humiliate him. According to Donald, "There was one guy, Winston, who was into bodybuilding and weights and he was a 'punch-you' addict. . . . He was always punching the little guys in the arm or shoulder to show you his strength."

Learning in school was incidental and peripheral to the main business of life. That business was to interact, to tease, to court the girls, and to fight. In the sixth and seventh grades, the girls would be attacked with romantic play episodes if the teacher left the classroom. This behavior, combined with frenzied attacks among the boys themselves, continued until the teacher returned. The favorite game in the gym classes was the violent use of basketballs to hit and "put out" one another. The teacher enjoyed this as much as the boys.

Violence in school merged with violence in the home. Donald described how a man shot a woman "five times right there near me." At age nine, Donald witnessed a neighborhood woman severely cutting another woman with a knife after an argument. The victim had been arguing with a teenage girl. At the height of the argument, the girl's mother ran out with a knife, and both she and her daughter attacked the victim. The mother was famous in the neighborhood for her knife-wielding exploits and was even rumored to have killed someone.

On one occasion the knife-wielding woman rushed into Donald's house to vehemently protest the aggression of Donald's younger brother against her grandson. During the intrusion, Donald watched the incident as he sat near his mother, who was taken by complete surprise as she stood ironing her weekly wash. In fact, she was so surprised she seemed to be in a state of shock. The woman, her famous knife in hand, yelled and screamed at Donald's mother, who hardly knew what was happening. Her voice was so loud that Donald's father rushed downstairs and surprised the woman, who thought he was away. He ordered her out of his house with such rage that the woman never bothered to speak to him—she quickly left. Donald's father was upset that his mother had not used the iron to defend herself. He dressed immediately and went to the local office of the justice of the peace to file charges.

Donald recalled the freedom he had as an adolescent and especially as a teenager. He and his brother (one year and two months younger) came and went almost as they pleased with very little restriction from their parents. Their parents were only concerned that the boys did not cause them trouble. There was little if any pressure (but some encouragement) to get good grades in school, to work, to come home for dinner, to go to bed, or any of the other parental coercions typical in mainstream lifestyles. Their parents' energies were consumed by the task of providing clothes, food, and shelter. So Donald's summer evening activities lasted until morning, long after his peers had been called home and the group had dwindled to a quiet twosome. Then Donald and his brother would return home for sleep.

Nevertheless, his parents reminded him that education was important for "good jobs" and professions. Academic excellence was one's own choice, and college was a word with little substance in his household. In addition, a few schoolteachers and Donald's newspaper boss (Lloyd D. Tobias, Toby) often reminded him of the value of education. Yet such ideas were remote when reinforcement was lacking.

As Donald and his peers became teenagers, their attention turned more and more to heterosexual relationships. Their games and their play often focused on exclusive time with females. He remembered his unrestricted experiments with sex in the summer evenings. Neighborhood families in which both parents worked provided convenient shelters for adolescent sexual experiments. Homes in which parents were seldom present, day or night, became "dens of iniquity." Donald's brother had an unpleasant experience when his girlfriend, who was eleven years old, was impregnated at such a house. He was thirteen years old; an older boy was responsible, but Donald's brother felt obligated to accept the fatherhood. The baby died.

Donald and his friends played several variations of hide-and-seek, but for most, the real game was "hide-and-pet." Although sexual intercourse seldom occurred, many youngsters were exposed to the "real thing" on some occasion. All of Donald's sexual education took place in these play encounters. He knew some of the girls who were impregnated during these times and remembered their maternal experiences. He recalled the youthful marriages precipitated by such encounters. Often the males would resist marriage in spite of their paternal status; but the status itself usually had a profound impact upon their future interests. School became even more confining, and one was anxious to fulfill one's role as a man. The adult world of menial work, money, street life, and heterosexual companionship beckoned them. Thus the cycle continued: poverty, undereducation, and institutional deprivation.

Donald had the ability to relate well with adults and the adult world. Because of this, it seemed to him that he had never been a child. Somehow, as long as he could remember, he had participated and functioned well in the adult world. He recalled that at the age of eleven it was his responsibility to travel the several miles from the Hill to the North Side by public transportation (the incline and the streetcar) to collect his mother's portion of his father's pay, so she would be able to go shopping before his father returned home on payday. Donald was sent downtown almost weekly to pay utility bills and insurance premiums for his parents and his mother's sister. It was also his responsibility to retrieve his aunt's check from the mailbox every week, cash it, and pay her various debts. When Donald's parents would leave the city or the state on kinship "call to duty," they would leave Donald in charge of his siblings. He recalled that as early as eleven years old he would help his father drive the car on the Pennsylvania Turnpike while sitting on a pillow to see the road. At the time, these duties seemed ordinary to Donald because he was able and expected to perform. As he recalls these periods, however, he is impressed with how much of his childhood was spent fulfilling adult responsibilities.

During this same period, Donald began to sell mail-order products from door to door in his neighborhood. He started with Cloverine Salve; after several successful orders, he began to sell other items. He subsequently sold a variety of Black periodicals and earned profits and prizes. He never forgot his first prize—a Monopoly game. Gradually he learned that he was endowed with a remarkable ability to sell. In fact, the quantity of a product seemed to be no problem; only his desire to sell mattered. Donald believed that, "If I wanted to sell it and I tried, I could sell it."

Donald's periodical enterprises brought him into persistent contact with life in the street. He spent many hours in the old Fullerton and Wylie nightlife area. He traveled Webster, Wylie Centre, Herron, and Bedford Avenues week after week. He frequented the barbershops, beauty shops, bars, speakeasies, gambling joints, poolrooms, private clubs, restaurants, shoeshine parlors, jitney stations, hat-cleaning shops, fish markets, and private homes. Because of these activities, he spent more time mingling with adults than with his peers. He enjoyed the sales activities and continued to be very successful. Again and again he proved to himself that he could sell as many periodicals as he wished. Donald accumulated a considerable amount of money as a result of these activities, but he had little time to spend it. There were many late evenings when he had sold several hundred periodicals but refused to quit and return home until he had sold the last item. The weight of the periodicals had been replaced by the bulk of coin; his entire body was tired from walking and carrying the merchandise, but he pushed on until the end. Week after week this process continued to be a personal challenge that brought him the admiration of his parents, his paper boss, and other adults, as well as the envy of competitive paperboys.

These activities allowed Donald to mingle with a variety of people in the Hill. He sold to the educated, the uneducated, the intoxicated, hustlers, gamblers, barmaids, bartenders, pimps, prostitutes, secretaries (in insurance companies and other offices), jitney drivers, barbers, beauticians, and theater attendants. He was rebuffed by the belligerent, the aggressive, the exasperated, and the defeated. Many a beleaguered and bellicose tavern owner or bartender tried unsuccessfully to keep him out of the bar and away from the patrons. Other proprietors and customers, whether they condemned or praised him, knew him and accepted him as a part of the scene. Some proprietors and bartenders accepted defeat after being continually outwitted by his tenacity. Some even became friends and customers after witnessing a boy who would use a series of strategic maneuvers to reach potential customers. These maneuvers would usually entail his getting in the door and to the rear of the bar before being discovered. Then, even if he were discovered, most of the patrons would already have been exposed to his wares; few proprietors were aggressive enough to stop a patron from making a purchase if he so desired. On some occasions, though, an exasperated bartender would insist that the patron follow Donald outside to make the purchase.

These regular appearances on the avenue and in customers' homes created close ties between Donald and some of his patrons. Some women almost adopted him, and he would always revel in the sound of their shouts that this was their "boy." One woman customer had to be "straightened out" by Donald's maternal aunt, Mattie Ruth Barnes-Franklin, because the customer had romantic designs upon him, notwithstanding the fact that he was fourteen years old and she was forty. Thus he was a regular part of the parade that marched from tavern to tavern, corner to corner, street to street, and encounter to encounter, wondering most of the time, "Will I find my love today?" He was one of the players in a human drama, most of whose participants had long been abandoned in the larger economic scheme of things. They played out their lives together in the "spit," sex, liquor, drugs, violence, and games of chance; even "foreigners" (whites seeking entertainment) would come and pay to see these acts but deny them any value when they returned home. Donald was often fascinated by the pomp, ritual, and ceremony of his customers on their public stages: the "high yellow" with their "good hair" and their private club, the "high society" and their favorite grill, the Friday night "big spenders" who were broke on Sunday, the flesh merchants, and the dream peddlers. The nucleus of this drama was Fullerton and Wylie Streets, which were later eliminated by urban redevelopment. After all, it was only a waste-land, a slum, an area of blight too close to the city's economic center—downtown Pittsburgh. So Donald's world was destroyed along with his house. He took his savings and contributed to a down payment on a house in the East End for his parents and his siblings. He was an unwitting part of an economic process that created urban deserts, forced people to invest in them, coerced residents to live in them, blamed African Americans for their existence, and then destroyed these homelands when it became profitable to do so.

Furthermore, as mentioned previously, Donald had extensive periodical sales routes in residential areas as well as along the commercial avenues. His job took him into the homes and social networks of his many residential customers, where he learned how they lived. Because many of them required credit even for such inexpensive items as newspapers, he also learned about their problems. Over a four-year period he became a familiar face; many customers became fond of him and demonstrated their affection with Christmas bonuses.

Many credit customers' payments were collected at their local bars, gambling haunts, or barbershop hangouts. To other customers, he loaned money for ciga-rettes, the numbers (lottery), milk, or beer, to be collected with their newspaper payments. Thus Donald was more than a paperboy; he was absorbed into the poor Black subcultural process, and as he recalled the experiences, one could believe that he liked it.

However, Donald stresses that his experience was not an isolated one. Many other boys participated in such lifestyles. Shoeshine boys with their homemade boxes traveled the same routes and competed for the limited money there. Other newspaper boys often raced him to a particular bar to hawk the same wares. Some boys combed the area to beg or roll the drunks or rob other young peddlers. Donald marveled that in all his years of roaming dark streets, alleys, corridors, and tene-ments, he was never robbed or molested. He consistently carried large amounts of coins and dollar bills without incident. For him, the dangers of the ghetto were never realized.

Donald's success as a newsboy brought him to the attention of Mrs. Robert L. Vann, president of the *Pittsburgh Courier*, which he sold among other periodicals (see *Pittsburgh Courier* 1947, 1954). Mrs. Vann made contacts with university officials and social agencies in Pittsburgh to secure him a scholarship to the uni-versity. He graduated with an A.B. degree. Donald's newspaper route supervisor and mentor made contacts in the periodical business world to secure him a whole-sale periodical distribution franchise. Donald expanded that franchise into a larger enterprise until he felt that the business had no further growth potential. Then he sold the business and returned to the university to continue his graduate studies.

Donald in Adulthood

As an older Ph.D. graduate student returning to the university at the age of thirty-three after operating a wholesale periodical business for fifteen years, I was especially stressed by the new lifestyle and my fellow students. Some of the students had earned master's degrees in anthropology, and I had no training in the discipline, for my A.B. (earned at age twenty two) was in economics. My fellow students and some of the faculty were younger than I, and all of them were white. I was Black.

One of the devices I used to cope with this new way of life and the tensions that accompanied it was to keep a notebook and a diary of my experiences. This account is based on those documents.

The department of my graduate study was controlled by men who had made their mark in the profession and in general academic circles. They had the power to make or break young scholars in the profession and, of course, the power to determine whether graduate students would continue. I soon began to realize that these men were very conservative and that I should avoid any controversial discussions with them that would reveal too much about myself. My fellow graduate students had warned me that I could create immediate hostility by revealing that I was sympathetic to Catholicism, Marxism, student rebellion, or antiestablishment change. This was especially true for me because I was the first and only Black in the graduate program of the department. I was advised to be very respectful and to accentuate my role as a student since I was older than most of the others. Later I learned about the unfortunate fate of those who were not sensitive to these admonitions. I was warned that the power elite in my department attempted to mask that power by appearing very protective of the female faculty and staff in the department. The message was clear. If I wanted to graduate from that department, I must learn how to "stay in my place."

The chair of the department was also a victim of the "power elite." He was chair in name only and was allowed to "push the bureaucratic papers." He was deprived of most of the authority of the position by the close working relationship that the power elite had with members of the higher administration. As a result of this dilemma, the chair was constantly attempting to clarify and fortify his position and role by creating rules and regulations. One set of those regulations caused me to act.

I had matriculated into the department under regulations stipulating that after the completion of a series of core courses, I would be advanced to the doctoral candidacy stage. Later, some of the "elite" professors who refused to teach such courses decided they would establish a set of preliminary examinations that covered all the important areas of the discipline. Each graduate student was required to pass these examinations instead of the core courses. I complained that such a regulation should not be retroactive and include students such as I who had come to the department under the core course regulation and who, indeed, had completed some of those requirements. My discussions with the faculty and the chair brought no relief, so I made an appointment to discuss the problem with the provost of the university. The provost promised me that he would investigate the matter and inform me of the proposed remedy. I never heard from him again. I was called into the chair's office, reprimanded for having seen the provost, and given the choice of following the new regulations or leaving the department. I chose to stay and spent many months attempting to persuade the chair and the power elite that I was not really a troublemaker.

Some of the faculty in our department had married upper-class women who were not disposed to be gracious to their husbands' students. These faculty would invite graduate students to their homes for social and academic occasions. I had to learn to tolerate the wives' attitudes, values, and comments about Blacks in America as yet another requirement of my graduate education.

As relationships with the families of faculty continued to develop, I learned that insensitivity from wives was only the beginning. My status among faculty children and other kin and even pets was often ambiguous. To have children who were my own children's (three sons) age address me by my abbreviated first name was disconcerting to me. I am often reminded of my graduate student experiences when I observe how the offspring of dominant parents among social animals treat the subordinate members of their group. In my household I felt in control of the family pets. In the households of certain professors, I felt that the family pets were in control of me. I am not yet convinced that my faculty did not enjoy the process of subordination I discuss below.

I will never forget how shocked two of my faculty were when I passed my comprehensive examinations on Africa. The senior member of the examination committee was the most powerful faculty member in our department. He was a Connecticut-born Yankee and an internationally known elitist. The two junior faculty members were sycophants of the senior member, who was an internationally recognized expert on Africa, and they could not effectively oppose his assessment of my examination. So they were anxiously awaiting the examination committee meeting to discover what he would say. For years he had developed a reputation for discriminating against women, Catholics, and Jews. He considered Blacks so "disadvantaged" that they did not deserve his attention. The junior members, who supported me, feared he would dismiss my examination without a fair evaluation. They knew that I was sensitive to discrimination and prone to act to defend myself. As the examinee, I was stressed by all of these factors as well as by the examination itself and the known history of the difficult comprehensive examinations given by the senior member of the committee for many years at another elite university. My department included faculty members who had taken their examinations from him, and they knew fellow students who had failed them. For years I had been told about these famous and "impossible" exams. To the surprise of the junior committee members, however, the senior member voted a strong pass for my examination. Why were they surprised? As a reader, you might be able to guess; I have several explanations; none of them reassures me.

The same senior faculty member had caused me some anguish in a seminar course. He, as most of my faculty, believed that my race and my "disadvantaged" background would not allow me to excel in my graduate work. They felt that if I worked very hard I could pass my courses, but none of them expected me to become a major scholar. Unfortunately, most of the fellow students whom they did expect to excel disappointed them. It became clear to me after only one semester that most of the faculty would rationalize one reason or another why my work was not excellent, regardless of its actual quality. In one course with a particular senior faculty member, all of the graduate students were trying to impress him because we realized that he could make or break graduate students if he chose. Each of us was required to present four oral reports in the seminar. I made a special effort to research well the four scholars that I had selected for my reports. This was my opportunity to use my age and the speech experience I had gained in the business world. I presented four rousing reports, and the professor and students reacted with enthusiasm. My final grade in the course, however, was not a reflection of these reports. Against the advice of my fellow students and some other faculty members, I went to the professor and questioned him about my grade. His response was that some of my reports were excellent but that some were not as good as others. Baffled by his comments, I continued to pursue the issue with others until I discovered that my fellow students and the professor had allowed me to choose two scholars (Ruth Benedict and Margaret Mead) that the professor held in contempt. No one had warned me that the only way I could do a favorably received report about them was to discredit their work in its entirety. The balanced reports I had attempted did not fulfill that requirement.

In another course a junior faculty member recorded a final grade for me that I felt was below what I had actually earned. I visited him and discussed my work. He advised me that my problem had been the final examination, which he had not returned for me to review. I requested my examination to determine why I had not done as well as I believed I would. After a thorough review of the examination, I discovered that he had not returned all the pages to me. I visited him again and requested the missing pages. He responded that there were no missing pages. That was the complete examination as he had received it. I asked him to review the pages with me to determine that the writing itself revealed that some answers were unreasonably abbreviated without the missing pages. He promised to look for the missing pages. A few days later, he called me to say that he had found the missing pages and that my grade would be changed to an A.

Another senior professor recorded a final grade of B+ for me in a seminar in which I thought I had earned an A. In fact, I had received an A in the only written assignment for the course, and on that paper the professor had written comments that suggested he was very impressed with my work. I visited the professor to discuss the grade, and he informed me that he would have given me an A if I had compared the society I had researched with another society. This would have given my work a comparative framework. I reminded him that nowhere in the requirements of his assignments to the class was there any indication that the students should work within a comparative framework. He responded that since our discipline was a comparative one, all graduate students should know that this was the way to proceed. The B+ would be recorded as a B because of the limitations of the recording system. I lost that battle as well as many others.

Many senior professors encouraged confrontational learning in their seminars. So the "best and brightest" students earned their grades and relationships with the professor by demolishing other students' ideas and class presentations. I was often the target of these humiliating attacks. On one such occasion, my attacker was so aggressive that another female student, full of indignation at what seemed excessive criticism, came to my defense. She supported my thesis with evidence that was unknown to me and silenced my attacker with ten minutes of rebuttal that I will never forget. My defender was Lebanese, and although we had no personal relationship, she was sensitive to abuse in any form. She found the environment intolerable and left to complete her graduate work at an Ivy League university.

Many of my professors had experienced tortured humiliations in their own graduate schools. Some of them had been converted to believe that the pain and suffering were just another rite of passage that their own students would experience to test their endurance and a part of the professional initiation. Being older and Black had already exposed me to enough pain and suffering. Believing that intelligent behavior was reasonable, I had many adjustments to make to the senseless cruelty of academic life. Some professors seemed to enjoy demolishing a paper that one had spent several months researching and writing. The final advice was "now rewrite it with my strictures in mind." I was often amazed that the paper could be demolished again after one had followed all of the instructions carefully. This time, on a second reading, the professor discovered flaws he had overlooked during the first reading. This process can be endless, especially if it involves a chapter in a larger thesis. For a Black who already feels persecuted, it can be difficult to appreciate that this process may make his work better. It is especially difficult to believe that this is the professor's motivation.

My final comments are for the ubiquitous cocktail parties to which the graduate student is often the reluctant invitee. Many professors invited the graduate students instead of hiring servants or having an affair catered. They expected us to come early to help prepare and to remain late to clean. They pretended to be doing most of the work themselves and even expected us to be grateful for the privilege of mingling with their "distinguished" guests. Cocktail parties were held for new faculty, departing faculty, interviewing faculty, faculty on external evaluation teams, and visiting faculty. They were held to reciprocate, cheaply, all of the dinner parties the hosts had attended. They were held when a new chair took office and for the old chair when he left office. They were held for holidays, birthdays, retirements, to Thank God It's Fridays, or just for a change of pace.

Most cocktail parties are similar and require no description here. My reason for discussing them is to describe my personal feelings on these occasions in order to reflect on my reactions in many group contexts of my graduate school experience.

In a group, conversations were usually directed to someone other than me, and people would often position themselves to avoid eye contact with me. It seemed that I was not expected to speak, and when I did, it was frequently as if I had not spoken, because the conversation continued without reference to what I had contributed. If we were standing, I had constantly to reposition myself as the movements of others, leaving and returning, tended to exclude me from the group.

For a long period, I felt that these cocktail parties were simply torture chambers. I was obliged to be friendly and talkative when no one seemed interested in talking to me. When I approached people who were talking to each other just to listen unobtrusively and to wait to see if they would include me, their body kinesis seemed designed to exclude me. I moved from one scene of rejection to the next until most people were relaxed from their drinks and only then willing to include me. Even late in the evening, I could be abruptly disillusioned when I wholeheartedly welcomed someone to my conversation, sensitive to my own recent rejection, only to have them communicate that they had walked over to talk to another person in the group. Last, when my wounds were just about healed, my hosting professor or his wife would communicate that I had stayed too long.

These cocktail parties are examples of social gatherings where some insecure people attempt to reach and maintain their mythological social levels. Their ubiquitous inferiority complexes coerce them to repel any symbol of perceived inferiority.

I have survived all of this. Perhaps I am stronger because of it. I am grateful for the strength since my profession and my society seldom allow me to forget that I am Black.

ANOTHER QUEST

The documentary approach causes discomfort among anthropologists who see in the discipline's past an all-too-frequent tendency to adopt a colonialist attitude toward "exotic" others or, in the words of one young visual anthropologist, "the dark, the naked, the breasted and the feathered." (Raymond 1991:A5)

The human inferiority complex that I have struggled with personally, professionally, and anthropologically is difficult to observe or describe. This chapter will narrate the personal relationships of another anthropology professor whose inferiority complex may become so clear as to ease some of the difficulty of description.

This is the story of Aud Procterman. As I have stated, many of those who enter the profession of anthropology seem to have a more severe inferiority complex than others. They seek to study people who are "inferior" to themselves. They enjoy associating with such people in a professional role that precludes contamination by these "inferiors." Cultural and social anthropologists enjoy the company of human "inferiors" who are the objects of their scholarly interest. Procterman had an unusual inferiority complex even for an anthropologist.

Procterman was reared in Brooklyn, New York, by Jewish parents who immigrated there from the Soviet Union. He had one older brother, and his father worked as a skilled tradesman. The family was poor, and the parents often argued about financial matters. These arguments contributed to Procterman's feelings that he was not loved by either parent but was merely a pawn who was frequently used in their disputes. For example, Procterman says that he was accepted into a prestigious art school with tuition assistance after he graduated from high school. His father protested that to attend would be a waste of family resources. He insisted that Procterman join the work force and provide some income to the household, but the mother was firm: Procterman would continue his education. The disagreement was not that the mother placed such a high value on her son's education, but, as Procterman says, "It was that she hated my father and that was her way of torturing him." Procterman's father was, indeed, tortured as he watched his unemployed son engaged in art projects that required his own earnings to be spent on art supplies. Procterman claims that his mother enjoyed this torture, and as I listened to Procterman recall the experiences, he seemed to enjoy the torture as well. What he seemed especially to enjoy were the tactics his mother devised to "get at" his father. She was a strategist in torture. He was an unloved child who seemed to be fascinated to be a pawn in his father's misery.

After graduation Procterman drove a bakery delivery truck over a large area of the state of New York. His artistic abilities were not sufficient to earn a living. He recalled how the long hours and the tedium of that job taxed his endurance. For him, the occupation was inferior, but he persevered as he has done most of his life. He married a Scottish woman (in three "marriages" he has never married a Jew) and released his frustrations on her by engaging in dangerous camping expeditions with her in areas where wild bears were common. He would recall with pleasure how the bears would enter his camps and tents and threaten their lives. He tested this member of a "superior" race until they were divorced.

Procterman decided to improve his life chances and escape his job by continuing his education. He matriculated at an elite university as a graduate student in anthropology. He was not considered a good student and was reported to develop catastrophes in his personal life whenever he had academic deadlines. He had difficulties passing his examinations and had a reputation for not enjoying the company of other students. Soon the students began to refer to him as "Murphy's madness" and "Murphy's mistake" because Murphy was his advisor and no one could understand why or how Procterman could remain at the university with such performances. But he persevered and finally passed his examinations after more than one attempt. Then he went off to the field in West Africa to rid himself of his "superiors" and to enjoy the company of his "inferiors."

Procterman's fieldwork consisted primarily of inviting men to his home in a city and interviewing them. Even in the field, Procterman avoided prolonged contamination with the "inferior." He did not do his research in the bush, as most anthropologists in Africa do. While there, Procterman met another anthropologist from the United States. She was an African American who assisted him with his fieldwork. They married and had two children. On a trip back to the United States when she was pregnant with their second child, Procterman informed her that he could never allow his mother to meet her because she was Black. He chose to torture the bride rather than have his mother torture him. They divorced and went their separate ways. She discovered that her career was delayed and negatively affected as a single parent abandoned at such a crucial moment. Procterman did not see or support his abandoned family.

Back in the United States, Procterman began his teaching career at Piltdown University as a single man. He claimed three areas of expertise: social structure because his department was dominated by Bigbabb (a world-renowned anthropologist) and this was Bigbabb's theoretical area; urbanization because he had done his fieldwork in a city; and "primitive art" because he had studied art and "primitives." Procterman was promoted to associate professor with tenure in 1967, supposedly aided by spreading rumors about his Jewish "rival" (a social anthropologist), namely, that his rival was teaching that Bigbabb's theoretical orientation was faulty and that the rival was performing poorly in the department's required experimental course. Procterman was also aided in his bid for tenure because he was bowing to every whim and directive of Bigbabb. This was in spite of Bigbabb's history as an anti-Semite, including membership in several clubs that prohibited Jewish membership. Bigbabb insisted on calling Procterman's Jewish rival a "New York Jew," notwithstanding the many times that he was told that this colleague had been reared in Connecticut where Bigbabb himself had been born and reared. Bigbabb believed that Jews were inferior, especially New York Jews. He called Procterman's research and his book "claptrap." (Another distinguished, more gracious departmental professor and friend of Bigbabb called it "journalism.") Bigbabb was oppressive to colleagues and to graduate students, but to Procterman, who always supported him, he was an academic pater who tortured "inferior" people.

As soon as Procterman became a full professor and chair, his expertise changed from social structure to social stratification. He was beginning to oppose being dominated. Notwithstanding his lack of research among African Americans and his failure to list African Americans as one of his areas of expertise, Procterman began to teach and behave as if he was an expert on "Negroes in the New World." His best friend was Black, and the only Black graduate student in the department was his advisee. Procterman dated Black women and considered himself an expert on Blacks at a time when such expertise was valued in the university where Black student revolts were common in the late 1960s.

These behaviors changed too when Procterman became a full professor and chair. Procterman had a hostile separation from his Black friend. He ceased to date African-American women, and he lost interest in his Black graduate student. He began to date a German-American graduate student in anthropology, the daughter of a wealthy "old" family. They married and traveled worldwide on "departmental business" and reportedly at departmental expense. At the wedding site, the home of the bride's parents, Procterman, leading a line of cars containing his anthropology colleagues, drove over the large lawn of the estate in a rite of degradation that was costly to the parents.

In the department, he began to recruit exclusively from "the best anthropology department in the world," where he had graduated. He assumed, erroneously, that as fellow alumni these recruits would support him. He also assumed, erroneously, that as a full professor and chair he could begin to dominate the department, notwithstanding the presence and power of Bigbabb. His newly found status made him overconfident. He ceased to associate with the socially "inferior" and began to identify ambivalently with the socially "superior." But his newly found status made him overconfident.

This overconfidence led to Procterman's ouster from the chair after two years and some months. He had begun to be less sensitive to Bigbabb's wishes and to those of his other colleagues. Some of these colleagues were quantitative anthropologists who represented a threat to the humanist anthropologists within the department. Procterman was considered a humanist anthropologist. He waited too long to accommodate one of them, Robustus, the recently appointed distinguished professor, with a new office. He attempted to seduce another from Bigbabb's research into his own project. Ultimately, he was trying to ease Bigbabb into retirement. All of these factors enabled some hostile departmental faculty members to maneuver him into declaring that he would resign. He thought that no one would offer to replace him because he had just arranged for the most eligible person to receive a free vacation. After Procterman announced his resignation, an acting chair was assigned, and the most eligible person agreed to accept the position at a later date, notwithstanding the vacation.

Few understood the personal impact of this upon Procterman. With his deep-seated inferiority complex he had struggled to prove that he was "superior." He published a reputable book on his African research. He maneuvered his way into an early promotion to full professor by serving Bigbabb. He was the chair of one of the major anthropology departments in the world, one that could boast of having three past presidents of the American Anthropological Association on its faculty simultaneously. He had married a wealthy graduate student from a Revolutionary War family, and he had purchased a grand house in one of the exclusive areas where academics and professionals resided. As one of his close friends and colleagues described him after he threatened to call the police on a friend's graduate student about overdue library books, "He was drunk with power." Of course, this was a graduate student whom Bigbabb had found wanting. Now Procterman was ousted from the chair. He could not write and publish because of his despair. He could not rise in academic administration because he had failed at administration. He had a young wife who had married him because of his prominence, which was now fading. He was distraught.

As his pain grew old, he attempted to salvage his reputation by becoming a connoisseur of foods, African art, and wines. With his background in art, he tried to be a gentleman and a scholar. He gave dinner parties for distinguished scholars, athletes, and community leaders. But without any recent publishing feats, his behavior became a source of amusement in his department. This period was aggravated by the presence of his young children, whom he tortured in response to his own pain. He had a habit of pinching the babies until they burst into cries and their mother would rush into the room and complain about these acts. She knew what had happened because of his history with them. This was a painful period for his household.

One of the benefits of all this was Procterman's renewed interest in his Black graduate student. Procterman had more time to supervise. It demonstrated to his wife that he yet had some academic authority. The student had continued to collect his data and was beginning to write his dissertation. Procterman had more time and interest in the work now, in spite of not being impressed with the student or his work. He had collected him during a period when it was fashionable to have a Black student. He had tortured the student as he must have been tortured during his own graduate student days. He would make promises to the student and later claim that he did not remember them. He would allow his sharp-clawed cat to climb over the student's lap, digging its claws into his skin and laugh when the student responded to the pain. The student did not dare to dispatch the cat or cease to return to Procterman's home for the torture. Procterman would tell the student that the cat was "mean" and that was why he enjoyed her. He would return dissertation chapters that had been revised according to his directions with new directives that contradicted the old. He behaved as if the student would never be able to complete the work. The student believed him. Procterman had lost confidence in himself as a scholar, and he was projecting this onto the student.

Something occurred to break this impasse. The student took one of his dissertation chapters to an anthropological conference. The audience was very responsive. In the audience was an editor of an anthropological journal. He requested the chapter for his journal. Procterman had published in this same journal, and the editor conferred with Procterman to get his approval. Procterman was ecstatic. Anthropology was giving him approval through his student. He assisted the student to prepare the manuscript for publication. He worked with the student until the dissertation was completed, and he sought out his own book publisher to review the dissertation for publishing in revised form. The publisher accepted with some major revisions. The student was ecstatic.

During this period of renewed interest in the student's work after it had been validated elsewhere, Procterman and the student spent many hours together working and relaxing. They became close friends, and the student became close to Procterman's wife and children. After the manuscript had been accepted for publication, Procterman told the student that the student's career would soar after the book was published. He seemed to be happy for himself and the student. After the book was published, he gave a large party at his home for the student and invited those whom he held in high esteem. The party was obviously as much for Procterman as for the student. Procterman believed that this disadvantaged Black student had succeeded beyond most other students in the department because he had Procterman as his major advisor.

Later, when Procterman had calmed, he changed his perspective about the future of the student. He told him that he should be satisfied with his present position at a small college, especially since he would one day be chair of the very small department there. Procterman was reevaluating what he desired for his student, but the student did not accept the message.

Approximately one year later, Procterman's university called his student and told him they wanted to consider him for a position in the anthropology department. This was a major shock to Procterman. His student was considering joining his own department. During the following weeks, Procterman never seemed enthusiastic about this development, but he did not display hostility until the final hour.

By this time, quantitative and humanist factions had been in close combat in the department for almost three years. A major question, now, was whether the quantitative faction was going to accept a student of Procterman, a humanist. This would mean another vote for the humanists in the department. The leader of the quantitative faction, Robustus, was to evaluate the student and report back to his quantitative colleagues. The chair of the department arranged for a meeting, in which the student won the admiration and quelled the fears of the leader. To the student, all was ready for the vote. On the night before the vote, Procterman surprised his protégé by announcing, "I will not lift a finger to help you." Procterman was angered by how little his help had been needed and by the support from the other faction. The student panicked and called his humanist supporters for fear that Procterman would attempt to rally the vote against him. They reassured the student that he had their support, but they were worried that opposition from Procterman would "open the door" for other hostile expressions. No one could explain Procterman's behavior to the student's satisfaction.

The vote passed, and the student entered the department as a nontenured associate professor. Procterman immediately began to behave as if he had done nothing unreasonable. On the contrary, he announced, without consulting the student, that they would be team-teaching a course together. Procterman's attitude seemed to be, "As long as you win, it is because you are my student and my client, but if you fail, you have lost a good battle and that is fine with me too." This egocentric position is, paradoxically, one that is frequently taken by those with severe inferiority complexes. The student tactfully declined the invitation to team-teach the course and taught his own courses. He also maintained good relationships with his quantitative colleagues, to the chagrin of Procterman. The student was maintaining support for tenure in two years, and he needed the votes of the quantitative members. Procterman never complained about his student's behavior, and he had plenty of opportunities because the student visited Procterman's home two or three times a week. The student continued to be grateful for Procterman's assistance and continued to need his support.

Yet, approximately two years later, Procterman voted against the tenure of his student without ever giving any indication that he would. For the first year of this period, the student had been away as a distinguished visiting professor at another university. He had returned and continued to maintain good relationships with his colleagues.

On the day of the departmental tenure vote, the student learned that he had one negative vote—Procterman's. He went to Procterman's house in disbelief. Procterman and his wife were waiting in anticipation. They both attempted to explain that the student had enough votes to get tenure in any case. Procterman's vote was supposedly a strategic maneuver to help the next candidate for tenure avoid comparison with a recent unanimous affirmative vote. That candidate had asked Procterman to lead her through the process. Procterman knew that she could not get all of the votes of the quantitative faculty. He claimed that he was protecting her with his negative vote for his student. Was he?

I do not believe that he was. Once again, Procterman was angry that his client did not need him. He was convinced that if the student did not need him, then the student had no basis to care about him. How could he be the student's patron if the client continually proved that he did not need him? In the heat of the discussion, he even told the student that if one member of the quantitative faction (whom he especially hated) "had voted against you, I would have voted for you." When everybody voted for the student, Procterman saw himself as insignificant, and he struck out against the student-client who had allowed this revelation. After all of this, Procterman still tried to convince the student that he was a decent human being: "Do you have any doubt that the university is going to give you tenure? I don't!" Even while the decision was being debated at the higher university level, Procterman was allegedly spreading the rumor that he, not the student, had written the student's book. This was reportedly discussed at the university tenure review meetings. All during this period, Procterman and his wife were pretending to be friends of the student.

Even if Procterman had voted no for the reasons he offered, the vote was unethical and unprofessional. A tenure vote is one of the most important votes in a professor's life. It is a vote on one's scholarly achievements and prospects and not a vote for the voter's political agenda. This should have been especially true for Procterman, who constantly proclaimed his ethics, honesty, and professionalism to anyone who would listen.

While Procterman was a departmental colleague of the student, he never entered his student's office. They were friends during all of this period, but Procterman never came in and sat to talk. There were other faculty who never entered that "polluted" office, but the student understood their behavior. He was Black, a junior member of the faculty, and doing research on African Americans. He was supposed to be avoided and especially not given the deference of being approached, but Procterman was his friend, his major advisor, his mentor, his patron, and, ironically, someone who wanted him to fail if he did not succeed by Procterman's assistance. Over the years, the student's office was ritually purified by the frequent gatherings of senior and distinguished colleagues. In all those years, Procterman never came in to sit and talk. Even when the student invited Procterman and his wife to the student's home with other guests for dinner, Procterman attempted to dominate the affair by lecturing the student on how the drinks should be served. Later, the other guests commented on Procterman's odd behavior.

Finally, the year the student (now a tenured associate professor) left the university, Procterman voted against his promotion to full professor in a vote that was in response to an offer of full professorship from another major research university. The student departed. Procterman never explained that vote. Perhaps there was no need. Years later, Procterman commented to a fellow advisee and mentor of the student about the student's continuing success: "We created a monster." The fellow advisee attempted to explain to Procterman that the student had entered graduate school at a mature age and was already "created" when they got him. A Black student who went further than Procterman was surely a monster; for once again, Procterman discovered his own feelings of inferiority documented and reinforced.

At one point, the student had been seduced into believing that there was a real friendship between him and Procterman, but Procterman was not capable of having a friend, a wife, or children who were African American. His inferiority complex was too severe. He had spent most of his life trying to become less inferior, and his student and others continued to document that he had failed. It is not the inferiority complex itself that is so devastating in this case, although I have stated that this complex leaves its devastation everywhere (Williams 1992a, 1992b). It is the drive (e.g., in Hitler, Stalin, Nixon, and Napoleon) to "wipe out that damned spot" with the lives of other people that was the terrible affliction of Procterman. Unfortunately, there are many others like him in academia.

Procterman's student did not understand that just as the loyal soldier is expected to die if necessary without questioning the general, the cause, or the command, the pathological patron expects the loyal client's support regardless of the personal consequences to the client. This kind of patron cannot tolerate an "inferior" client questioning his judgment or his motives. The patron, like the general, must be right because he is "superior." As all of the soldiers who have died in lost, forgotten, and erroneous causes, the client will be out of sight and out of mind when and if the patron realizes his folly. Generals, like despots and pathological patrons, expect the destruction of lives to achieve their own successes. They have little doubt about the respective values. The value of "inferior" people is well understood by those who exploit them. What is power if not the capacity to decide your "inferior's" fate? Any "inferior" who grows to challenge his "superior's" power has, indeed, become a monster to him.

Somehow Procterman's student had never learned how to be an appropriate "inferior" for Procterman. Procterman never realized that the student was not challenging his status or his authority. The student just did not understand Procterman's kind of patronage—the kind that Procterman had learned from his mother, from his own graduate student experiences, and from his years as a close observer and sycophant of Bigbabb. Procterman was fulfilling his societal role— showing the student where a Black's "place" was located in the academy.

I emphasize the example format of the descriptions in this chapter. The pervasive feelings of inferiority are one of the fundamental problems of our time. These feelings make the rich, powerful, educated, famous, and exalted insecure with all their privilege, entitlement, and empowerment. The wealthy greedily reach for more. Great scholars seldom believe they are great enough. They plagiarize material, falsify scientific data, undermine their colleagues, and envy their scholarly awards. Jealousy runs rampant in the halls of the rich, powerful, and famous. I have met many "great" men and women, and none of them have felt they were great enough. None of them had the capacity of personal security to be comfortable in association with those perceived to be inferior. No amount of upward mobility seems to make people comfortable with their inadequacies as well as with those of others. No amount of personal aggrandizement and embellishment allows them to accept their animal selves and those of all their species and kingdom.

As Baritz (1988:318) observes:

Freed from civilization's shall-nots and from poverty's constraints, the new Americans, especially those born in the late Forties and Fifties, may now enjoy the perquisites of status and liberation from the obligations and limitations imposed by love. While a rose, an infant or a sonata does not produce advantageous cost-benefit ratios, this cold new world evidently does. Although extreme individualism necessarily shades into isolation, although a hypertrophied rationalism must become callous, although commodity fetishism can never be satisfied, all nevertheless apparently justify the abandonment of place and intimacy. The cost of success, then, is a redefinition of pleasure and thus also of pain. The fathers knew there was risk and pain in love and life. Fleeing this human adventure, the children calculated their progress toward a better life—the contemplation of all that success may produce, life as work, the happiness produced by objects, the envy of strangers and the freedom to float above the struggles of others, in warmth and comfort, alone.

Chapter 3

The Domestication of Human Insecurity

My studies of the "genuine" African American who denies, defies, and defiles American values (DDDAV, pronounced "did-did-dav") have culminated in my concept of DDDAK (pronounced "did-did-dac"; see Williams 1990, 1992a) for humankind. These have been adaptive human emotions. Since the beginning of human culture, humans have denied, defied, and defiled their animal kinship. That energy and that vector created culture and, eventually, modernity. But the technological sophistications of modernity no longer permit this approach to humanness. They threaten the endangered Earth. DDDAK is the human (with his/her unique perceptive ability) response (including fear) to his/her animal heritage and destiny (death). Humans fear what they are (animals) and what may happen to them—hunger, violence, homelessness, meaninglessness, loneliness, illness and death. Thus humans substitute myth (including superiority) and power (to enforce and validate myth) for their history, their present, and their future. Superiority requires comparisons and contrasts (see Veblen 1987), so humans create "inferior" ("lower") animals and "inferior" people (classism, racism, ethnocentrism, sexism, sectarianism, ageism, nationalism, and speciesism, CRESSANS. (Williams 1992b:4)

I argue that you cannot fundamentally lift the status and well-being of your social "inferiors" in a society founded and built on inequality without undermining the old structure of the society itself. Fundamental change such as that requires a new social foundation for the society. If you would transform the social inferiority paradigm that permeates the society's superstructure, you must lay a new social foundation. DDDAK must be replaced with a fundamental respect for life and Earth. So all of the piecemeal efforts to treat the symptoms—sex education, condom distribution, sexual license, body exposures, Ruth Westheimer, explicit media sex, and homosexual spouses and families—will merely create social dislocations in a defunct social system. The Ecological Revolution is the globalization that is the planet's manifest destiny. But to the extent that it is a mixture of actuality, idealization, and illusion, the Ecological Revolution is also mythology.

INTRODUCTION

Globalization (complex relationships between national societies, individual selves, the international system of societies, and human nature; after Robertson 1992), world systems theory, and ecological sanity require social scientists to understand, explain, treat, and transform human divisiveness. I argue that human divisiveness is a fundamental characteristic of human culture and cognition whose adaptive value is diminished and defeated in a world-system (non-Marxist) formation and world ecosystems deformation (Cartmill 1993, Smedley 1993, and Thomas 1983). It is the central social problem of our time (see Baumeister 1993).

If humans are to approach an imagined world community as a utopian reality, they must understand and treat human divisiveness. As human divisiveness is a component of the existing malleable human nature, such an attempt at resolution requires a conception of a new universal culture (in contrast to a globalization of locality).

Human perceptions of humans originated and developed within the contexts of "lower" animals and plants. Being animals themselves, humans focused on "lower" animals to develop and form their own identity. I discuss three aspects of that struggle for hegemony: sex, death, and digestion in man, a Janus-faced animal (Koestler 1978) who has the mark of the beast and a mind that contemplates God.

As humans distinguished themselves from "lower" animals, they disdained animal characteristics wherever they discovered them (Parker et al. 1994). Freud 1949 and elsewhere) has treated the human struggle for separate animal identity under the yoke of sexual instincts and reproduction. This book represents another effort to suggest an explanation for the origins of culture. That origin will help to explain who we humans are and where we are going.

A fundamental issue of human origins is the distinction between human nature and human culture: Does the cultural process form and constitute human nature, or does it regulate an innate, panhuman, and universal animal that is human? Cultural idealists and materialists of the Hegelian and Marxist schools have usually joined with empiricists such as Locke and Hume, and social behaviorists such as George Mead, in supporting the first position. But from Plato throughout medieval and modern times, others have "contended that an ontological or metaphysical knowledge of human nature is possible and that there are innate factors of mental structure and function which are not derived from experience and culture"(Bidney 1964:154).

THE DENIAL OF THE SPECIES

No other animal except humans has incest rules, adultery, and "inferior" populations. Freud attempted to analyze the nature of the human animal and to disclose the basis of human anxieties. He contributed much to the development of that body of knowledge. But Freud emphasized human sexuality and aggression (see Laqueur 1990). I will expand my own explanations to include the entire human animal. Freud focused his discussions of human anxiety on the terrors of animal sexuality, especially among children (Oedipus complex). I attempt to broaden the discussions to include the terrors humans have of their close kinship to other animals and other "inferior" humans (Stannard 1993). Myrdal (1969:103,1078) illustrates the point (see also Blumer 1958):

In drawing a parallel between the position of, and feeling toward, women and Negroes we are uncovering a *fundamental basis of our culture* [emphasis mine].

We are not under any obligation, of course, to extend civil courtesies, equal justice, suffrage, and fair competition to animals, however much we love them. Kind treatment of animals is not a "right" of theirs but is rather construed as an obligation to our own humane feelings and to those of our equals. In so far as the Negro can be placed lower in the biological order than the white man and nearer to the animals, he is also, to an extent, kept outside the white man's social and moral order. The white man's entire system of discrimination is then in no need of moral defense. The Negro becomes deprived of the "natural rights of man," and will, instead, have his protection in the civil kindness toward inferior and dependent beings, which behooves a Christian society. He will be asked not to insist on "rights" but to pray for favors.

[This was] the thought of the older South—the sincere and passionate belief that somewhere between men and cattle, God created a tertium quid, and called it a Negro—a clownish simple creature, at times even lovable within its limitations, but straitly foreordained to walk within the Veil. To be sure, behind the thought lurks the afterthought—some of them with favoring chance might become men, but in sheer self-defense we dare not let them, and we build about them walls so high, and hang between them and the light a veil so thick, that they shall not even think of breaking through.

Another analogy may be found in the status of women and children. They, too, were— in a considerable measure—wards of the adult males, particularly in the period when the race dogma was being built up. They did not enjoy "equal rights" but had to rely for their protection upon kindly considerations from their superiors. Their status was also partly explained and justified by biological inferiority or lack of maturity. The Negro can be classified as nearer the animal but still a man, although not a mature man. Unlike children, he can be assumed never to grow to full maturity. Not only the individual Negro but the Negro race as a whole can be said to be "undeveloped" and "childish."

Race is a "scientific" expression of DDDAK (see Shipman 1994). The Civil Rights Movement represents decades of unequal tensions between the conscience of power and the power of conscience. "Inferiors" continue to pay a debt they have never owed (Ryan 1971). Even in scholarship, "inferior" (Black) social scientists and those African Americans in the humanities tend to research and teach about "inferior" (non-white) people (Williams 1992b). After Emancipation, "scientific" inferiority (race) replaced structural inferiority. Some African Americans respond with the following.

Social distance is a pervasive characteristic of social organization in the United States. So one feature of the poor Black subculture, where mobility is rare, is the effective control of disruptive levels of social distance within groups that tend to cohere and persist. Zion (a church group, see chap. 4) is one of these groups, but there are others surrounding Zion, and their style is different at some levels.

In Zion, orality is flaunted in the form of food symbols, reference to the mouth, and the blatant exercise of verbal expression during worship. Testimonies, prophecies, speaking in tongues, the holy kiss, and the constant refrain during sermons are a consistent exercise in orality. Such exercise effectively disavows the standards of poise, dignity, and composure that characterize middle-class behavior, especially during worship.

This defiant behavior (against mainstream values) is also evident in the members' movements during religious services: running, hollering, screaming, jumping, waving arms and hands, dancing, and violent shaking during spiritual possession. This, too, totally disregards mainstream standards of behavior within or outside church. These patterns of behavior are not incidental features of Zion; on the contrary, they are a cherished design of this group. They are meaningful instruments of solidarity. They defy mainstream standards of approved religious conduct and defile the very conception of religion held by most socially mobile Americans. Relative to other groups in the ghetto, Zion is restricted in the range of signs and symbols it can organize, utilize, and manipulate, but those at its disposal are intensively exploited.

This defiant behavior is not exclusive to Zion but is the behavior of the Black ghetto within which it exists (Powdermaker 1939). Any discussion of the alternative groups that surround this church requires some attention to the nature of their solidarity, which is a competitive alternative to Zion's. Black ghetto-specific behavior is rich with evidence that these people are in a fierce struggle to keep social distance among themselves at tolerable levels. Whether rapping, jiving, running it down, copping a plea, signifying, or sounding (Kochman 1970), poor ghetto Blacks manipulate defiant signs and symbols—oral, anal, and genital—that defy, defile, and deny certain standards of mobility in the wider society. To protect his redistributive social network from the disruptive symbols of social mobility of the wider society, the poor Black attempts to level any tendency of hierarchy among his group with the use of defiant symbols with oral references—"suck," "sucker," "suck out," "eat," "eat me," "eat my," "blow," "tongue," "kiss," "kiss my," "gum," "teeth" (defiled), "mouth" (polluted), symbolic lips (defiled), and symbolic tongue (polluted)—in his daily unoffensive communication. He also manipulates genital symbols—"fuck," "fucker," "sack," "make," "some," "get over on," "stuff," "cock," "pussy," "hole," "cat," "poontang," "poodle," "a little bit," "grinding"—in the same manner. And anal signs and symbols too—"ass," "asshole," "butt," "sweet," "nice," "punk," "faggot," "girl"—are basic conversational vocabulary (Gover 1961).

The poor Black will also nickname his children for food—"Sugar," "Peanuts," "Peaches," "Beans," "Butter," "Duck," "Cookie," "Honey." He will publicly manipulate his anal and genital zones; he will use terms that are polluted and value-laden in the wider society—"mother," "sister," "father," "brother"—as common expressions of greeting and communication as well as verbal games ("dozens"). These are not historical accidents so much as mechanisms of survival and adaptability. Oppressed groups will organize, utilize and manipulate signs and symbols to defy the values in the symbol system of the oppressor (Abrahams 1962, Bailey 1965, Berdie 1947, Boas 1966, Dillard 1972, Dollard 1939, McDavid 1951, Stewart 1965, 1966). I have found similar evidence in prisons, ghetto schools, detention homes, and among the Black Muslims, where defiance becomes an instrument of solidarity for those whose lives are oppressed. (Williams 1984)

THE DENIAL OF THE BODY

The social inferiority of flesh (e.g., in the food chain) has a long history (Featherstone 1991, Laqueur 1990, Sennett 1993, Shilling 1993, Williams 1981b:14,41; 1992b:157,185). Blood and body parts have been essential foods for the gods. The Aztec gods required fresh human hearts. The Christian God received a bleeding Jesus on a Calvary cross as atonement for the sins of his followers. Those followers continue to sing and believe today, "We are saved by his blood. We are healed by the wound in his side." Abraham reluctantly agreed to sacrifice even his son Isaac to the Hebrew God. And this is but one example of the Jewish *idée fixée* on blood. The gods of war have required rivers of human blood and many mountains of their bodies. Christians make a universal distinction between the spirit and the flesh. The flesh is always the inferior. Thus sex, death, and digestion are denied, defied, and defiled in human experiences. I ask my students, "How many of you are sexually active either with partners or through masturbation?" No one responds. I ask, "How many of you have made your wills or funeral arrangements?" They laugh at me. "How many of you have bad breath or flatulence?" No one does. Of my hundreds of students, few have accepted the animal characteristics of sex, death, and digestion.

From an ecosystem perspective, humans are part of the animal kingdom. It is illustrative to examine human efforts to deny, defy, and defile our kinship to our fellow animals (see Tiger 1969, 1979b; Tiger and Fox 1971). Note the range and variety of animal names that we attach to humans in order to degrade them.

We describe the struggle of humans by referring to the dog: going to the dogs, every dog has his day, the dog days of August, dog-eat-dog world. We denigrate humans by calling them: bitch, ass, horse, cow, pussy, cocksucker, pig, chicken, turkey, pigeon, coon, fox, wolf, guinea pig, cat, hippopotamus, whale, crocodile (after while), alligator (later), hog, parrot, monkey, ape, gorilla, chimp, snake, weasel, worm, insect, asshole, rat, bear (hugger), crawled out from under a rock (moisture-laden insect), and even water buffalo (news from the University of Pennsylvania 1993). Those animals we admire are not used accordingly (e.g., stork, ostrich, sheep, bison, bird [e.g., the eagle, "Wild Birds Unlimited," and the Audubon Society], deer, cheetah, leopard, tiger, lion [king], elephant, rhinoceros).

Like most mammals, humans eat, eliminate, have sex, give birth, nurse, wean, become pubescent, engage in violence, and die. But because we refuse to be animals we surround these natural animal functions with elaborate ceremonies and rituals that recreate them in the image of gods (see Boyarin 1993). Jesus' mother even gave birth without intercourse. There is no report of his sex life, and, as we humans aspire to, Jesus conquered death in heaven.

Human ritual and ceremony extend to eating. Many of our "best" people continue to dress for dinner, eat only with the "appropriate" people, bless the food, thank God for it, and use special utensils and dishes. Eating is restricted by elaborate manners that involve the amounts eaten and the seasons in which a food is to be consumed and where it is to be eatern (Rifkin 1992). There are health, sex (aphrodisiacs), and sport (muscle-building) foods. Most food must be prepared and protected appropriately. "Lower" animals eat it as they find it.

Our sex lives are ritualized and ceremonialized. Many children were reared believing that babies were delivered by animals or other creatures. They were taught that the sexual organs were taboo. They were not to be handled, displayed, or discussed except in special circumstances. Children and adults were told to refrain from sex most of their young lives and even during the height of their sexual years if they had not yet united appropriately (joined by God) with a partner. When sex was permitted, it was designed for circumscribed purposes. It was confined to restricted visibility (see Friedl 1994), people, places, times of day, positions, and acts. Like elimination, it was a strictly private activity. Paul Rozin (personal communication, 1993) has pointed out that of all the orifices of the body, the vagina and the mouth were the most protected from a dead sanitized insect.

Elimination is mysterious (Loudon 1977). Freud (1949) suggests that we stood erect to avoid olfactory contact with other people's feces; I suggest that we also wanted to be taller and different from most other animals (DDDAK). But Freud suggests that we abhor the smell of other people's feces while not that of our own. Gordon Allport (1958:302) says that this is merely the biological self-centeredness that allows survival. In any case, moving one's bowels is a private activity. Many people appear to have the urge to write and publish (on stall walls) their most animal ideas while sitting in private moving their bowels. Public restrooms seem to release sexual inhibitions, and the "anal retentive" appear reluctant to use them. Often young single women are reluctant or embarrassed to admit to their male dates that they have to eliminate feces unexpectedly, and vice versa. Women have powder rooms to powder their noses. Men have restrooms, men's rooms, or bathrooms, not rooms to move their bowels. People in movies generally do not eliminate, and we seldom see the equipment.

For many years husbands were not allowed to view the birth of their children. Not even a woman's husband could see his wife's vagina in full view and well-lighted, performing one of its natural functions. Some women were reluctant to have their vaginas stretched by birth and chose surgery (C-sections). Vaginas and breasts have in some cases been transformed from functional animal organs into aesthetic and creative materials (analogous to Michael Jackson's grabbing his penis, Goya's nudes, or Gauguin's "native" paintings) for sexual allure and beauty. Meanwhile the quest for sexual pleasure has contorted accessible naked faces into objects that perform like genitals in movies, illustrations, and advertising films.

Lewd, offensive, and obscene speech and gestures are often associated with sex, death, and digestion because there are some things you cannot explain about virgins, the hungry, the dying, and those in urgent need to eliminate by means of ordinary words and pictures.

THE DENIAL OF SEX

I grew up believing that the stork brought babies and that any unnecessary contact with the genitals was immoral. Even when I learned that babies were inside mothers, no one had explained to me how they got there or outside. Girls were admonished constantly to keep their dresses down and their legs closed and never to allow boys to see even their underwear. Girls were not permitted to play in the summer sun without their chests covered even through all the years that their breasts were undeveloped. Underwear was required to cover the breasts, genitals, and buttocks but not the legs, feet, arms, armpits, neck, or head. Even nursing mothers were forced to hide during feedings.

Parents pretended to be asexual by taking every precaution to have their sexual activity out of sight and sound. Children (especially girls) were taught that sex was an activity only for those in love, joined by God, and attempting to create families. As such, sexual activity was rigidly defined by times, places, privacy, positions, and genital contact points. Such definitions denied the animal sexuality of humans and domesticated human sexual activity. Carl Withers (West 1945:177) described the relations between the sexes in rural Missouri:

The strictures on modesty, especially concerning the exposure of sexual organs to the sight of others, are very rigid. Most married couples would consider it immodest to un-dress completely before each other in a lighted room; many married couples are said never to have seen each other undressed. Siblings must never see siblings of the opposite sex (except very small children) undressed, and children, as soon as they can bathe and dress themselves, begin to conceal themselves carefully from the eyes of parents. Boys of any age strip off freely in each other's presence in a room or at a swimming hole, and boys micturate before each other, but not before adult men, without turning their backs. Adult men ordinarily turn away from others when micturating.

Modesty is often carried in Plainville to extreme ends of squeamishness. Two grown sisters living in town who share a room and sleep in the same bed were said by a neighbor woman never to undress for bed at the same time "without either turning out the light or setting up a screen between them." One woman told her married son as an oddity—he said he would not have thought of it so—"As long as your father and I have been married, we have never once gone to the toilet together."

In my youth I could have expected these same attitudes in the urban Northeast (Pittsburgh).

During my youth, because sexual activity was so narrowly defined, "old maids," old people, nuns, priests, and others who had no family goals were expected to abstain. The social pressures were such that many girls required that boys at least say "I love you" before intercourse. Most girls confessed to love before participating. Even today in an age of presumed sexual license, my students complain of parents who are too open about their own sexual activities. Parents are attempting to be mature and modern, but the students are very uneasy about discussing sexual intercourse with people within their incest range.

Today sexual intercourse is associated with a variety of sexual diseases, many of which are incurable, resistant to treatment, and lethal. Many people will discuss their ailments with you but not if their genitals are affected. Other results of sexual activities are abortions, teenage pregnancies, teenage mothers, welfare mothers, single parent families, fatherless homes, domestic violence, child abuse, and many other problematic situations. If society cannot deny or control sufficiently, it can at least malign sexual activity. I am reminded of all the negative terms used to describe females by identifying them solely with their vaginas. I argue here and elsewhere (Williams 1992b) that by associating sexual activity with females, humans have cast women as inferior throughout human existence. Juries find it difficult to believe that a woman who is considered a "tramp," prostitute or libertine, or who is the wife of the perpetrator, can be raped. Chastity belts were never worn by men. If a woman is chaste too long she becomes a spinster, an old maid, and "different," but if she enjoys sex with several partners she becomes a "tramp." If she sells it, she is a criminal. If she becomes pregnant, there are laws controlling the fetus. There are no such controls over the genitals of men. "Sleep is the only freedom she has ever known."

Society has criminalized most perceptions of sexual activity: date, spousal, and statutory rape, deviant sexual intercourse, fornication, adultery, sodomy, incest, degrees of sexual assault, and sexual harassment. Even if you refrain from sexual activity you, can be arrested and imprisoned for not concealing your genitals— indecent exposure, lewd and lascivious behavior. If you can manage to engage in sexual activity without being guilty of a crime, you are warned that one in four of you will contract a venereal disease in your lifetime. Even masturbation has a negative image among many in our society.

Genitals are the most dangerous body parts, and many a rebellious person (e.g., Michael Jackson) demonstrates their "courage" by holding or touching that area (covered of course) in public. This human mystification of sex is responsible for many of our collateral social problems: incest, child abuse, alcohol abuse, drug addiction, prostitution, rape, deviant sexual behavior, 50 percent divorce rates, depression, dating services for profit, singles' bars, bar pickups, sexual violence, and orgies at fraternity and other "parties."

Allan Bloom (1993:14) gives us a "requiem for romance" as he laments the increasing loss of sex denial and transformations in the social construction of sex.

The word "love" now applies to almost everything except the overwhelming attraction of one individual for another. And sex is a timid pseudoscientific word that tells us only that individuals have certain bodily needs.

There is an appalling matter-of-factness in public speech about sex today. On television, schoolchildren tell us about how they will now use condoms in their contacts—I was about to say adventures, but that would be overstating their significance.

On talk shows, young collegians tell us about how they decide whether they have been raped in their various encounters. There is nothing in these tales of the now impossible complaint about outraged virginity.

Sex is spoken of coolly and without any remains of the old puritanical shame, as an incidental aspect of the important questions of disease and power. The sexual talk of our times is about how to get greater bodily satisfaction or how to protect ourselves from one another.

The old view was that delicacy of language was part of the nature, the sacred nature, of eros and that to speak about it in any other way would be to misunderstand it. What has disappeared is the risk and the hope of human connectedness embedded in eros.

Ours is a language that reduces the longing for another to the need for individual, private satisfaction and safety. Isolation, a sense of lack of profound contact with other human beings, seems to be the disease of our time.

There are great industries of psychotherapy addressing our difficulties in "relationships"—that pallid word, the very timidity of which makes substantial attachments impossible. One has to have a tin ear to describe one's great love as a relationship. Did Romeo and Juliet have a relationship? The term betokens a chaste egalitarianism; it levels different ranks and degrees of attachment.

THE DENIAL OF DEATH

Death comes equally to all of us and makes all of us equal when it comes. Death among Americans specifically and humans generally is often an occasion for rites of solidarity and of denial (Metcalf and Huntington 1992). Human deceased are usually prepared for their final social appearance, placed in a variety of social contexts for the ceremonies, and ultimately given a solemn good-bye ritual for their last journey, one for which the other guests are admonished to prepare in order to meet the departed again ("souls" are taken by God).

These human rituals and ceremonies, like those surrounding eating, bathing, eliminating, procreating, and healing, are designed to document, validate, and reinforce humanness. Such rites are necessary because the activities that they accompany are equally distributed among the "lower" animals. Death, especially, is a difficult cognitive exercise (Becker 1973) for humans who feel that they are made in the image of God.

I argue that much of the difficulty for humans in death and dying resides in a denial not only of death but also of their animal kinship. Such a denial extends to the kinship of "lower" animals, of all other living forms, and of even Earth itself. The myth of eternal life has been a successful survival strategy for humans. It has helped them dominate the Earth and most of its forms of life. Today, however, because of transformations in humans, human technology, and human populations, the strategy has become obsolete. Values and attitudes about death and dying will change in a global population that will learn to cherish Earth (topophilia) as cradle and as grave during the Ecological Revolution of the twenty-first century.

Ernest Becker (1973), an anthropologist, wrote a Pulitzer Prize–winning book titled *The Denial of Death*. Because of the subject, most anthropologists and anthropology students have never heard of this celebrated anthropologist. Of those who know his work, most think he was a psychiatrist. Becker and others (e.g., Bowker 1993, Metcalf and Huntington 1992) have explored this subject thoroughly. Becker's concept of human heroics is analogous to my concept of human feelings of inferiority. For Becker, heroics underlie the human struggle for self-esteem. Most people are aware that they deny and fear death. The case need not be made here.

Humans begin to plan for life as soon as there is birth, but they seldom plan for death (vs. life after death) until urgency requires it. People have to be persuaded to make their wills, arrange their funerals, and donate their organs. The persuasion is often not successful. Much life insurance is sold as an investment, not as one's final debt liquidation arrangement. People abuse their bodies and accept unnecessary risks to health and well-being as if they are ordained to live forever. Death always comes as a shock unless the person is sick and dying slowly. Why should death be any more of a shock than birth? We know equally well that both are coming, although we seldom know when. Most people will go to any extremes to delay the inevitable. They will try irrational cures, spend their entire estates, and often deny the increasing certainty to the end, all the while knowing that birth, struggle, and death have no detour.

THE DENIAL OF DIGESTION

The mouth is a digestive organ. Like the mouths of most animals, the human mouth is full of bacteria. Yet humans behave as if their mouths are clean and sanitary. Within their "clean" in-group, they think nothing of kissing one another, sharing their mouth-contaminated food, drinks, smokes, and bottles. They dread the idea and the act of putting anything "dirty" into their mouths. Yet any food emptied from the mouth is treated as a pollutant. The entire process of digestion is animal, but acts of "love" even with the identical animal organs (e.g., urination and "making love"—animal waste and the "fruit of the womb") have distinctive conceptions.

As a child and as a parent, I can remember vividly the ritual and ceremony at the eating table (see Lévi-Strauss 1979b).

Wash you hands before you eat.
Pull your chair to the table.
Sit up in your chair.
Put your napkin in your lap.
Take your elbows off the table.
Say your blessing.
Don't drink before you eat.
Don't take more than you can eat.

Cut up your meat so you can eat it.
Use your knife and fork.
Don't play with your food.
Don't talk with a mouth full of food.
Don't reach across the table.
Don't mix all your food together.
Don't drop food on the floor.
Wipe your mouth, chin, nose.
Don't eat like an animal.
Don't lean into your plate.
Take your lips out of the glass.
Don't slurp your soup.
Eat your salad, vegetables.
Chew your food well.
Wait until you are served (dessert).
Don't be greedy.
Watch your table manners.
You can leave the table if you don't know how to behave.

The ingestion of food is an animal act that for humans must be another carefully circumscribed behavior. Once the food is ingested, it becomes polluted. You do not belch or vomit it without the disgust of your associates. The longer it remains in your body, the more disgusting it becomes. Feces and urine, then, are most disgusting (see Loudon 1977). There are few places to deposit them. We have bathrooms, powder rooms, potty rooms, lavatories, restrooms, ladies' rooms, and men's rooms but no feces and urine rooms. Whenever we deposit them, our greatest convenience is to push a button and make them disappear. The closest association we make with food and its elimination is to keep our toothbrushes in the bathroom. The level of feces disgust is probably ranked: a burglar (enemy), an adult stranger, rat, dog, cat, an adult friend, an adult family member, a child, your own child, a baby, your own baby, your own.

Consider the observations of David Scheffel (1991:182) about a Slavic community in Canada:

The analysis of dietary rules is of some importance in the context of sexual behavior. Indeed, in several respects, proper sexual conduct parallels orthodox dietary practices. Just as vegetarianism is considered more admirable than the consumption of meat, so too a life of restricted sexuality is valued more highly than an existence dominated by carnal desire. The example of the pious, chaste, and solitary *inok* (hermit, monk) is used rather often to describe ideal Christian attributes. The Old Believers do not credit many people, however, with the strength required for attaining this ideal stage. As with their diet, the people of Berezovka exhibit sexual attitudes which are designed to curb excesses without resulting in a complete suppression of sensuality.

In agreement with this strategy is the insistence on regulated sexuality, a condition defined as the conjugal relationship between two members of the opposite sex. Unregulated sexuality, such as masturbation, sodomy, pre-marital and extra-marital intercourse, is considered aberrant and sinful. Although the material collected on this topic is sketchy, it is apparent that pre-marital relations do occur sporadically, in spite of (in particular) the desirability of female virginity. Early marriage functions as one of the precautions against pregnancy and social disgrace. At the same time, it expresses local unwillingness and inability to postpone sexual gratification.

Regulated, that is, marital sexuality, is regarded with a mixture of pleasure and fear, resembling the attitude towards the consumption of tasty food. As long as obsession and gluttony are avoided, copulation and eating are accepted as normal processes of life. Both realms are controlled by rules of abstinence and moderation (*vozderzhanie*), which ensure that behavior which is on the borderline between purity and defilement does not become excessively dangerous. This applies primarily to periods of increased ritual significance, such as fasts, as well as to the night preceding a church service, when sexual activity must not take place.

Despite the clear parallel between food and sex, the latter domain is subjected to several further precautions, which demonstrate its riskier nature. As I have already indicated, the iconostasis at home is equipped with curtains that can be closed when sexual intercourse takes place. Given the delicate subject matter, I refrained from a systematic inquiry into the extent of and justification for this custom. But even the incomplete evidence at my disposal demonstrates quite conclusively that what makes intercourse distasteful to the eyes of the holy figures is the animal-like passion which often accompanies it. Like excessive drunkenness, sex can be "hot" and "wild," the opposite of the ideal of restraint. But unlike alcoholism—or, for that matter, the drinking of blood—marital sexuality is not an infraction against the "law" but rather an institutionalized "breach of decorum." Hence it seems that the drawn curtain should be seen as an admission of guilt in a permitted but improper situation.

The guilt is alleviated somewhat by shifting the responsibility for sexual desire onto the woman and her primeval ancestress, Eve. The Old Believers, especially the men among them, are very fond of narrating the story of Adam's fall, and they never fail to draw the conclusion of the female gender being naturally inferior. Although Eve too is held to have been created in God's image, her status is claimed to have been intended to remain below that of Adam. This postulate is proven allegedly by the creation of the woman from the body of the man, and, as if this were not enough, from his left rib. Whenever the creation story was narrated, I would be encouraged to verify it by counting my ribs to see that one on the left side is missing. The fall of Adam is attributed to his foolish willingness to allow a creature that was in more than one sense his property to act autonomously. Since Eve allegedly lacked the moral will and ability to follow God's commands, she snared Adam by attracting him to her beautiful body. Ever since, the woman has been used as bait by Satan, and her lasciviousness must be subjected to strict controls imposed by the inherently more spiritual man.

The most important visible symptom of the greater animality of women is their periodic discharge of blood in menstruation (*miesichnaya*) and childbirth. A menstruating woman is regarded as a source of defilement of the ritual domain, on account of which she is barred from the chapel. This condition does not seem to affect her natural purity, as she is allowed to engage in the usual duties, including the preparation of food. Childbirth, on the other hand, requires that the mother be segregated from the family and use her own set of dishes. The period of impurity lasts for eight days if the child is a boy and forty days if a girl. A prayer read over the mother by the *nastavnik* at the end of the purification period restores her previous status.

The onset of menopause signals the loss of the woman's natural attractiveness and, especially when combined with widowhood, some elevation of her ritual status.

Like Jung, I assert that "man does not live by bread alone" but by all the mythology that fills his daily life. Chief among those myths are his being made in the image of God who somehow made man a higher being than all the other animals (Genesis 1:26). He even gave man the dominion over the other animals to use, abuse, and destroy them (Genesis 1:30).

Freud used a psychological model to delve into the unconscious terrors of man and the story of his origin. Lévi-Strauss used a linguistic model to examine the deep structure of human meaning. Jung used a mythological model to probe the collective unconscious (or Adolf Bastian's concept of the "psychic unity" of man). All of these have been critically examined and discounted. But the failures of the models do not prevent the scholarly probes or discourage us from continuing to seek the truth about the nature of man. My own paradigm awaits the next decision of its inadequacy. The truth about the nature of man can no longer wait.

THE ECOLOGICAL REVOLUTION

Nonhuman primates have to compete for food, sex, safety, and territory. They have endured their positions in the food chain. But as the transition from nonhuman to human primate occurred, brainpower was a crucial component of humans' increasingly selective adaptation. We became more self-conscious and self-aware (Parker et al. 1994). We began to perceive ourselves as separate, superior, and distinct from the other animal species. Eventually we denied, defied, and defiled our animal kinship. This process of perception was the beginning of human culture, and it continues to develop to the present. The process has been successful. Humans have spread throughout the Earth, and they dominate the animals and other resources.

But perhaps, like the dinosaurs before us, we have become too successful. We are overwhelming the resources of the planet. We are undermining the global web-of-life. But unlike the dinosaurs, we have culture and the capacity to change rapidly (the Ecological Revolution). Our global ecosystems must be protected, and we are now aware of that need. What we must learn quickly is that such protection requires a major transformation in human values and attitudes. DDDAK must be discarded. Humans must accept their humble places in the biosphere. We must change people in order to protect their environments. In this book I have tried to use evolutionary thought to examine some of these issues, as suggested by Daly and Wilson (1988:297):

The human psyche has been shaped by a history of selection. There is no serious controversy about this proposition; the only "alternatives" to selectionist explanations of adaptation are religiously motivated creation myths. The interesting question is not whether this is so (it is), but "so what?" How can students of murder (or any other social phenomenon) use evolutionary psychological ideas to stimulate their research and improve their understanding? We do not for a moment imagine that the analyses we have undertaken are the last word on this subject; quite the contrary. What we hope we have demonstrated is the potential of evolutionary ideas as metatheory for psychology and criminology, and we hope that other students of human action will be inspired to let their imaginations be informed by contemporary evolutionary thought.

Sexism has probably existed since the beginning of human culture. With the male inferiority complex developed from DDDAK, and the woman there to exploit, man soon began to treat her as an inferior. He continues today. She no longer wears a chastity belt, but she does not control her vagina. Women who never share their vaginas with men are viewed as freaks (spinsters, old maids). Women who share them too soon or with too many partners are immoral. A husband (as Evelyn Nesbit and Stanford White discovered) may never forgive her if she shares it with someone else before him. Yet she is perennially encouraged to display (e.g., brassiere and shoe designs) her sexual assets as a constant reminder of her perceived animal inferiority. Meanwhile men have few of these restrictions applied to them. Notwithstanding that women have been oppressed longer than any other human group, and many of them are aware of it, they have also collaborated longer with their oppressors. They have oppressed one another—race against race, class against class, religion against religion, nation against nation (imperialism), and abortion against pro-life. They have proven that "a house divided against itself cannot stand." Even in the women's movement, the feminists and the gender scholars contaminate their effort with the base alloy of hypocrisy. With the Ecological Revolution, DDDAK and sexual discrimination may end. Women may be treated as equal partners in the human enterprise.

The painful sacrifices of social change and the dynamics of social interaction will never allow a utopian human existence. The Ecological Revolution will not usher in a utopia on Earth. But it may allow the continued existence of human life on Earth and may revolutionize the nature and character of human relationships. The myriad artificial categories of human populations will be eliminated, and the human species will work, play, and disagree together in the common enterprise of protecting Earth and exploring the universe.

THE STONE AND THE STEEL OF SUPERMAN

We in the United States will find it especially painful to accept the Ecological Revolution. DDDAK is the basis for the constitutional human feelings of inferiority, and individual inferiority complexes result from such a constitution. But American culture and society places special emphasis on self-reliance, success, and competition. This effectively ignores that the defense industry (among others) is the welfare program for the rich and the middle class. Such values build on, reinforce, and substantiate DDDAK far beyond those in some other cultures and societies. Our culture and society often select and reward individuals who have intensive feelings of inferiority. These people are high achievers and may gradually become the leaders of a lost generation. Nothing demonstrates the inferior feelings of Americans like their behavior with their automobiles. They exploit them to achieve a false superiority with power, speed, luxury, prestige, competition, and aggressive prowess. The car has taken us from the confinement of our front porches to the city and coast to coast. It has conquered the land and invidiously challenged our neighbors.

The automobile is one of the most popular symbols of the human inferiority complex. The car is a powerful machine (steel and plastic) that deludes us individually and collectively about our animal superiority. Such an irrational effort to document our power and prestige is evident in American society's domination by the automobile. Its disasters dominate the morning and afternoon news as helicopter traffic watchers report on most of the major television channels. Parking is one of the most serious concerns at many city halls, businesses, and universities rather than services, profitable practices, and teaching. We fight wars for their oil and fund research to run them on alcohol, electric power and natural gas. They dominate entire human communities (e.g., Breezewood, PA).

The automobile dominates our vocabulary, resources and lifestyles. We have (stone) freeways, highways, overpasses, high occupancy lanes, ramps, bridges, and tunnels for them. There are car tows, car shows, drive-ins, washes, deodorants, jiffy lubes, stereo, tape deck, security systems, and cd player shops, traffic police, traffic signs, parking signs, parking enforcement patrols, private parking spaces, driveways, garages, traffic signals, air conditioning shops, upholster shops, detail shops, parking structures, attendants, meters, meter maids, ticket machines, violation computers. There are chauffeurs, car ticketers, carhops, 3 in 1 car jockeys (car pool deception), car jackers, car bombers, and wreckers. They can ticket it, service it, repair it, inspect it, insure it, license it, regulate it, finance it, advertise it, remodel it, "trade it in," chase it (police), race it, steal it, strip it, and annually update it.

There are "throwaway cars," minivans, vans, pickups, sports cars, luxury cars, status cars, prestige cars, foreign cars, station wagons, hatchbacks, sedans, coupes, four-by-fours, front wheel drives, economy cars, limousines, stretch limousines, and giants (recreational vehicles) that you can live in. Cars have pollution bulletins and alerts, research and design departments, and experimental models.

Automobiles can be "loaded" with equipment: bars, refrigerators, telephones, televisions, radios, carpets, cigarette lighters, compact disks players, reclining seats, reading lights, vanity mirrors, food and drink holders, air conditioning, removable tops and roofs, spotlights, alarm systems, and customized designs. You can buy them, lease them, rent them, trade them, sell them, borrow on them, steal them, and be bankrupted by them. The fronts of them resemble human faces, and many owners will fight or kill you if you "cut in front of them" or otherwise humiliate their cars. Some cars (e.g., Jaguar XKE) appear phallic to their owners. Some people are accused of loving them more than their partners, spouses, children, and siblings. Some owners sleep, eat, watch movies, shop, romance, and have sexual intercourse in them. Others wash, wax, and store them. In the Ecological Revolution, humans will abandon internal combustion automobiles as vanity machines that do serious harm to the Earth.

The Ecological Revolution will see the selection and rewarding of a different kind of *Homo sapiens*. Many of them are downwardly mobile in our present society. They are more at ease with the Earth, its forms of life, and its diverse humans. They accept death, sex, and human waste as part of the living experience. They do not require the presence of inferiors to feel wholesome and successful as human beings.

The Revolution will not be created by thoughtful humans but by a series of ecosystem disasters that threaten life—all life—on Earth (eco-crises). Humans will be forced to rear their children to respect the Earth as cradle and tomb (see Dubos 1968, 1980). Children will learn that the Earth is the source of life. Mother Earth deserves the same treatment as human mothers who bring life into the world and nourish it in a chain of being. The life that the Earth sustains is a component of that chain. All life has purpose. We must understand and respect that purpose and that existence. A "good" education is to learn to understand nature, society, and self, as well as the relationships between them. Life is to be destroyed only to sustain life in a reasonable and well-planned food chain. Children will learn to love and respect themselves as beautiful components of the life of the world and not as "superior" forms of life in competition with "inferior" forms of life. With the technological sophistication of modern society, the struggle for existence is a myth to support ruthless violence to life on Earth (e.g., the "smart bombs" in the Gulf War). Humans need a model of human behavior that allows them to feel good about themselves without depreciating other humans and other forms of life. After killing hundreds of thousands of Iraqis (and thousands of Kuwaitis) on the battlefield, General H. Norman Schwarzkopf said on CNN television (Feb. 27, 1991) that "they're [the Iraqis in Kuwait City] not a part of the same human race that we are!"

The Ecological Revolution will bring some pleasures. DDDAK not only forced our control over the "lower" animals (e.g., in the form of zoos, safaris, pets, circuses, research animals, recreational hunting, and animal farms), but it also influenced our control over humans. Just as wild animals needed to be controlled, so did potentially "wild" humans (e.g., "savages"). As we "break" wild horses, we also "break" humans by socialization—order, orderliness, rules, regime, bureaucracy, schedules, and sanctions. Such controls grew more and more elaborate as humans became more and more "civilized." So in modern society most humans have lost much of the freedom of body and the freedom of spirit. We have domesticated animals and domesticated people. We have become slaves to our technology (e.g., stone, steel, and plastics) and bureaucracy. Such losses are evident in human behavior such as military formations, corporate behavior codes, chorus lines, assembly lines, rush hour traffic, classroom behavior, fashion cycles, dress and uniform codes, television addictions, holiday shopping, tourism, weekend and vacation routines, dating, and marriage decisions. But the losses are far more pervasive than these. Many people work at occupations they hate (and TGIF), live with people they dislike, recreate in activities where they feel trapped, dare not express their feelings, and have lost all hopes of executing their dreams in life. Some of these people live vicariously and cathartically through the violent lives of others at football games, boxing, bull fights, cock fights, dog fights, baseball games, hockey games, movies, plays, television (sex, violence, and death), novels, sports magazines, sex magazines, pornography shops, car races, horse races, dog races, gambling casinos, detective stories, music recordings, and video cassettes. Others are born or drift into lives of poverty, crime, drugs, neurosis, and quiet desperation.

The rich, famous, and powerful conspire to deceive us into believing that they are free and happy. But money, fame, and power have their own burdens and shackles. And we conspire to prove that they are as miserable as we are (by means of tabloids, tabloid journalism, exposés, and other scandal publications that we support). Modern society creates victims of the masses. Many people are good at their jobs, but no one appreciates their work. They have abilities that no one recognizes. They do not get promotions, awards, testimonials, and banquets. They do the same things day after day, year after year, and they know they are likely to be doing them when they retire. They grow up going to schools that are highly regimented. They live in communities that are intolerant of differences. They are reared in families that expect them to be "normal." But they do not want to live and die that way. Nonconforming behavior, however, is strongly discouraged at most stages of life. Free spirits and bodies are admired in the abstract but punished in the real.

The Ecological Revolution will allow all forms of life, including the human, a greater freedom of existence. Without the drive for superiority (DDDAK), there will be more room and space for self-expression and self-realization. As Ferguson (1992:82) explains, the Ecological Revolution is a visionary myth:

If globalization as an historical process only emerged fully formed in the 1980s, now, in the 1990s, ideas about planetary interdependence embrace an ecological dimension. The one-world, Gaia, philosophy at the heart of "Saving Planet Earth" links culture and economy to perceptions of a world ecosystem and its protection. Not only are we enjoined to "think globally and act locally," but also to realize that eco-crises such as "global warming require the rise of the global politician, buttressed by a global citizenry, whose vision extends for decades" (O'Riordan, 1990).

The utopian ideas embedded in this myth are transcultural and synchronic, displaying the power of myth to reinvent itself across space and time. In fact "Saving Planet Earth" combines ancient (and sometimes sacred) beliefs about man's intimate relation to nature with modern ideas of eco-activism. Narratives about the environmentalist project to rescue the planet from self-destruction, echo archaic myths of the "eternal return," and such sentiments, according to Eliade (1968), appeal to our primitive longings for cyclical regeneration and new beginnings.

But (wo)man does not live by bread alone, and adaptive mythology is a human hallmark.

AN INTERNAL REVOLUTION:
THE HUMAN SEARCH FOR SECURITY

Like past cultural revolutions, the Ecological Revolution will be precipitated by external events. The discovery of seeds, combustion chambers, fossil fuels, atomic fission, and computerized weapons have brought humans to the twenty-first century. The discovery of imminent human extinction will govern our behavior in that century. But unlike the Agricultural, Industrial, Atomic, and Potential Revolutions, the Ecological Revolution will require rapid transformations in human attitudes and values. The human search for security will be rationally reconstructed.

Children will be socialized without a need to control, dominate, compete with, or exploit "others." CRESSANS (classism, racism, ethnocentrism, sexism, sectarianism, ageism, nationalism, and speciesism) will disappear from the Earth. This requires that parents and adults recognize the necessity of these transformations and commit to executing them. Parents in the United States attempt to send their children to the "best" schools, churches, camps, vacations, neighborhoods, communities, sports teams, stores, malls, colleges, and families (for social relationships and marriages). These parents vicariously share the "superiority" in such efforts and enterprises. But the same parents virtually ignore the kind of Earth they are forcing upon their children and grandchildren since they do not expect to share that with them. This is a pernicious example of selfishness. The national debt, AIDS research efforts, pesticides in food production (versus integrated pest management) ozone depletion, and environmental toxic waste (e.g., lead) are other examples.

Perhaps the stages suggested among the dying (see Kübler-Ross 1970) are useful projections for the initial stages of the Ecological Revolution:

A. Denial
    1. Deny Ecosystem Deformation
    2. Deny Human Mythology
B. Anger
    1. Realize Ecosystem Disasters
    2. Recognize Imminent Human Extinction
C. Bargaining
    1. Self-Realization
    2. Discover Human Nature and Dilemma
    3. Rationally Reconstruct Human Nature

D. Depression
E. Acceptance
   1. Embrace Transformations
   2. Eschew the Inferiority Complex

It comes as no surprise that the initial efforts for the rational reconstruction of human nature find usufruct in the conflict-management dynamics of death and dying.

The internal revolution will be partially shaped by new perceptions within the changing society. Perceptions of vulnerability and unworthiness will be radically altered. Those perceptions will elicit education, language, mass media, and family for the major transformation required. The socialized will unlearn old behavioral patterns and help to teach new ones to the young. The entire process will be aided by that greatest of all animal motivators—survival.

DISCUSSION

My general hypothesis is that humans have evolved and ultimately dominated Earth because of a species-specific inferiority complex (Williams 1992b). I suggest that different human populations have variations in the intensity of those inferior feelings (e.g., men may have greater feelings of inferiority than women). Some of those variations are determined by the tolerance of human characteristics that are shared with other animals (e.g., death, sex, and digestion). Is human identity dependent on "lower" animals and "inferior" people?

Robertson (1992:165) makes my case for me: "At the same time, contemporary sociology is rapidly recovering from many decades both of disciplinary "professionalism" and ideological narrowness. A number of its practitioners are returning to the high ground of the history, structure, and future of humanity, but leaving far behind Comte's assumption that global unicity facilitates and necessitates a "positivistic" science of (wo)mankind."

I am searching for fundamentals. I subscribe to some of "the mythology about globalization" (Ferguson 1992), especially those of "the new world order" and "saving planet Earth." But I would repeat that (wo)man does not live by bread alone. Humans live by means of mythology. We must discover the myths that are necessary and adaptive in the twenty-first century. My new world order is couched in a new cultural revolution that is ushered in by the Earth-impact of modern technology in the control of "primitive" humans. The cognitive development of humans was rapid only for the last 100,000 years, probably since the development of language. It occurred in a global field. The Ecological Revolution requires another leap in human cognitive development. The Ecological Revolution is another definition of the global situation—utopian realism. It gives globalization cognitive purchase.

Some recent social transformations reflect the complexity of human behavior given our understanding of DDDAK. More than twenty years ago B. F. Skinner (1971) warned us of the chaos and social destruction that might result from increasing demands for and tolerance of freedom. This was at a time when many of the social "inferiors" in American society were clamoring for their constitutional promises. Even though Skinner's arguments were faulty, his predictions have proven themselves. Efforts to give social "inferiors" more "freedom" while maintaining a dominant "elite" have undermined the social contract and the social cohesion of our society. Amitai Etzioni's solution is communitarianism (personal communication, 1993). Etzioni states that the voluntary compliance that supports our social-moral infrastructure in the United States has been collapsing. People are constantly exposed to the hypocrisy of those in authority. Both authority and the discrimination that characterized the country into the 1950s were dismantled. We now neglect and abuse our children, rape our dates, and in half of our families fail to instill moral values in our children. Family values, crime, community, and schools have become political terms that stifle debate rather than moral ones that invite it (Carter 1993). People have a strong sense of entitlement versus a sense of community and responsibility. They want to be guaranteed a jury trial but do not want to serve on juries. They want good health care but continue to drink, smoke, and engage in irresponsible sexual behavior.

CONCLUSION

The rational reconstruction of human nature reflects the potential for evolutionary ideas as metatheory for the social sciences generally and for anthropology specifically. This is an approach that allows the imagination to be informed by contemporary evolutionary thought.

One hundred and fifty years ago, another social scientist, Auguste Comte, attempted to create a new moral and social order when he thought his social world was crumbling. His attempt has been criticized ever since. I, like Durkheim, do not wish to invent a Comteian new religion.

The exact expression employed by Durkheim is: "Religious interests are merely the symbolic form of social and moral interests." Straining the analogy somewhat perhaps, I would be inclined to say that Durkheim's book on the elementary forms of religious life represents in his work the equivalent of the *Système de politique* positive in the work of Comte. Not that Durkheim describes a religion of humanity. At a certain point in his book, Durkheim says explicitly that Comte was wrong to believe that an individual could make a religion to order. Precisely if religion is a collective creation, it would be contrary to the theory to suppose that a sociologist could single handedly create a religion. Durkheim did not wish to create a religion in the manner of Comte: but insofar as he wished to demonstrate that the object of religion is none other than the transfiguration of society, he laid a foundation comparable to the one Comte had given to the religion of the future when he asserted that humanity, having killed transcendent gods, would love itself or at least would love what was best in itself under the name of humanity. (Aron 1970)

I now want to revisit the theme that when human societies fail, humans are capable of creating new social and moral orders. The social cohesion of the global village appear about to fail.

As Comte, Marx, Durkheim, and Weber grappled with social theory to under-stand the social transformation of their century, social scientists today are grap-pling with a period in human history when the social and moral order seem to require new and better social cohesion. The Ecological Revolution will be ush-ered in and sustained by such cohesives: environmentalism, reverence for health, respect for all life and family, community, and occupational memberships. Many of these social cohesives will become sacred as they are identified with the suste-nance of society itself. This new moral order will create a relative respect for the authorities and leaders who administer it effectively. Much of that moral order will emanate from the new reverence for nature, Earth, and universe. DDDAK will die as humans will embrace their animal kinship as children of the mother of all families, life, societies, communities, and global villages—the Earth.

Comte will be revisited for some of his insights on new social orders. Rousseau's request for human dignity will be obsolete because humans will be a respected component of the web-of-life on Earth. Like Herbert Spencer, I envision a world in which humans will behave to save humanity. This world is not unlike Comte's religion of humanity. But the Ecological Revolution will be forced upon human-kind by the pressure of human survival. It will create a way of life close to Max Scheler's (1961) vitalistic pantheism (notwithstanding his philosophical predis-position for hierarchical "panvitalism"). As Coser 1971 summarizes Scheler (1961:18, 20):

Scheler's analysis, then, leads to this message: It is not given to any epoch, to any culture, to any human type to encompass a full vision. Only, perhaps, a slow harmonizing of all world perspectives might lead to a panhuman synthesis in which all the variant views would finally be merged in the construction of a general human culture. But such a culture can only emerge if the various peoples and men will accept from each other, value state-ments of which they themselves can have no direct intuition. This can happen only, for example, if Western man, driven by his Faustian urge to know and hence to dominate the world, comes to see in the passive, accepting, yielding world-view of the East a necessary complement to his own. Such ultimate harmonizing is possible only if scientific views are seen as partial, restricted and limited visions of the world, only if we become aware that a world-view which seems to have given us an unprecedented amount of dominance over nature has in fact led to a pervasive narrowing of our vision. Just as other forms of knowl-edge, science deals with but a partial aspect of reality, and it is a disastrous error to assume that everything ignored is less real than what it considers.

As it is, Scheler's emphasis on the vigor of biological drives; his assertion that the vital sphere is in some way more "real" than the others, that the *élan vital* always prevails over the mind, which is powerless in itself; his glorification of vital values and contempt for "merely" utilitarian values; his assertion that what is most needed for the West is a "re-sublimation in which Westen Man has been imprisoned for so long," goes too far. All these are based on a number of assump-tions that have repeatedly been used by modern apologists of irrationality as engines of revolt against reason. Here Scheler stands in the long line of those modern thinkers who have rediscovered the persistent strength of the irrational in man and society, but who too often claim that these underground powers are somehow superior to the life of reason.

Furthermore, under the Ecological Revolution there will no longer be an "elite" to misappropriate to itself symbols of "honor, dignity, and rank" unwarranted by biological inheritance, achievement, individual merit, and especially by the short lifetime of just another earthbound animal. The "elite" will cease to lead by exemptions rather than by example. The cowboy mentality will end:

As Jean-Paul Sartre did not fail to notice, the cowboy was the first existential hero: the stranger, the outsider, living by an absurdist code that—though his fiancée pleads with him—could only end in death. For his ambition to master the Earth, his need to snap the primordial bonds of family and community, his identification of freedom with the restless itch to "move on," sprang from his secret love for the infinite, which finite Earth cannot contain. The lover of the infinite must inevitably be killed. (Novak 1972c:95)

Anthropology and other social sciences will play leading research and advocacy roles in the human dimensions of these global transformations. They will provide the social framework for humans who do not live by bread alone (Deut. 8:3, Matt. 4:4, Luke 4:4), but live also by dreams with their eyes open (Carter 1993). Unlike Benjamin Kidd (1908), I do not believe that religion and other human mythologies will destroy rational behavior in humans. But when those beliefs interfere with human survival (e.g., DDDAK), they must be transformed into new and different cosmologies. Societies can maintain their coherence only through common beliefs. In the recent past those beliefs have been shaken by science, mass media (especially tabloid television, violent movies, and sensational journalism as well as by rapid data collection and dissemination), and hero and heroine bashing. I agree with Durkheim that humans continue to need a morality inspired by the scientific spirit—social commitment. The biophobia and biophilia (Kellert and Wilson 1993) hypotheses may, indeed, encourage the human biocentric (Ecological) Revolution (see Patten and Jørgensen 1995).

We need new and different stories, not those about fame and fortune, not those about upward mobility, consumerism, power, and achievement, but new stories for a new century and a new human era. DDDAK and change have undermined the dreams of socialism, communism, and capitalism. With the end of DDDAK, environmentalism will usher in and sustain the Ecological Revolution. Environmentalism and biopolitics without ecological imperialism will become the basis for a new social and moral order, a new cohesion for a global community.

Chapter 4
Food, Animals, Death, and the Body

Zion is a Black Pentecostal church in Pittsburgh whose members form a closely knit community of individuals in both sacred and secular association. In order to maintain and perpetuate its social boundaries and strong solidarity, Zion uses symbolic expressions, in the form of references to food, animals, and rural southern life, as idioms of its distinctive identity. The analysis and description of Zion's symbol system is a useful analytical tool for understanding this group's cultural character in the urban context. But it is also an insight into how oppressed populations utilize mainstream taboos to socially construct subcultural identity and solidarity.   —*Melvin D. Williams*

In the study of the urban setting, the anthropologist may take as one approach the analysis and description of the cultural character of identifiable groups. We frequently use the terms "subculture," "microculture," "symbol subsystem," and "community," but more research is required into what these phenomena constitute in the urban context by means of the ethnographic record.

This chapter describes some of the communicative symbols that are created and employed in the Zion church in Pittsburgh. Food, death, animals, and the body are behavioral metaphors in this church. This symbolic code helps to create, determine, and delineate the interactional system among its members. One method of substantiating and delineating subculture in modern society is by an identifiable subsystem of symbolic expression—in other words, a communication code.

Zion is a church of ninety-one active communicants that was established by migrants from the rural South. The members interact intensively in religious and social spheres. The Zion group represents a revitalized perceptual field of the rural South, a racially excluded minority, and a distinct religious ideology. These factors underlie a unique organization of symbols used by people who perceive themselves in a strange, alien, urban context. Thus a subsystem of symbolic expression emerges in Zion which coexists with the conflict and solidarity that characterize the dynamics of behavioral interaction among its members.

Symbolic expression at Zion takes as one of its forms a communication code that serves to create images of both the biblical story and the traditional lifestyle in the rural South of the United States. The verbal expressions of the membership are liberally laced with references to food, the farm, the rural landscape, human anatomy, animals, death, the physical world, and the supernatural. Sermons, testimonies, prophecies, songs, and casual conversation are rich in images with which the members can identify and reinforce the cohesion of their religious community. The foods they eat and conceptualize are traditional. The animals they refer to for examples and analogies are reminiscent of life in the rural South; and the idioms expressed in terms of human anatomy, the rural landscape, death, the physical world, and the supernatural are subtle messages with which the members of Zion constantly validate the values that underlie their interaction. Believing they are a different people, a "despised few," "poor folks," and "outcasts" in relationship to the wider society, they use this perspective to validate their own existence by means of a distinctive system of meaning for those things with which they are familiar. The pressures they perceive from the wider society culminate in a self-conception full of traditional idioms which they constantly express. Visitors attending a service at Zion or listening to a conversation among its members are apt to miss the subtle communication or codified messages that are expressed by means of references to traditional characteristics of farm life and synthesized with religious terminology.

FOOD

Food is a pervasive theme in the conceptual framework of the membership. One of the familiar pleasures of rural surroundings, food is incorporated into their new way of life. Zion has salvaged the values of the "good food" of the rural South and recast them into a new symbol subsystem. Food is accordingly fashioned into a symbol of communication and solidarity. It is to the land of "milk and honey" that they all aspire, in the "sweet by-and-by." Even the ruler there can cook: "Jesus can cook, not just preach and heal. He cooked for Peter and fed five thousand." He is a "sweet Jesus." "Taste him and see that the Lord is good." Jesus Christ is "bread in a starving land."

One of the criteria for identifying an in-group is the food they traditionally consume. It is constant reaffirmation that "we are different; we are unique; we know about food." The outsiders "don't know what I am talking about"; "he don't know about that." Even the young and the "city folks" "don't know about that." Certain items are persistent symbols of identification. When you are criticizing the sale of food in the church as a sacrilegious activity, you emphasize that "hot dogs" are being sold in the church. But when you are encouraging the congregation to spend the entire day at church and have "fellowship in the kitchen," you emphasize the sale of fried-chicken dinners, stewed-chicken dinners, fish dinners, fish sandwiches, chicken sandwiches, collard greens, cabbage, cold watermelon, chocolate cake, and sweet-potato pies. They say, "Nobody can cook fish like Mother Jackson," and this distinguishes her in the group. They believe that stomach disorders can be healed "through cooking." They say "a lot" of their members "can smell a pot of beans and tell how long they have been cooking." A person gets his strength from having been bred on "collard greens and drinking the pot liquor." The pastor may tell the congregation, "I know you love greens, Kool-Aid, pork chops, and black-eyed peas," which is his way of emphasizing that he knows the nature of his membership and the leadership they require. Members say, "you can look at them and see they're used to eating cornbread and cabbage," thus attempting to validate their "fleshy" physical appearance.

References to food pervade the conceptual framework of the group. They describe some of their fellow members as being "so sweet that honey is falling out of their mouths." Someone has a "butter-mouthed tongue" if he practices well Zion's themes of love and fellowship. Solidarity is expressed in terms of reliable members who can digest "strong meat," "cornbread," and "black-eyed peas at night." A "strong" sermon, one that has a chastening effect on the congregation, is equated with ham hocks and contrasted with ice cream, which is "smooth and sweet." Members are told to "stay out of the kitchen if you can't stand hot grease" ("don't come hear me preach if you can't endure a strong sermon"). A pleasant or "weak" sermon, one in which the preacher entertains the congregation and they "shout off" (dance), is characterized as a "sugar tit" sermon or a "sugar-coated message" in contrast to "pork chops and beans" that will disturb one's sleep or a "spoon of hot soup that will burn all the way down. You don't need a bowl." And the trials and tribulations of life are described in terms of "drinking your cup of vinegar."

Styles of behavior among the congregation are exemplified by foods. A "sweet dumpling" or "pumpkin pit" is an agreeable sister who goes along with the leader's program. Such terms characterize a dependable member who causes no conflict, in contrast to the "sour peach" who is disgruntled and dissatisfied. These sweet dumpling members are considered vulnerable as well as valuable, for there is a fear that some other pastor may attempt to persuade them out of this church into his own. This fear is often expressed in supernatural terms, and thus dumplings, the food, are frequently the object of potential witchcraft. This fear is a reaction to the extreme anxiety, stress, and tension that are created by a threat of schism in Zion or even the loss of a few of its dependable members to another church.

A sour peach has its animal analogy: It is said that a sour peach looks "like a toad frog when you put salt on his back." Such a member is perceived as being disruptively ambitious. Temptation is exemplified by crabapples. One's personal qualities, abilities, and achievements are often identified with apples; hence the expression "don't pick apples off my trees" to mean "do not exploit my assets for your own ambitions."

The preacher (who is anyone "called" by God to reveal his will) is sometimes called a "chicken eater" in a derogatory sense (in reference to his expropriation of members' resources). The description "tender meat," in contrast to "strong meat," alludes to youth and all those who have not been in the membership long and so cannot endure open exposure to conflict in the church. Thus food is a basic theme in the idiom of Zion-as-nourishment, as an instrument of identity, as a mechanism of communication, and as a means of solidarity.

Judith Goode (1992) says it well:

As one of the basic human drives, the need to eat provides many opportunities for communication. Human groups select raw foods from nature, transform them through cuisine, compose meals, create cycles of meals to punctuate seasons and stages of life, and create rules of etiquette for meal performance. With each of these steps they use food to mark social status, power relationships, and group identity. Food transactions and sharing underscore major social relationships. Domestic events reveal relationships of dominance and subservience between gender and age groups. Community food events have the potential to display relations of cooperation, exchange, solidarity, and sometimes conflict within friendship and extended-kinship networks. In many societies large public feasts and transactions as well as patterns of preference and avoidance communicate relationships of inequality and exclusion between major class and ethnic groups. Finally, many cultures use food systems as elaborated domains of meaning to express important messages about relationships to sacred forces.

Sex and death have analogous human denials as people transform nature into culture.

ANIMALS

References to animals, too, provide a consistent theme in the communication among the members of Zion. The eagle, for instance, described as "a powerful animal that flies high and looks low," is used as a symbol of leadership. It is said to be the only animal that can look directly into the sun and fly so high that it can get above "the storm." Foxes and their dens (referred to as "foxholes") are conceptualized as threats to the task of leading "contrary people." The behavior of geese is utilized to validate leadership in the pastor's analogy: "When I was a little boy down in Kentucky and geese would go back, there was always one just a little ahead of the rest. That was the leader." The members of Zion consider the faithful and dependable among them as sheep and the "confusion-makers" as goats. They say, "Where there are sheep there is always a goat around," or "A goat is the only animal that will eat dry paper" (an indication of inferiority and gullibility), and this is especially significant when you consider that what the members of Zion eat is both literally and figuratively well defined. A goat "sits up in church and sleeps." A goat will lead the gullible sheep up on a mountainous stump where the wolves can get them. "The goat smells like a polecat; he's a stinky thing." The goat is frequently associated with "worldly" people. The members of Zion describe the harsh initiation ceremonies in the fraternities of sinners as "riding the goat." In short, the goat is the epitome of evil in contrast to the sheep, an analogy drawn from the New Testament (Matt. 25:33).

The wealth of the Lord can be measured in terms of cattle. The members say, "My God is a rich God; he has cattle on a thousand hills." The nature of evil is described in its many varieties by the use of animal references. Persecution by the agents of the devil is "being beat up by crocodiles." When the agent of God persecutes you for interfering with his program or his leader who administers that program, "God has turned his bloodhounds loose on you," or "That's why you in the hog pen."

The pastor explains contrary members with the example of the pig litter. In his sermons he sometimes tells this story:

When I was in Kentucky we use to raise pigs. You all know anything about pigs. The mama would have a litter of ten or twelve little pigs. They would all grow normal but one. Wouldn't nothing grow on him but his head. He had a great big head and a little body and he would be gruntin' all the time. He would eat all the time but he would never be satisfied so he was gruntin' all the time. Down in Kentucky we used to call him a runt. You couldn't sell him because you couldn't fatten him up like other pigs. The only thing that would grow on him was his head. So we would kill him for hog head. Everybody doesn't like hog head. We've got runts in the church. We've got people in the church who are just like runts. They mumble and grumble all the time. No matter what you do for them they are never satisfied. They don't grow in the spirit. Nothing grows on them but their head.

The members illustrate humility by the example of the dog who lies on his back with all four feet up. Failure is described in terms of one who fishes all day (to win souls, or natural fish) and does not even catch a bullfrog or a tadpole. The pastor reacts to division amid the congregation or a threat of fission in the church with this animal analogy in his sermon:

You can get someone in the church to go along with you no matter how wrong you are. You can be killing someone's influence and someone will say, "You can count on me." You didn't even catch a bullfrog or a tadpole. It looks like a fish but if you give him time he won't be a fish, he will be a frog. I'm talking to those Mississippi, Louisiana, South Carolina, and Virginia folks. You city folks don't know what I'm talking about. Some folks want to put on airs, a front, and ain't got two dollars. I never did like this front business. I was raised where a shirt was so stiff it looked like a fly would not be able to hang on it. But if you take that coat off there was nothing there but a front with strings to tie it down. You'd be surprised at the folks you think are wonderful ain't nothing but a front. You ought to be a sound minister and not trying to act like somebody else. You will just pick up his faults. . . . Launch out in the deep. Get away from these folks who can't go where the clean fish are.

A wolf in Zion is a "church buster." He has canine teeth to tear the flesh of the sheep, and he is always hungry. He does not heal and comfort but isolates and destroys. If you are not careful, the wolf will teach you his language (how to create division in the church). Even the discussion of men suitors in Zion is described in animal terms. The pastor tells his congregation, "I am going to bark at these foxes in my chicken pen." He rationalized this action by telling the members that any good hen will take her roost under her wings when there is danger about.

Finally, the Holy Ghost and fire that one must have in Zion are described as a house aflame with heat so strong that the spiritual rats and roaches who would otherwise be attracted by the trash, garbage, and rubbish (gossip and other sins) cannot dwell therein (see Leach 1972).

The members of Zion have integrated the images of familiar animals and foods into a distinctive perceptual field (for a statement on urban study using this material, see Williams 1973b). The nature of this familiarity in Zion determines identity and enlivens communication. Moreover, it affords the potential for the organization of, participation in, and manipulation of rural symbols within the context of contemporary urban life. Such distinctive symbolic expression underlies this group's solidarity and defines the nature of subculture and community as useful concepts for understanding the interaction in this church.

DEATH

The concept of death, too, is a standard vehicle for communication among the members of Zion. A familiar human crisis out of their past, death is sometimes exploited for the solidarity of Zion. It is the chasm that must be crossed by every member of Zion to reach the "land of milk and honey." When death occurs, it is an opportunity to demonstrate loyalty to a member of one's alliance, category, or church; or to demonstrate one's love and fellowship with the survivors by one's presence, labor, and food. Death is the final, full, and complete exposure proffered a member of Zion. The members organize the funeral as a final tribute of membership and as a rite of intensification of Zion's values. Thus the members will praise the financial support, the loyalty, and the alliances of the deceased while giving him his final exposure. It is an earthbound reward for one's services in Zion. As the chairman of the deacon board put it, "I has done much that will only be told when I is dead."

Death has a character all it own, as indicated by the phrase "death is still riding," used to admonish anyone who opposes the pastor's program or a particular member's self-interest. The members are warned periodically by the pastor that "death is still calling folks in. You got to go when God gets ready."

Death is a time of fear, and that fear is used to coerce loyalty and financial support from the members. These admonitions are designed to bolster the humility that fosters solidarity in Zion. Death is made a frightening phenomenon, contrasted with "blood running warm in your face." The members say, "You don't know when God is going to move; you don't know when we're going to be shot down in the street"; "you don't know when bombs are going to fall." The pastor proclaims, "I am scared of hell." He warns the members: "You may have cancer now, you don't know, God is a killer. He'll kill you in your home. He'll kill you on the operating table. . . . My wife worries about me because I fast a lot. Some of us leaders will have to give our life. Some of us are going to lose our life. Times are going to get worse. You don't know when God is going to call you on the carpet."

In this way death and the fear of death are used to mitigate against potentially disruptive conflicts in Zion. Death is a sanction threatened against unruly members and those in conflict. The members testify, "I see somebody [dying]." After the timely death of his adversary (Elder Jodie), who was plotting to split his territory after splitting his church, the pastor attempted to vindicate himself: "I didn't plot and plan how to overthrow anybody. I didn't pray and ask God to kill nobody. If God wants to kill 'em, he knows how to do it."

Death is a time of victory if the deceased was your competitor, as in this case. The pastor exclaimed that God was "on my side." He explained that he had "let God fight my battle." This can have the effect of demonstrating the supernatural power of the victor, especially after a long struggle between two adversaries such as Jodie and the pastor. This indication of supernatural power adds significantly to the victor's charisma, and thus to the loyalty of his followers. One of Elder Jodie's close associates reacted thus to such an indication by the pastor:

There's no TV time here. Elder Jodie's time was not cut off because of his controversies. Don't sit in judgment here. There's only one umpire in this game and that's Jesus. *It is better to have fellowship with men than to lead men. Don't get so excited over leadership that you lose fellowship. Drink your cup of vinegar. Accept someone you can't accept. Love someone you can't stand. Dexcuss, argue, fuss, but stay together* [emphasis mine].

Death is a time of practical adjustments in the system of ranking among the members of Zion, especially if one dies holding an important position, and there are always those "who can't wait to move to the head of the class." The emotional intensity of these prospective adjustments makes death a powerful symbol. Even the pastor expresses his anxiety about events that will probably occur after his death.

After I leave some grievous workers will come in among you, will rise up among you, speaking perverse things; watch everything rising. When I am laid out don't have all those folks who didn't support me having something to say over me, who worked with me. I want to be laid out in the new church. It makes me vexed to see all these folks talking over you at the funeral who helped to kill you and couldn't stand you when you were alive, who did everything they could to make things hard for you, then get up talking about sleep on, sleep on, we love you but God loves you best. . . . People put you in a way-out cemetery so they can forget about you. You live in Homewood but they don't bury you in Homewood; that's too close.

The pastor and the members make frequent references to "this life" in contrast to "when I am gone off the scene." They believe that some of their ambitious enemies pray for them. But they assure these enemies, "Don't think I'm going to flunk. You can't look me down to the undertaker."

Death is used to motivated lethargic members. They are told to "get up and get in the prayer line cause it might be your last chance." The congregation is often rebuked and intimidated by the pastor with "those old saints, the end is near." Death is the life crisis that Zion frequently uses to proselytize the living before it is "too late," for it is that moment in Zion when one's soul is either saved or damned. But Zion is the answer to death, for through its membership one can have everlasting life.

Even love and fellowship are reinforced in terms of death. You must be careful not to kill a man's joy or influence, for "he that would kill a man's spirit commits worse than suicide." Members are queried about their lack of enthusiasm during the services: "What you doing all week that you come to church dead." Members say they don't like a dead church. Leadership is explained in terms of the good shepherd who will give his life for his sheep, while a hired servant on salary (Zion's pastor does not get a salary) will flee when the wolf comes. The members assure one another that death is God's remedy for "contrary" members: "These folks grumbling and complaining, many of them you won't see no more." They believe that death is one of God's instruments for punishing: "I want to live so God won't put his bloodhounds on me."

The concept of death pervades Zion's ideological framework. It is a sanction for misbehavior; a threat for social control; the entrance to eternal life; a ritual of solidarity and intensification; and an idiom of communication. Death is a familiar phenomenon to all, even Zion's wide range of membership. It is a secular and sacred life crisis with a prescribed place in Zion's scheme of things.

THE BODY

Components and features of human anatomy constitute another rich source of symbols for the members of Zion. The human body seems a distinctive focus. They want it to survive after death so they can "walk the streets of heaven" and are obsessed with its being crippled and diseased, "bent over" and "crooked." The sexual potency of their bodies is a concern, for it may lead to "evil" or distraction from keeping their "whole mind and body" in Zion. This concern is expressed in constant references to the anatomy and demonstrated in body actions that are permissible in Zion's services: running, jumping, hand-clapping, singing, dancing, screaming, swaying, foot-tapping, rapid shaking, "speaking in tongues" during spiritual possession, and feet-washing. The constant response to the minister as he delivers the sermon often includes waving one's handkerchief in the air as a symbol of solidarity in Christ. Bodily expression is important for these people, and the restrictions imposed upon this expression by their religious code result in a concentration upon these expressions of body position, conditions, movements, and features that are acceptable within the doctrine of their church.

The members believe that the body and all its parts are unclean. Concern with the body and its needs, desires, and pleasures is evidence of a "carnal mind." To be rid of this unclean body one must be "born again," for this is a denial of the "old" body with all its sins: the "new" body has been washed clean with the blood of Jesus. The members believe that all of man's troubles arise from his "interest in bodily pleasures" instead of his being motivated by the Spirit of God. This concern with the problems of the human body in relation to its propensity for evil spreads to verbal symbols rich with references to anatomical terms. Obsession with a human body that is forever threatening one with evil activity (illicit sex, illicit conversation or gossip, smoking, intoxication, swearing, and competitive behavior) compensates for the body's cultural deprivation and becomes a continual rite of intensification for the commitment of self-denial and an effective form of social defiance. This body orientation is a built-in mechanism for intense excitement among the membership when the "backslider falls away" because the temptation of "worldly" pleasures is too great. The member will be forgiven when he subsequently returns to the church, but this reputation, packed with vivid images of sin, will never be forgotten. He will be referred to with considerable delight as "that devil" for his susceptibility to temptation, yet he will be a validated member in Zion, especially if he is among the elite or core members.

Human anatomy is ripe with vivid images that can be called up even in the context of religious themes couched in anatomical terms. The verbal accounts of Zion's development are rich with stories of the transgressions of present and past members; periods of time are marked by such events. There is no animosity, but an excitement even in the recollection. A missionary informed me that a trustee, "that old man," would teach me "bad habits." "He's done more than you've ever thought about." She seemed to be able to document it with personal experiences, and she received considerable delight in recalling escapades of his past life in his presence. Thus the notions of pollution related to the human body seem more complex in Zion than what Lessa and Vogt (1972:196) describe: "Notions of pollution and taboo are not more than rules which protect men and societies from ambiguity and dissonance; they create and preserve boundaries by which moral and social order may exist." These notions provide evidence that in Zion ambivalent entities have potency that may be both worshiped and feared. "Whatever is taboo is a focus not only of special interest but also of anxiety" (Leach 1972:211), and anxiety, kept within tolerable limits, is a mover of men.

The pastor and members frequently refer to parts of the body, body positions, and conditions of the human body. Some of the old members remember Elder Baxter, whom they described as a "rough" preacher who referred to women's "backsides" and their "hind part." Elder Jodie was later called a young Elder Baxter because he made constant references to females' "thighs," "miniskirts," and "sweetheart" relationships. His sermons were usually full of anatomical symbols:

Big folks are hiding in the mountain. The devil's got folks with a downhill drag. Deacons are sitting in a corner with the bishop's wife, and the bishop's in the corner with the deacon's wife. Nobody's mad but the devil [mad because of his biting criticism]. Burn off the miniskirts, God. The more I talk about miniskirts the higher they get, but God's going to burn them off. People lay on their hair so much it won't grow. Get up and go to church. You stay at home looking at naked women on TV, but miniskirts is gonna put TV out of business. Women, hide your thighs. When you get married, then look at the thighs and anything else you want. Mother, you are going to hell if you don't put that little girl's dress down. I didn't get a chance to say much, but a spoon of hot soup will burn all the way down. You don't need a bowl of soup. Words fall from my mouth and hit folks right here [pointing to his heart.] You should leave any church that's not going to give you this word of God. Stop laying home on your lazy self. If you're mad, tell the usher to give you your hat. If you got a robe on [in the choir], take it off. No, you better not; you might have a miniskirt on under it.

Wigs and miniskirts are frequent subjects of conversation in and out of the pulpit. Many texts are taken on the subject of homosexuality. The members often refer to the fact that there were not two men or two women "in the garden [of Eden]." The pastor preaches, "It's not natural for a man to be burning for another man." There are frequent discussions about sissies, women-lovers, men who "burn" for other men, and women who "burn" for other women. In a congregation where it is the ideal to greet members of both sexes with a holy kiss and a hug, this insistence on appropriate sexual "nature" creates some problems. As one male member put it, "When a man hugs me I want him to hurry up and turn me loose." The pastor advises his congregation that there are two places to look if you want to know a person's sex, and he quickly adds (in his timidity about that subject) that his wife told him that.

He uses analogies that consist of references to nudity: "When you're naked you're not comfortable. Time the door moves you jump. But if you got your clothes on you say come on in. Some people are naked spiritually and they're trying to hide it, they don't want folks to see them." The Bible is referred to as the "naked word."

Many descriptions of preachers are couched in anatomical terms. When a preacher "preachers hard" the members say he "rared back, laid his head on his shoulder." A preacher suspected of illicit affairs is referred to as a "common law, slipping around, lopsided preacher."

The symbols of mobility in American society concentrate on disguising or manipulating the features of the human anatomy. These disguises and manipulations are designed to create appearances that fit into the schemes of American standards of beauty, poise, and polish. But the members of Zion take the opposite approach in their verbal references to the human anatomy. They emphasize the frailty, disease, inadequacies, and common features of the human body. In their references to human anatomy, they make no effort to disguise or manipulate physical features to adhere to some standard of beauty. On the contrary, the Zion membership uses the human body to demonstrate the fundamental equality of its members, who must "carry around with them" a frail and troublesome body. These references to human anatomy are successful idioms of solidarity. They are persistent messages to the members that Zion is for "common people," the "despised few," and a Zion mechanism to combat the social distance that results from a ranked organization structure.

Even their religion is translated into concepts of human anatomy. The members say that God knows everything about you, your "down-setting and your uprising." The power of the Lord is symbolized by "His mighty hand" and his ability to "blow you away" (kill you). He can "wash you on the inside," and his ability is described by the saints with an analogy to "natural cleanliness": "Some people don't wash good. They're in too big a hurry. They jump in the tub and jump out, but God starts on the inside." They remind one another that "you must get your eyes off one another and see Jesus." Praising the Lord is referred to as "lifting Him up." Members are taught to "turn your face toward heaven and tell God what you need." The power of God is described as "His mighty hand, and he is said to have "scooped the [Red] Sea out with the palm of His hand." The pastor describes God for the members: "God's so big there's just enough space in heaven for Him to sit down and use the Earth for a footstool. He's got big feet. You can lean on God. He won't give way. He's a sturdy crutch. He's a good leaning post. He has a voice like thunder and when He open His mouth lightning comes out."

The members say, "I want to be so much like God till I walk like Him, till I talk like Him." They conceptualize communicating with God as "breaking through to God."

The pastor advises the members about the church doctrine in anatomical terms: "Some people say my mother always told me I was born with a hot temper. She said I came here kicking and fighting. But you suppose to be born again. When Bishop Jenkins left me at that old antiquated church, they wouldn't believe you were saved unless you rolled on the floor [in possession]. But you can be saved by faith. Only faith is necessary. You don't have to hit the floor."

A "knock-down" sermon is one that "hits" (criticizes) most of those present. The members distinguish between an "honest-heart sinner," who makes no secret of his actions, and a "sneak church sinner." The latter are described as the "half-handed, eagle-rocking church folk" (note that the eagle is used to represent the leader).

Conflict in Zion is frequently described in anatomical terms. A reaction of anger is characterized as "having rocks in your jaw," to "puff up," "swell up," "get hot," and "blow your top." The pastor says that angry members "draw up like a knot and if you don't get your way you look like you're sitting on a spoke." The members say that they have "no confidence in the flesh; some folks can't see no further than their nose; and a lot of folks have forked tongues, they can't talk out of both sides of the mouths." The pastor often uses the family to make analogies to relationships within Zion, and these relationships, too, are described in physical terms. The marriage ceremony is "jumping the broom," avoiding the finality of being swept away forever, by means of potential offspring. But "a wife means more than rubbing your head." "A whole lot of folks just rub your head when they want something." The pastor continues: "Sometimes you can't believe your own folks calling you honey bunch and pie today and tomorrow they got a club for you. Make all the friends you can but don't try to buy'em. Don't try to buy me. You make me think, you think I'm soft. Give me all the gifts you want, but don't try to buy me with gifts."

The members are often admonished by the ministers not to "put their mouth on the leader," that is, gossip about him. They are told that if they make their "bed hard they are going to have to turn over in it"; that you should not come to church to look at one another; that there is no little toe in the church, there is only one whole body; that you should have clean hearts; that you should greet your sisters and brothers with a holy kiss and hug instead of "backbiting" (note reference to body and teeth). The pastor explains:

You can wear yourself down dealing with contrary folks. The spirit is willing but the body is not able. When disease is upon you, it is sin 80 to 90 percent of the time. These ulcers, cancer, and opium are from sin. Self can be dangerous because to exalt in self is sin. You must get self out of the way if you are to receive the blood of Jesus. Folks pat self on the chest so much and really think they're somebody. I have no confidence in the flesh. You don't have to pull no strings, pay nobody off, slide nothing under the table to advance in this church. On February the fifteenth, I came into the church. I didn't ask to be ordained. I didn't ask for any office. But I got it anyway. Somebody tried to block my ordaining. I lean on God, not them.

Members who create "confusion" are described as having "something wrong with their heads," "their head not functioning right," or being "confused in the heads."

The problems of daily living are described in terms that refer to the human body. The pastor advises the members:

You need supernatural help because some men will desert you. But God will be with you though all men forsake you. Peter said, "I don't know the man," when asked to speak for Jesus at the cross. This is happening today, and the days are hard with all the odds against you. Everything seems to be going against you. The waters won't behave themselves and the sun won't shine. All the leaning posts are falling away, but you must trust God. Everybody is looking for you to fail. Nobody is expecting you to make it, but you are advancing through handicap. You battle with the adversary day after day, year after year, wear yourself down, and you get weak physically but stay strong on the inside. They have done me wrong but I'm not bound. I haven't upset the city, but they are accusing me. All I have done is preach Jesus.

The members describe anger as feeling "something moving on me." The trials and tribulations of a member's life are described thus: "Saints are knocked and buffeted about in this life, but hold on with your little strength." Persecution is described as "being stoned to death." Stubbornness is "being hardheaded," and education is something that "swells your head." Members of Zion are "walk-around folks." Humility, meekness, and passiveness are Zion ideals, but in actual relationships they recognize that "being saved don't mean to let folks walk over you all the time." "God gave you five senses and there's a time when you should stand on your feet and speak up. You can be too soft. You got to know when someone's on your territory. Jesus said if you're going to be my disciple you're going to have to deny yourself. You got to know the differences between Jesus and me. Ourselves is our greater hinder. It is like the tongue. No man can master the tongue."

The pastor describes the women who do day work thus: "Men are the head.

They may be a weak head, but he is the head. God didn't intend for these women running around catching these buses. If she helps you to get out of the hole, you ought to call her in afterwards and say you can sit down now, honey. A whole lot of people don't want to sweat. The book says by the sweat of your brow. They want their hands clean. They want a sweetback job" (note reference to taste and anatomy).

All the ailments of the limbs are referred to as "being crippled" and "bent over." The sick are "shut-ins." A saint testifies, "When my bronchial tubes were stopped up and I could not breathe for myself, I needed an artificial respirator and Jesus got them tubes." Another testifies, "I had a sore throat yesterday. God is a throat specialist." Body deformities are frequent themes of discussion: "This old flesh gives us a lot of trouble. It wants to peak out on you. It takes a lot of care." But you do not need to get a "hand" from a "hoodooer" (a voodoo practitioner). You do not need to "run somebody down; you don't need to lay somebody out." "Keep you hand in God's hand and you will get what's coming to you."

Spiritual growth of the saints is described with anatomical vividness: "Some children are born, and this ain't no reflection on nobody, with a head bigger than their body. And mom says, 'Come on Hon, come on Hon,' and Hon can't come because he's unbalanced. You got to have a big head with a big body, feet, and big hand. . . . Saints suppose to grow, not just their head. It is easy for your head to grow, especially if God is blessing you."

Saints are supposed to close their "weak and watery eyes so they don't see too much." They are supposed to hold "their tongues so they don't talk too much." Their arms are "too short" and their strength "too weak." They need the Lord. Stubborn members are characterized as "stiff-necked folks," "carnal folks with carnal minds." "They will take your head off."

The pastor slows the pace of his scripture reader by saying, "Don't carry me too fast, let me hear what you're saying, don't carry me too fast." The members describe lethargy as "looking funny." Members are consistently described as being spiritually "weak": "We need tarry meeting because all of us are weak and some here need the Holy Ghost. Somebody helped us. Tarried at midnight until sweat ran down. Brought me out of the muck and mire" (note reference to nature, midnight, and moisture).

Membership recruiting can even be described in anatomical terms: "just before you break is there any among you who is not a member of the church? [Four people acknowledge, and the pastor leaves the pulpit and comes down into the congregation.] I want to shake your hand. Now I'm not trying to shake you in the church."

If dissident members are allowed to come back into the church without "humbling themselves," they are characterized as being allowed to "come strutting in." To give organizational support is verbalized as "to stand by me." Not only does God talk to his "chosen few," but he even whispers to them at midnight: "Some folks put forth all the grand plots they can think of to put people against you. God is the one that whispers in your ear, sometimes late at night, and tells you to live on when the doctors have given you up." Success for the members is described as being "lifted from the dunghill and set on high," or being removed from the "muck and mire."

Even geographical references can be translated into body features. The immediate Pittsburgh metropolitan area is described as "this neck of the woods." Leaving the church before the sermon is over is termed "running out on me." A capable minister is described as being able to "walk around." When the membership is not listening, the pastor chides, "When people turn a deaf ear to you, you have to have enough grace to keep your feet on the ground."

The members' conception of Satan is couched in terms that suggest he has a human anatomy. The relationship between members and the devil is sometimes seen or described in pugilistic terms. Thus they caution one another to "hold on," when the devil is getting the best of them and to be aware that with all their prayers the devil is "still hitting you below the belt." The pastor says, "I fight hard not to let nothing get in my heart against those trying to hurt me." The devil has a body which the Lord can "bind." The devil can also enter a member's body and "bind" that member's spirit, in which case the devil is told to "Loosha, Loosha" ("Turn loose the body and the spirit of this child of God"). You have to "shake yourself loose from the devil." The devil is ordered to "get behind me," and the Lord is beseeched to "go before me."

Some saints who have been "saved" and return to the "world and sin" are called backsliders; they are said to be able to fall on their face and "get up in the morning and we're somewhere talking our way into hell," that is, they ask for forgiveness and are forgiven while members are gossiping about them. The members refer to those who participate in gossip as "busybodies." Those who are in need of prayer are told to "get on their knees." Those who come out of the baptism pool frightened are described as having come out "kicking." The act of praying for someone is "laying your hands on them" (see Finkler 1994). Unpleasant experiences are bumps or knots on the head from which God can teach you a lesson. According to the members, all such communication harks back to a period of rural life in the South where such expression was common, accepted, and valued; one who used them was "a good talker." It is revived in Zion to express and identify the dynamics of interaction that occur there.

Thus human anatomy is pervasive in the membership's conceptualization. It was an available resource for conceptualization in the rural South. It is the subject of ritual pollution in Zion's religion (see Douglas 1972). The members have contorted it into a unique symbol system for communication and codified messages which underlies their solidarity.

SUMMARY

When the members describe their disgruntled and dissatisfied members as "sour grapes" and "sour peaches," they are translating into their idiom a powerful feeling of antagonism, for taste is tantamount to experience among these members. When they tell you that those members who are verbal experts in love and fellowship have a "butter-mouthed tongue" and honey flowing from their mouths, they are communicating a vivid reaction in their own idiom. These people endow foods, taste, and eating with a range of meaning that suggests the explanation I have attempted. Food is transformed from a biological necessity to a social drama, and "sweetness and power" become collaborators in biophobia and the human search for security (see Mintz 1987).

There is also a constant effort to validate the inclusion of the "poor," the "outcasts," and the "despised few" in Zion. This is Zion's reason for being—it is a shelter for poor Blacks from the rural South. This effort takes a variety of forms, some of which I have referred to in this chapter. I have mentioned for this purpose the terms, expressions, and symbols of orality. Largely denied the verbal manipulation of those genital terms and symbols that demonstrate a defiance for social mobility in other Black subcultures, the members interact with other oral terms and symbols that demonstrate the same defiance. The holy kiss, the butter-mouthed tongue, the honey-flowing mouth, speaking in tongues, screaming while possessed, testifying, prophesying, confessing, and eating (all in the association of other members) are constant ceremony and ritual in intimate oral exposure to combat and defy the very social distance inherent in Zion's social organization of elite, core, supportive, and marginal membership. Many of the members' verbal expressions are codified messages of orality—"Don't put your mouth on me" (gossip about me), "God opens his mouth and lightning comes out," one can talk another "down to the undertaker," and one must be watchful of those who "fix big meals for them." A common gesture in dyadic conversation in Zion is to cover the mouth so as not to offend.

Even with rigid restraints upon genital and anal references, the members manage to evade subtly the letter of the law. Thus references to the genital, the anal, and especially the oral characteristics of members are weapons against social distance in Zion and defiance of social mobility in the wider society (see Jankowiak 1993).

DISCUSSION

While Zion is an example of how the denial of sex, death, and digestion can be manifested and exploited, such denial, defiance, and defilement of the animal body has far greater ramifications. One is the lifelong abuse of the greatest machine known to humans—the human body. The other is the care and control of the body by "certified" professionals who torture and exploit the bodies of "others" for profit and prestige. Humans are socialized to believe that the body is alien and must be cared for and controlled by "certified" agents as are electric wires (electricians), pipes (plumbers), wood (carpenters), and masonry (bricklayers). For the human body there are even "certified" specialists for its different parts and different "treatments" for these parts.

In the Ecological Revolution, humans will take their cues from Zion and celebrate, not deny, the body. The female, gay, Black, and "ugly" bodies of the world will be the global membership cards and the universal metaphors of (wo)man. These common denominators of humanity will replace the failed myths, hegemonic discourses, and pathological pursuits of power. The body will be recognized as the human victory and no longer be perceived as the human fall from grace.

Health care and war (defense) are two of the main human industries of the twentieth century. One purports to save the body; the other promises to save the world for the body. Both industries are designed for profit and prestige.

Finally, with the end of DDDAK, the health-care, death-care, and sex-advertising industries will no longer be able to torture and exploit the human race for profit and prestige.

Chapter 5

The Body and the Beast

Humans are animals that perspire, and perspiration has its odor. We secrete from the eyes, ears, lungs, bronchial tubes, skin, sinuses, nose, sexual organs, and colon. We salivate, masticate, expectorate, regurgitate, urinate, defecate, masturbate, fornicate, gestate, exudate, suppurate, lacrimate, fight, kill, sleep, hemorrhage, die, and decay. Yet we reject our animal kinship and even subordinate other humans arbitrarily defined as "inferior" to prove our superiority.

Females have the additional animal functions of menstruation, gestation, labor, and lactation. Furthermore, who knows the animal character of the male better than the female. She carries him for nine months, ejects him during labor, nurses him until he must be weaned, copulates with him, has her eggs fertilized by him, cares for him as he ages, and finally buries him. So in this process of DDDAK, women are a major threat to the image of men who are made "in the image of God." The only means men have for demonstrating their artificial superiority to women is by symbols and force (Foster 1994). He subordinates her with expressive symbols of inferiority (Hollander 1995, Johnson 1995). He is reinforced in these expressive efforts by her additional animal characteristics. I repeat for emphasis, she menstruates, lactates, is impregnated, gestates, breeds, and rears her brood. By her presence she constantly reminds the male of his vaginal origin, seduction, sedation, and animal kinship. A woman conspiring with a snake represents one of our society's most vivid symbols of evil. (Williams 1992b:73,114)

As I have stated in the Preface of this volume, racism, classism, and sexism are problems of human identity. Other such problems are ethnocentrism, sectarianism, ageism, nationalism, and speciesism. Humans define themselves and thus create meaning for birth, struggle, and death—or sex, death, and digestion—all of which are "lower" animal characteristics that humans deny, defy, and defile in themselves. In the twenty-first century, human divisiveness and their destructiveness toward Earth will force them to learn to accept their animal kinship and to cherish their miraculous bodies in order to live harmoniously with "races," classes, genders, and even with Earth itself. To accomplish this, humans must cease the historical denial and domestication of human insecurity. That insecurity has created the denial, defiance, and defilement of our animal kinship. Such a state of denial renders humans incapable of dealing with their own lives, health, and planet.

I present an evolutionary discussion of how the human state of denial began and evolved and attempt to describe how this former adaptive strategy has outlived its time on Earth. I state in conclusion a tentative evolutionary solution (the Ecological Revolution) to human divisiveness and human extinction. That solution will eliminate all the artificial and contrived categories of human inferiority, denigration, and degradation. Humans will finally discover the pervasive influence of DDDAK in the creation of these categories: the poor, homeless, wretched, delinquent, illiterate, addicted, and CRESSANS.

GENDER

As a boy I was taught that my body was "born in sin" and "must be born again" to save my soul, that it would take the blood of Jesus to clean my dirty body, which would return to dust (but not my soul). One of our highest ideals is the development of the mind (e.g., "a mind is a terrible thing to waste"). Meanwhile, most of us spend much of our lifetimes abusing our magnificent bodies. An "intellectual" is expected to have a "puny" body, while those with athletic bodies are suspected of underdeveloped minds. Thus we have attempted to separate the body from our highest values, and we have associated the body with our lowest denigrations.

Understanding gender requires an examination of the mythology about the human body. That mythology is the basis for much of the hegemonic manipulation of sexual dimorphism and the hierarchical misinterpretations of human anatomical characteristics (Tuana 1994). The social science efforts to reclaim the human body (Beck 1975) may assist in undermining the ritual and ceremony of human sexuality that enchants entire populations into gender values that create social inequality. The brief discussion here is designed to contribute to that effort.

As stated above, women are considered inferior because of their animal characteristics. We have institutionalized that inferiority by highlighting women's animal attributes. We coerce women to grow abundant hair on their heads and to style it so that it bounces as they walk or draws attention to their eyes and lips by dropping around them (e.g., Veronica Lake fifty years ago and Claudia Schiffer's bangs). We encourage women to wear rings in their ears and makeup that distorts the appearance of their eyes and eyebrows. Male surgeons "remodel" their faces, and optometrists style the "fashion" frames for their eyeglasses, many of which (e.g., sunglasses) are worn for attention. Women are socialized to put blush on their cheeks, powder on their faces, and lipstick on their lips. They wear necklaces and low-cut apparel to show their necks and cleavage, bras to lift their breasts, and halters to expose their waists and navels. Women's clothes are designed to expose the contour of their buttocks (note the recent problems with panty lines) and the proportion of the waists to the buttocks. In cold weather they wear brightly colored sweaters that extend below their coats and attract attention to their buttocks. Miniskirts and "hotpants" expose the thighs and legs, and stockings, socks, pantyhose, and coloring attracts attention to the size and proportion of their legs. They wear split skirts that alternately expose one leg and thigh and then the other as they walk and skin-tight spandex athletic suits. The shoe industry exploits the exposure of their feet with toes (painted) and heels exposed, and the height of the shoe's heel is designed to tilt the buttocks. Most women "need" a variety of shoes (e.g., Imelda Marcos) for such variable exposures of the feet.

Businessmen wear our most common and "respected" clothing. They do not attract attention to their ears, eyes, cheeks, or lips. They wear uncomfortable shirts that cover their necks and ties that attract attention away from their nipples. They do not expose their waists or their navels, and they wear coats (inside buildings during the summer) that cover their buttocks and genital areas. The coat lapels are shaped and designed to enhance the "masculine" physique and the neckties they border. They wear pants that have no space for their genitals; on the contrary, the pants are cut as if they have none. Their apparel does not expose their thighs or legs, and their shoes do not expose their feet or tilt their buttocks. They have institutionalized their "superiority" by denying and disguising their animal bodies. This can be lethal to men as it is often accompanied by the denial and defiance of body symptoms of injury and illness. This is especially true of problems in the genital area (e.g., prostate pathology), and it subjects them to premature disabilities and death.

I am not suggesting that we change the clothing (mere empty expressive symbols) that I have briefly described here but that we must change our attitudes and values about the human body.

In all of this, woman, whose body structures and functions (described below) are perceived as being more similar to those of the "lower" animals than those of men, are kept among the "inferior" (Ortner 1974, Van Leeuwen 1990). De Beauvoir (1953) documents the impact of DDDAK on human females. Ortner (1974) elaborates on the universal perception of the inferiority of women, but she does not strike to the heart of the matter, namely, the perceived similarity between women and "lower" animals, and she creates ambiguity with the term "nature." But de Beauvoir examines the physiological structure, development, and functions of the human female; her review, and my own, illustrate that such obvious parallels to the lives of "lower" animals would condemn human females to the "inferiority" that DDDAK demands.

In the Ortner (1974) paradigm, "man is to woman as culture is to nature." If one replaces the ambiguous term "nature" with the word "animal" the equation becomes plausible. Females are perceived as symbolic animals. Their reproductive organs are controlled by men as if private property. The most severe sanctions have been applied in the South when white females have intercourse with other "races." And why not, when white females are physically capable of eliminating race in the United States by miscegenation. Society socializes and sanctions white females to maintain "race" at all costs. Moreover, society goes to great lengths to conceptual African Americans as "lower" animals. I have a large collection of

African-American memorabilia that demonstrates what efforts white America is willing expend to "document" the animal inferiority of Black Americans.

Sexual "inferiority" is only one component of the human inferiority complex created by DDDAK. Race is another. Human beings compensate for perceived animal deficiencies by releasing aggression on suitable scapegoats. DDDAK and our ever-present animal bodies create an appropriate framework for legitimating the practice of racial discrimination. As we struggle to prove that we are not "lower" animals, we are constantly made aware that we cannot escape our own animal-based feelings of inferiority by projecting and displacing that "inferiority" onto others. These projections and displacements are a part of the human condition, but they do not resolve the human dilemma. We have the mark of the beast—an animal body—and a mind that contemplates God.

THE FACE AND THE FUTURE (DEATH)

The human obsession with the face (as in "saving face"), a primary locus of the ego, wastes thousands of hours of anxiety during a lifetime. If we were only as anxious about the cells of our miraculous bodies, how much healthier our lives would be. Many people enter a restroom before meeting others, not to eliminate but to secure their faces. You see them stopped at traffic lights adjusting their rearview mirrors to see themselves. They damage the exterior mirrors on vehicles of strangers by clandestinely forcing the mirrors into a position to see themselves. Many people carry a mirror at all times, and most people never get stranded far from one.

The face is not the person. The face is one of the contrived components of the body for identity. Yet most people take better care of their faces than they do the remainder of their bodies. In the Ecological Revolution, mirrors will cease to exist. People, like other animals, will no long require facial images to deceive themselves and others.

Humans are also obsessed by their future. Men are not content to have sexual intercourse today. They attempt to guarantee it for the rest of their lives. They design it as a property right. They contract for it "until death do us part." When in danger of losing it, they become violent and maim, stalk, and kill in their attempts to secure it. They seldom accept the loss and with emontional maturity seek a new sexual partner; a replacement is usually available. But they pine the loss of the one that got away as if they had a right and a privilege to keep her, and as if they were justified in expecting that her availability was guaranteed to them throughout their future.

I have already described how humans deny, defy, and defile death, the one certainty of their future. Death is the ultimate submission ("inferiority"), as Bishop Sampson Jr. (see p. 68) said to Bishop Jackson, do not come here (to get "TV time" at Elder Jodie's funeral) to exploit the death of Elder Jodie as a victory (superiority) for yourself, merely because your life is extended beyond his. Bishop Jackson was attempting to merge excellence and superiority into longevity. He was trying to proclaim, as do many humans, that burying your enemies is the ultimate revenge. So disgruntled employees kill their persecuting "superiors" or supervisors. Abused spouses kill their abusing ("superior") partners. These behaviors reflect the perception of death as a great equalizer, a forced and final submission to the ultimate "inferiority." I suspect rape has a pathological relationship to this perception.

This perception of "superiors" and "inferiors" ignores the fact that humans are all equal, all of the time, not just at death. This perception of inequality creates the fear of an ultimate submission and a final, absolute, and complete "inferiority." So humans struggle with their end of life rather than celebrate the end of their struggles. Death hangs over our heads as a lifelong burden rather than being accepted as our ultimate salvation. Even those in Zion who worship for life-after-death cannot avoid the human fear of death, a fear that is a cultural overlay of a survival instinct. Thus it is difficult to be rational about death. Shakespeare was incomplete when he asked, "Who would bear the whips and scorns of time?" (*Hamlet,* Act 3, Scene 5). Fear of death entails not only a fear of the unknown but also a fear of inferiority. (Note the stigma, aura, abandonment, and denial that surrounds the "terminally ill" when it could be argued that all humans are "terminally ill.")

But humans are equally obsessed with other future necessities. Most humans spend most of their lives preparing for the future. They will never collect and store enough resources to secure that future in their own minds. They never have enough money, land, power, personal possessions, status, recognition, fame, success, prestige, and rank to feel secure. There is always more, and that forces them to feel less (secure). Human insecurity has evolved since the origin of (wo)man and requires an evolutionary understanding of the resulting human divisiveness—race, class, and gender.

THE RECLAMATION OF THE BODY

Human have never been secure with their bodies (Sheets-Johnstone 1992). Those bodies look similar to those of the "lower" animals. Thus humans stood erect, acquired language, made tools (to extend the reach and grasp of their bodies), and engaged in myriad body-modification activities: corporeal art, circumcision, clitoridectomy, cutting, piercing, tattooing, adorning, footbinding, body building, hairstyling, body painting, implants, body disguising (clothing styles), and body hiding (see Foster 1994). In the Ecological Revolution, humans will cast off DDDAK and take their bodies back from:

1. physicians and medical schools, with their pathological model of the miraculous bodies that perform most of their cures for them;
2. nurses and nursing schools, with their inventory paradigm of magnificent bodies that they "handle";
3. medical technicians and their technology that is often unnecessarily invasive and destructive to precious human tissue;

4. hospitals, the temples of postmodernity, that propagate the propaganda of eternal life simultaneously as they probably terminate more lives than they make eternal;

5. religious practitioners, who create evil and sinful bodies that they then exploit rather than transcend;

6. funeral directors, who create a "beautiful" facade of life after social institutions have ignored the beauty and destroyed the life;

7. cemeteries, where we celebrate the sacred waste rather than the former sacred life;

8. psychologists and psychiatrists, who artificially separate the body from the mind and emotions and create subsequent mysteries that only "professionals" can pretend to comprehend;

9. the pharmaceutical, sex, alcohol, and consumer industries, whose chemicals, potions, and fantasies poison and debilitate our cells, tissues, and organs. A healthy immune system is the greatest pharmaceutical industry ever known.

10. gender, by which bodies are programmed, abused, raped, stalked, exploited, and ranked (see Foster 1994); and

11. others that give us vast misconceptions of our unique bodies.

We live in a society that invests billions of dollars in disease (e.g., hospitals, medical research, medical schools, nursing schools, dental schools, medical equipment, and pharmaceutical industries). Consumers spend other billions of dollars in taxes and medical services to support the health industries. The United States is projecting bankruptcy in part as a result of the skyrocketing "health care" costs due to Americans' backside conception of health care rather than a frontside conception (see Temple and Burkitt 1994, Tiger 1979a).

Backside "health care," like most of society's resources, is very scarce among the poor. History proves that, regardless of how the poor and their lobbyists campaign and complain, the pattern of withholding "health care" resources from the poor will not change much. But in this period of "health care" reform, the poor will receive an identifiable pittance, and with that minor resource they can, with some ingenuity, create a revolution in health care among themselves.

The poor and their communities can discard the backside conception of health care and initiate, especially among their children, a frontside conception. True health care is not the factitious care of our miraculous bodies. It is not "prevention." It is the concerted effort to refrain from the careless and malicious destruction of our bodies. It is the development of attitudes and values that ceaselessly attempt to support the body's health and well-being. We can accomplish this among the children.

In the Ecological Revolution all of the agencies that have contact with children (e.g., Head Start, day care centers, public schools, Youth Services Corporation, and Job Corps centers) will be mandated to provide frontside health care and health education. The mandate will give force to the principle that no education is more valuable than the care of one's body. The best health care system is a very healthy body.

In any facility that cares for children, there must be color-and-numbercoded toothbrushes. All children must brush and floss their teeth upon arrival and departure and after meals. Children will be taught how and why they must care for their teeth and their mouth tissues. Chewing gum and all foods that are destructive to the teeth or other body tissues will be discouraged and lobbied against. Hands will be washed on arrival, after every activity, and at departure. Children will learn that the hands distribute harmful bacteria. Feet will be washed frequently. Children will discuss how these and other important organs are abused. All children will receive their inoculations and explanations as to their purpose. Pregnant teenagers will be required to have prenatal care, sexual guidance, and parenting classes. The food pyramid will be described and explained every day. Children will learn the meaning of nutrition and how everything that they eat and drink is used by the cells and organs of the body. Pain will be explained as a body warning system. Children will discover how easy it is to abuse the body if they eat and drink garbage and swill. And they will learn how to identify it. Every child will exercise every day, and exercise will be explained as being as important as food for the muscle tissues. Children will be required to lie down and rest for a period each day, and they will learn that sleep is as essential as exercise for a healthy body.

These teaching and behavioral programs (in the schools and the homes) will continue as the children move through elementary school, and by the time they reach junior high school they will believe and behave as if the body is the real temple of postmodernity. Violence to the body in the media will disappear as the harm it causes becomes apparent. Children will learn a new version of the Golden Rule: "Your body is as sacred a temple as mine." All human bodies are in the same species, and contrary attitudes and values will not remain with the children. The children will carry the new principles of health home and chide their parents and siblings for any abuse of the body. Parents and siblings will learn from these new age children. The new attitudes and values about the body will eventually permeate the entire community. The Revolution will have begun.

After the Ecological Revolution, humans will remember how they used to abuse their bodies from birth to death in sports, diets, fashion model industries, sleep habits, pharmaceuticals, exercise deficiencies, and sexual activities as they simultaneously complained about and wasted billions of dollars on health care costs. That memory will allow them to understand how they almost destroyed their Earth as a human environment as well. Contempt for our bodies and contempt for our Earth are made from the same fabric of irrationality. We will remember how the Eurocentric, Afrocentric, and feminocentric (and others) perspectives evolved into a biocentric one.

THE BODY AND THE BOUNDARY

Language is inadequate for communication about the body (Csordas 1994). It uses categories that do not exist except within the symbol system itself. It enables humans to lie, and it has failed to prevent some of the greatest "misunderstandings" among humans ever recorded (e.g., the Holocaust, massacres, wars, genocide, murders, abuse, slavery, divorce, violence, and litigation). Perhaps language was never designed solely for communication. Humans communicated long before language evolved (see Greenberg 1968). Language did allow humans to rank "others," however, and it continues to perform that function (Collins 1975).

Reclaiming the body could be perceived as an extreme behavior, but extremism is not my intention. The act of reclaiming the body allows us to cast off the "beasts," but it must not create another boundary or another caste of "others" (see Game 1991). It must not create mirror-gazing or another form of narcissism. Earth creates and reclaims all bodies. Those bodies are similar in our species and alike in our animal kingdom. Respect for our own bodies should extend to respect for all life. The social organization of the wolf, the weaving of the spider, and the architecture of the bee will receive human respect in the Ecological Revolution. Our bodies are a part of the natural order. They have no boundaries. They do not belong to us. They begin with the engagement of two other persons' egg and sperm. They develop in and from the fluids of mothers and eventually from the direct sustenance of Earth. They grow and mature only with nurture by other people. They procreate by sexual intercourse, and in the end they return to the Earth that sustained them.

So the body is neither a boundary nor a "beast." It is one of the greatest inventions of nature. If it is treated with great respect, nature will care for it and protect it (see Sheets-Johnstone 1992, Temple 1994, Tiger 1979b). Such care and respect for all of nature's bodies may prevent the human misunderstandings that I noted at the beginning of this section. The body's role as "meat" for athletic coaches, whoremongers, and dining tables will cease in the Ecological Revolution.

CONCLUSION

This book presents an overarching theory that posits the behaviors described as responses to the natural universe. Human nature appears as a social divisive that allows a species like ours to survive and increase. Fear of our animal bodies fosters other fears and insecurities about where we belong in the animal world. We saved ourselves by heroics (Becker 1973), breathing life into our gods, developing contempt for our bodies, and ranking everything we discovered below us. We saved ourselves from cosmic humiliation (Miller 1993). But now we must confess our sins and find our species' security elsewhere. We are exposed. Our secrets are no longer hidden and underground. DDDAK forces us out of the closet. We are not independent and autonomous but have mutuality and reciprocity with life on Earth and Earth itself. The little children, abandoning the mythological beast, reclaiming their own bodies, and controlling the fantasies of face, ego, and futures, will lead us into the Ecological Revolution.

Race is one (race, class, and gender) component of my evolutionary discussion of human divisiveness, and I argue that biophobia is the origin of that divisiveness. Without succumbing to reductionism, I am reminded that Kroeber (1923, 1948) stated that psychology would provide the laws of human behavior. Not only financial markets, industry, and services but also human insecurities of postmodernity are permeating the peoples of the globe. "Smart weapons," consumerism, and greed are transnational. When race is fully understood, many of these other social problems will no longer be mysteries.

In the beginning there was the body (see Wrong 1961), and the body made humans. The biological determinism question is an old one, and it is not one with which I wish to grapple. But biology was there in the beginning, and it will remain to the end. Yet Wrong's (1961) quotation (in a footnote) of "Paul Goodman's observation that anthropologists nowadays 'commence with a chapter on Physical Anthropology and then forget the whole topic and go on to Culture'" continues to be pertinent. Other animals were also present in the human environment. These are some of the significant stimuli to which early humans responded. I argue that they responded with fear, arrogance, condescension, and elitism. Those responses were adaptive and successful then but not now. Culture is no longer required to "conquer and control" nature. Nature is not our constant enemy. I have attempted to use geology's principle of uniformity to demonstrate that the present is the key to the past. One of the goals of anthropology is to understand the meanings of being human. That is also one of its major missions. Biological anthropology is one of the significant recognitions that the study of the body is necessary to comprehend humans and human behavior. I argue that the relationship between biological anthropology and ethnology is much closer than has been stated. The concept of race is one approach to observing that relationship.

Prehuman primates had many disadvantages relative to other animals with whom they shared environments. Note that many of humans' closest kin, the great apes (humans share more than 99% of their DNA sequences with gorillas and chimpanzees), have been driven into small pockets of the Earth and are threatened with extinction. Humans survived and became successful adapters in most areas of the world. Their "big brain" was the precursor in this adaptive strategy. As the human brain increased in size and complexity, this 2 1/2 pounds of electrified neurotransmitters (that are affected by their total environment and affect human behavior) made humans increasingly more self-conscious of themselves and their relationships with other animals. The developments of face (ego), family (incest taboos), and future (eternal) were simultaneously accompanied by an obsessive fear of being just another animal. That fear is the basis for humans becoming "superior" and "higher" animals by ceaseless demonstrations of that "superiority." That fear has become maladaptive in postmodernity and must be relinquished in the Ecological Revolution.

In the beginning was the body (i.e., sex, death, and digestion). And it was adaptive: The biophobic prehuman created the ego and culture. With an ego (see Updike 1989), a face (ego-invested rather than a part of the head with all those holes), and a future, humans developed families, religions, communities, ethnic groups, nations, and first, second, and third worlds. Today our technological capabilities have created a global village and disabled most of our social institutions (including race). Survival into the twenty-first century requires new social institutions that are compatible with a global village and biocentric human beings. Race is a vestige of a human biophobia that is three million years old and obsolete in the twenty-first century. If humans are not the products of a lethal mutation, the war against the social "inferior" will end. People will celebrate their bodies and their animal kinship. They will end body-bashing sports and diets. Human societies are complex adaptive systems (see Waldrop 1992). The potentiality of the whole human race is born again in every new baby. One of our next adaptive transformations is the Ecological Revolution.

Race is a global concept (Count 1958). Race is determined by gene pools (Shipman 1994). The phenotypes of race are biologically determined. But humans are biophobic (fear of sex, death and digestion). Any human differences that are gauged by biological processes (race, gender, and age) are especially potent. Differences among humans are archetypically exploited for social hierarchies. Race mythologies are as powerful as human biophobia.

The phenotypic differences of race have been ranked and distorted into sociocultural mythologies of "others." Thus race is a biological basis for ordinal ranking and excluding human populations from full membership in the human family. The unilineal evolutionists were casualties of biophobia. Their theories were debunked, but such arguments have little impact upon the archetypal emotions of humans. Most humans probably share the feelings the unilineal evolutionists had when those theorists concocted their arguments that some races are members of human subspecies. People living in the jungles with "lower" animals and "living like those animals" cannot be full members of the "civilized" human family.

Scientific jargon about the human body will not communicate to the layperson nor educate children who are not familiar with those terms. Small children must learn the body basics without the terms that conceal shame. If I were to explain to a layperson or to a small child the human inferiority complex that underlies race and racism, I would proceed in this way.

All people have body functions and traits about which they are taught to be ashamed (e.g., blemishes, skin color and eruptions, sizes, "defects," "deformities," proportions, hair characteristics, perspiration and digestive odors, vomit, saliva, tears, and nasal mucus). Note the negative attitudes attached to secretions from human orifices.

Children grow into teens bombarded with humiliating comments about those characteristics about which they have been taught to be ashamed. In my youth we were "put down, dragged, razzed, signified on, laughed at, ripped on, rapped on, capped on, put low, played the dozens with, and dissed." Children learn to describe one another as "ugly, fat, skinny, nasty, stinky, dumb, stupid, crybaby, clumsy, bird brains," and unworthy of social inclusion. They refer to one another using genital, buttocks, feces, and urine referents. They tease one another about all body "defects" and functions. These socializing experiences reinforce the shame that children have already learned. These patterns of humiliation create and develop feelings of inferiority, and those feelings are accentuated as they enter pubescence and their bodies begin to "explode." With constant reminders of their shortcomings, people attempt to demonstrate and prove their "superiority." They develop the need to reinforce their own personal pride and confidence by comparisons to those who are "inferior" to themselves. They attempt to valorize their socially depreciated bodies by fashion, style, and graven images. Society encourages these behaviors by teaching pre-adults that they are outranked by adults and by enforcing professional statuses that outrank other adults. Adults continue to feel inferior and to humiliate one another for anxiety relief and invidious comparisons. These lifelong feelings and habits create divisive humans. More than sixty years ago it created Hitler and Nazi Germany. Today we have Vladimir Zhirinovsky, Rwanda, and Bosnia. If all children could be socialized to know and to feel that a human body is far more valuable than a top-of-the-line Rolls Royce, they would believe that "I'm okay!" (Branzei 1995). All the children in Mr. Rogers' "Neighborhood" are made to feel okay. "It's You I Like," not your hair or the clothes you wear.

The children of the world must be saved from:

1. working parents
2. teenage parents
3. inadequate parents
4. poor parents
5. negligent parents
6. abusive parents
7. illiterate parents
8. ignorant parents
9. inadequate foster parents
10. inadequate child agencies
11. inadequate schools
12. inadequate social workers
13. inadequate counselors
14. inadequate teachers

Most efforts to confront the pain and suffering of racism (see Kaus 1992, Shanklin 1994) have been confined to the symptoms rather than to the malady. Humans must remove biophobia from human culture. It has been adaptive for three million years. But in postmodernity biophobic human culture is destined for extinction (Babbie 1994). The advent of biocentrism (Gross and Levitt 1994) will remove and replace Eurocentrism (Herzfeld 1992), feminocentrism, and Afrocentrism (Asante 1987).

Below are some brief examples of the pain and suffering created by race in America (see Clark 1965, *Ebony* 1965). Throughout this discussion a central point requires reminding: racism is not the product of evil men but the result of being human. Hitler could exist only because there was a large German population that wanted to feel better about themselves at any cost to "others." Hitler merely showed them how. Those kinds of populations still exist. It is easy and simplistic to blame their leaders (e.g., the spokespersons for the Nation of Islam, David Duke of Louisiana, Tony Martin, Leonard Jeffries), but the problem is that large population hungry to hear about the evil of "others." That population will always find someone to give them the message. The solution is to wipe out that damned spot that requires the production and reproduction of social inferiority among humans. Until then the death of despots, the laws of equal opportunity, and the ideals of diversity and multiculturalism are mere band-aids on the malignancy of the human biophobe (see Baker 1994, Shanklin 1994).

Part II
Race, Class, and Gender

Chapter 6

Human Insecurity and Racism

Race is folklore and mythology that provides a window into the souls of 'white' people and other insecure humans.
                                                        —Melvin D. Williams

Ota (or, as in the publisher's advertising, Ota Benga) tells several important stories. It details the intersection of turn-of-the-century anthropology, imperialism, and popular culture and underscores the centrality of race to the construction of American national identity. Though the authors do not emphasize sufficiently the long-standing importance of popular amusements for popularizing anthropology, dating at least to the exhibition in European capitals of the "Hottentot Venus" in the early ninteenth century, their attention to biographical detail is a notable contribution to this literature on science in the service of imperialism. (Rydell 1993:109)

As with most scholarly issues, racism can be examined from many perspectives: idiosyncratic vs. institutional, attitudes vs. behavior, self-conscious vs. unintentional. One can document how racism operates or simply assert its importance and impact. One can distinguish it from discrimination, segregation, prejudice, ethnocentrism, classism, sexism, sectarianism, ageism, nationalism, and minority relations. Racism can be defined in terms of power, skin color (colorism), biogenesis ("scientific"), and "civilization." All of which is to say that these brief pages make no claim to a definitive statement on what is racism or why it exists. On the contrary, they represent a brief statement of my own approach to understanding racism.

Teun A. Van Dijk (1993), Philomena Essed (1991), Richard Jenkins (1986), Winthrop Jordan (1974), and William Wilson (1973), among others, have discussed the problem of racism. For example, Van Dijk asserts that the upper classes are as racist as the lower, and Wilson contends that racism always occurs when two or more groups have continuous contact and one or more become dominant.

No studies have determined whether some people or groups are more racist than others, but all humans seem to have the propensity. Situational and contextual factors account for the form racism takes and its intensity (see Katz and Taylor 1988).

Canada, Somalia, Russia, and the former Yugoslavia threaten to disintegrate along the fault lines of geographical identity, among other divisions. Within the national borders of the United States there are distinct geographical and other identities: rural America, Appalachia, the Deep South, Yankee country, suburbs, and inner cities (see Williams 1993a). Cities are divided into tenderloin districts, downtown, uptown, across-the-tracks, slums, and "cultural" districts.

W.E.B. Du Bois said that the problem of the twentieth century would be the problem of the color line. The problem of the twenty-first century may be the problem of the human line—separating the one human species into various populations defined as different, and then ranking those populations to exploit the "inferior" ones.

Racism, like sexism, probably began as soon as humans acquired the ability to distinguish populations among themselves. The first primates in the human evolutionary line—*Australopithecus afarensis, africanus,* and *robustus*—may have competed to the demise of one or more of them. Louis Leakey announced that *Zinjanthropus boisei* (later named *Australopithecus boisei*) was the hunted and *Homo habilis* hunted him. *Homo erectus* was followed by *Homo sapiens* and in some ecological niches could have been displaced by force, just as it is speculated by some that Neanderthals were displaced by Cro-Magnon humans. All of these human populations looked different from one another, but were they any less human?

Humans are a very insecure species. Evolution involved traumatic psychological experiences as the great perceptual powers of humans emerged within "common" animal bodies and with common animal needs. Those perceptual powers enabled humans to contrive an image of themselves as "superior" animals within the animal kingdom. That contrivance, and the human hegemony developed to validate it, were successful adaptive mechanisms to survive, persist, develop, and evolve, as well as to tolerate the ambiguities of existence. That contrivance also carries the cognitive baggage of inferior feelings among humans because humans must continue to live with animal bodies and animal needs, despite cultural evolution and revolutions. These inferiority complexes endow humans with the obsessions of producing and reproducing social inferiority among themselves, including the obsession of creating "inferior" geographical areas. Geographical space is pressed into service to collaborate in the polarization of people, locally and globally. A sociobiological origin of inferior feelings is assuaged by geopolitical power and control, both economic and political.

Racial prejudice is learned from generation to generation. If it were not passed on, it would disappear. Racism can be implanted in a child as early as age three, and by age eleven subtle racial stereotyping is begun. L. A. Hirschfeld (personal communication), a psychological anthropologist, has found that children as young as three have a complex understanding of society's construction of racial categories. Children do not sort people into different races based only on physical differences. Although they do sort people into a range of groups based sometimes on skin color, hair texture, clothing, and so on, Hirschfeld's work (1996) suggests that society's "racial" assignments provide more of a signature of "other" than do physical differences. For children, race does not define the person.

Paul Rozin (1992 and personal communication), a psychologist, has studied the evolution of the human emotion of disgust from "uneatable" foods to social relationships (see the "Abomination of *Leviticus*" in Schultz and Lavenda 1995:418). The emotion of disgust has been transferred from uneatable (causing gaping) to untouchable (polluted populations). Rozin notes that the French are less fearful of uneatables and untouchables than are Americans, who tend to believe that you are what you eat and with whom you socialize (see Douglas 1966, Douglas and Isherwood 1979).

RACISM AND REGION

In the continuing quest to understand human behavior and especially to comprehend human divisiveness (e.g., classism, racism, ethnocentrism, sexism, sectarianism, ageism, nationalism, and speciesism), geography should not escape the scrutiny of scholars. Humans attach themselves to social and material objects for social meanings and for security. Geographical places are salient human attachments (Altman and Low 1992). My studies suggest that identity by geographical location is not the source but the result of human divisiveness. (Williams 1992a, 1992b, 1993b). Certain human characteristics (e.g., phenotype, kin, "intelligence," agility, articulation, and activity) result in social and psychological attachments that culminate in the utilization of hearth, home, university, community, city, country, and continent for human divisiveness.

As Michael Novak (1972a:85,87) explains:

The most striking aspect of Nordic racism was its scientific support. *Science* magazine, for example, commended Madison Grant's often reprinted *The Passing of the Great Race* (1916) as "a work of solid merit." The author, an anthropologist at the American Museum of Natural History, wrote solemnly:

The Native American has always found and finds now in the black men willing followers who ask only to obey and to further the ideals and wishes of the master race, without trying to inject into the body politic their own views, whether racial, religious or social. Negroes are never socialists or labor unionists and as long as the dominant imposes its will on the servient race and as long as they remain in the same relation to the whites as in the past, the Negroes will be a valuable element in the community but once raised to social equality their influence will be destructive to themselves and to the whites.

Except for "the foreign laborers," he adds, America would have remained "exclusively native American and Nordic."

There was a myth, for example, that the old Anglo-Saxon immigrants came as craftsmen—skilled, literate, and virtuous. Recently, even Margaret Mead compared the idealism of the early American immigrants to the crassness of the later immigrants, for James

Baldwin's benefit. Ordinarily we think of Mead as a woman extraordinarily without prejudice. But when she talks about the idealism of her Anglo-Saxon forebears, as contrasted
with the barbarity of those who came later, she shows she is as human as the rest of us. She
writes: "I think you have to discriminate between the people who came here early for
political and religious reasons—the ones whom we still think made the country and whom
we still talk about and use as ideals, and who did come here to live their kind of life the
way they believed in—and the great many millions of immigrants who came here in the
nineteenth century—simply because they were driven out at home and they would have
starved if they stayed there."

And she tells James Baldwin: "I don't have as good rhythms as you have, but my rhythms
go back ten generations to England."

THE ECOLOGICAL REVOLUTION AND THE
FRONTIERS OF ANTHROPOLOGY

Xenophobia and "inferior" people and places are products of human origins
and history. The production and reproduction of social inferiority permeates most
human activities. Those same activities are rapidly destroying the Earth's biosphere. Humans must change. Scholars must create various maps for such transformations. I have proposed my own cartography elsewhere (Williams
1992a,1992b).

Humans will continue to develop models, myths, movements, and magic for
themselves, but those developments will cease to be divisive within the species
and destructive to the ecosystems of the Earth. They will continue to strive but not
in a manner that demeans who and what they are or where they live. The geopoli-
tics of the past with the destructive exploitation of spatial identity will be replaced with "the moral commonwealth," and the Ecological Revolution will usher
in "communitarianism."

Throughout the twentieth century the social sciences have focused on the symptoms and ravages of social problems among selected populations. This has allowed them to avoid examining their own human divisiveness and that of their
species. The avoidance is the result of the reluctance of humans to see themselves
as a species in unflattering ways. I believe that the future analysis of social problems will involve anthropologists examining human divisiveness from the four-
field (cultural, biological, linguistic, and archaeological) perspective. That divisiveness is social and biological. It is often executed with language. It is almost
three million years old.

Anthropologists in the United States have been reluctant to investigate contemporary American problems such as racism. Such research removes some of the
"glamour" from the discipline that is noted for studying distant peoples in far-
away places. Anthropologists have a history of cooperation with authority, colonial or other, and authority has usually, if not always, been racist. But there are
psychological and cognitive anthropologists studying the origin and development
of racism in children. The research of Lawrence Hirschfeld (1988, 1996) at the
University of Michigan is an example of such fieldwork.

Racism is only one example of human divisiveness (see Miller 1993). That divisiveness is, in part, the result of human feelings of inferiority. Both the perpetrators and the victims of racism harbor feelings of social inferiority. The Ku Klux Klan, skinheads, and Nazis are frightened for their own economic and social insecurity. Racism reinforces those feelings because it treats symptoms, not causes. The bipedal animal with no feathers has a big brain that has constructed superiority (e.g., gods, "upper" animals, and "elite" people) for itself as a successful adaptation to survive on Earth. But the Earth is different (endangered) today and humans must change (the Ecological Revolution). We must no long confuse the losing human species with the lost generation. Humans have become an overspecialized species. Just as human populations attempt to dominate and control other arbitrarily defined human populations to neutralize their potential power, human populations have tried the same strategies on the Earth itself. Such efforts have been so successful that humans are neutralizing the Earth's ability to regenerate and recreate itself, causing destruction of entire ecosystems.

Let me use a simple analogy. Human fetuses evolve so successfully that in the twenty-first century they are able to dominate and control their mothers with complex chemical and hormonal techniques. But with their small underdeveloped brains and nervous systems, the fetuses are not able to determine how to use their powers to guarantee being carried to a healthy and successful term. The fetuses, small and full of feelings of inadequacy, cannot resist using their evolved powers, and instead of being carried to term as they have been for three million years, they are carried to extinction. The universal "other" is obsolete. The "other" is we "for whom the bells toll." Humans must look into that mirror (e.g., ethnography) and see themselves, not "others."

The propensity to exert power over and control "other" populations has dangerously enveloped the Earth itself. The strength of that propensity can be seen in the racial determinism of Houston Stewart Chamberlain, the Comte de Gobineau (1984), and Friedrich Nietzsche (see Stewart 1915 and Sorokin 1964). Franz Boas (1966) had to battle that propensity for much of his anthropological career. Today, as we enter the twenty-first century, scholars are rushing to examine the genetic basis for criminal behavior in a world that is about to self-destruct from CRESSANS and other intraspecies hostilities. Conflict-resolution programs are growing and developing in major universities. We do not have the time or the resources to waste studying deviant behavior when normal human behavior is about to destroy us. Our future examinations of racism will require us to return to the discussions of Leslie White (culture is autonomous) and Alfred Kroeber (culture is superorganic) to assess the possibilities of social transformations that contemporary society may require in order to eliminate these forms of discrimination and conflicts. But can we eliminate racism and other social problems that threaten human survival, or are the seeds of human extinction incorporated within the essence and creation of human culture (i.e., universal)?

There is a dialectical tension between the extremes (overstatements and understatements) with which we often describe human behavior. The truth of that behavior lies somewhere in the middle ground, or processual field, too complex for our usual words, categories, and concepts. My pages here reflect that tension. Humans have a limited ability to conceptualize complex human behavior. Our perceptions often fall at extremes (poles) and be come snapshots of intricate processes. Reality lies within the behavioral field identified and bounded by the poles. The nature-nurture debate is an example of the phenomenon. As Jencks (1992:20) has stated: "The ongoing quest for internal consistency that I see as the hallmark of any successful ideology makes realism extremely difficult."

I do not propose a coherent alternative to divisive behavior. Such complex prescriptions for an unpredictable future are folly. Monocausal explanations for social behavior merely reflect the limits of human conceptualization.

Racism is the focus of much nonanthropological social science because most social scientists and the people they serve have an obsession with race. Race is highly visible and extremely stable. It must have ceaseless attention because the majority of the globe's population is people of color. They could become a threat if not kept subdued with feelings of inferiority, self-hate, and divisiveness among themselves. Race is a faithful companion that guarantees to "superior" people that the mirror on the wall will continue to proclaim them the "fairest of them all," in spite of the depths of depravity in which they find themselves. Actually, race is only one of the myths of human divisiveness. It allows people and populations with fragile ego structures and poor self-esteem to concoct superior perceptions of themselves for the purpose of exploiting others (see Rosenberg et al. 1995). The Ku Klux Klan in the United States, and the unemployed Nazis in 1930 and 1993 are examples.

The study of the Black and the poor requires a new theoretical approach that considers cultural and evolutionary parameters. Racism is a distinctively human behavior. It persists in spite of wars, laws, and education to prevent it. It resists analysis, notwithstanding centuries of efforts to understand and explain it. It is pervasive, even though those who practice it deny it. To understand it one must come to terms with some basic characteristics of human behavior. Such an understanding allows us to comprehend not only racism but also many other social problems that find their genesis in "the imperial animal": classism, sexism, imperialism, and religious intolerance. My approach to the study of race and ethnic relations will show the relationships among culture, society, human nature, and race and ethnic relations (see Goldberg 1993); we must understand, identify, and explain the institutions, values, attitudes, and human characteristics that continue to allow humans to label, legitimate, license, and lobby the inferiority of other humans.

This anthropological approach to race and ethnic relations will provide a new and heuristic meaning to the concepts of race and ethnicity. It may provide the integrative catalyst for the diverging fields of anthropology. Much of the biological basis for the concept of race and ethnicity has lost its credibility (Shipman 1994). But race and ethnicity continue to have social, historical, political, and economic impacts on those populations that are distinguishable by phenotypical, political, geographic, and historical characteristics. Ethnic groups have cycles of prominence that display fission and fusion relative to the strength and intensity of nationalism or larger political bonds. These groups persist with social, historical, political, and geographic significance in many contemporary societies. The transformations in the former Soviet Union and Yugoslavia give a dramatic contemporary view of the dynamics of ethnicity. Racism is a result of the acceptance of race as a standard for identifying separate human populations, the development of cultural values, and the nature of the evolutionary human experience. My approach would bring unity to these disparate vectors by beginning the analysis of the relationship between the human body, human nature, biophobia, and social boundaries.

Racial and ethnic intolerance is global. Examining this intolerance from a holistic, evolutionary, and global perspective will give us new insights into the history and the future of humankind. Such an examination requires a review of the possible origins of culture so that we may better understand the unique behavioral and historical development of *Homo sapiens*. It will review the theories of Freud, Jung, Lévi-Strauss, and others who have attempted to comprehend that origin and development. It will trace the salient features of human history and contemporary modernity to explain the nature of humans, with their pervasive racial and ethnic perspectives. It will allow us to compare and contrast discrimination based on race, ethnicity, religion, social class, and gender. In this approach the comparisons will be generic because the genesis of the discriminations is the same—culture and human nature. The understanding of human nature and its development will enable us to comprehend, explain, and resolve racism, classism, sexism, imperialism, and religious intolerance. Are these discriminations fundamental to the character of human culture? Are they, like modernity and its other social problems, characteristic of civilization? These are some of the questions with which my approach would wrestle.

What are the social transformations that contemporary society may require to ban these forms of human distinctions, discriminations, and intraspecies hostilities? Can we eliminate them and other social problems that threaten human survival, or are the seeds of human extinction incorporated within the essence and creations of human culture? These are some of the issues that this approach demands we explore. Perhaps the dinosaurs had the seeds of their extinction incorporated within the essence and creations of their adaptive success. But humans have culture, which is malleable. If we learn quickly enough, we can transform the nature of humans.

Like the ugly, stupid, short, weak, poor, and other undesirable humans, polluted artificial races enable feeble humans with great feelings of inferiority to live with themselves. The production and reproduction of social inferiority and the conceptualization that, like water, social inferiority tends to reach its own level, threaten an overpopulated and polluted planet.

It is the onslaught against the Earth that will force humans to eliminate racism. If we are to save the Earth, humans must cease their passions to control and dominate it. Humans must minister to their inferior feelings and heal themselves. Such wellness will eliminate CRESSANS and the human divisiveness that creates racism.

How can we begin? Humans must be socialized to respect life and the biosphere. Every person is a genius. Every person must be nourished and supported to allow that genius to grow and develop. If we had not destroyed millions of people in ghettos, prisons, wars, and genocide, they might have cured AIDS, cancer, inferiority complexes, and Alzheimer's disease. People must appreciate themselves and others without artificial inferiors. With culture, humans can create such a global village and then make rational reconstruction of human societies. With the endangered Earth, humans have no choice.

Freud studied the relationships between social problems, human identity, and the denial of human sexuality. Ernest Becker (1973) added the denial of death to the discussion. I (1992b) have expanded these to the holistic denial of human-animal kinship (documented by Darwin). These dilemmas of human identity are the basis for racism. The solutions are at the frontiers of anthropology, although the identity afflictions of the practitioners make progress very slow.

Academic disciplines and other modes of organizing knowledge continue to restrict the views of students and scholars about the relationships of human behavior. Anthropology's four-field approach was once a concerted effort to combat such restrictions. But the informational deluge of modernity, the technological prestige of assembling it, the misuse and misunderstanding of ethnography, and the scholarly supremacy of restricted access to a narrow and highly specialized "knowledge" all threaten interdisciplinary efforts. After the Ecological Revolution, anthropologists will cease to project and displace their own social problems onto "others." There is nothing wrong with ethnography as a social science method. Reflexivity and "other voices" treat the symptoms of the researchers. The problems are with the readers and writers of ethnography. They read and write about "different" people: "primitives, savages, simple societies, classes, races, ethnic groups, genders, sects, ages, nations, and others." They exploit "others" to reinforce their own fragile selves. After the Ecological Revolution, anthropologist will write about and readers will read about humans in order to find themselves. The new social scientists will study humans so that readers and writers can look into the "mirror for man" and see themselves, not "others" (Said 1978).

CONCLUSION

Let me close with St. Clair Drake (1987) who, after more than fifty years of research, could not fully understand racism.

It is my hope that some other serious students of the Black Experience, as well as a broader circle of readers, will be stimulated to read more widely than I did and to search for answers to some of the questions that neither I nor anyone else has yet found. While comparative history and anthropology make some contribution to this discussion, there are questions about attitudes toward blackness that require research designed by psychologists and psychiatrists.

Chapter 7

Human Insecurity and the Black Middle Class

BELMAR, 1997

I have returned to the Belmar neighborhood several months every year for the past decade to observe the social and physical transformations there. The economic decline in Belmar that I described in 1981 continues sixteen years later. It will not reverse itself until the values change in America and in Belmar.

The alterations in family, church, and neighborhood life had a major impact on educational goals, single-parent families, teenage pregnancy, and the unemployables. The spirit and the activities seem dominated by the young men and women who ply their trade in drugs. The children are surrounded by and sometimes inducted into these drug activities. They see and know the dealers and their cars. They admire their clothes, shoes, money, cars, loud car stereo systems, and business acumen. One twenty-one-year old male dealer called to a nine-year-old neighbor as he stored his drugs in the trunk of his parked-car business location, "Milton, watch my stuff. Don't let anybody mess with it. If you see anybody messing with it, let me know who it is."

The neighborhood continues to lose its "core members" (those who invest in their community without expectations of immediate returns). Even Deacon Griffin (Williams 1981b:55), who was middle class and resigned to "live out his days" in Belmar, has moved. If he could see the traffic in front of his former house today, he would have no regrets. The neighborhood seems alive with young adults, and many older residents appear overwhelmed by the drug networks, activities, control, noise, and the dominating impact on them and their children.

INTRODUCTION

I have studied Belmar, an urban, Northern African-American neighborhood, for almost twenty years (see Williams 1981a, 1991). During most of that period of ethnographic research, my work concentrated on the low-income residents. But throughout that period I have also worked among and observed the middle-class residents. I still do. There are several middle-class enclaves in Belmar. But these enclaves are surrounded by low-income residents. Most middle-class residents are reinforced by one or two middle-class neighbors. The remainder attempt to separate and distinguish their houses by elaborate remodeling, yards, shrubbery, and fences. These neighbors interact predominantly with one another and within social networks outside Belmar. Many are forced to live here because of government and community job requirements, inability to sell for prices that will recoup their investments, and old age that makes relocation high-risk to health and well-being. Most of these middle-class residents are entrepreneurs, middle managers in corporations, government workers, and university employees. Their houses are easily identified by their well-maintained appearances. They sweep the sidewalks and streets in front of their homes, demand city services, and complain constantly about the loitering teenagers, young adults, and low-income residents.

Black "leaders," poverty programs, public policy agents, government intervention, private investments, housing code enforcement, school desegregation, and political realignments in Belmar and Homewood (the larger region containing Belmar) are cosmetic factors that do little to address the problems of the neighborhood. Houses continue to decay and to be replaced by lots full of debris. Pool halls are replaced by drug streets, street corners and houses (crack houses). Other gathering places and activities—for instance, the library, taverns, store corner groups, wino groups, street-mechanic groups, street and schoolyard game groups, bicycle groups, and the swimming pool—seem to wane in the face of major economic enterprises in street drug traffic. Even vandalism, burglary, and robbery appear to have decreased as money seems more available in the drug traffic. The rubbish and garbage that the residents remove from their property in the early morning after the busy night transactions reveal the new and more expensive eating and drinking habits of those who work and litter there.

Most of the middle-class residents have lived in Belmar long enough not to fear the neighborhood, but the recent increase in drug traffic and its salespeople is beginning to alarm some of them. This is true notwithstanding that this activity has not been accompanied by violent crimes against them. But the activity has increased the noise, the automobile traffic, the loitering, the eating and drinking on the streets, and the debris that must be cleaned from the streets and sidewalks each morning. Many of the middle-class residents resent having to walk through gangs of teenagers and young adults crowding the streets and sidewalks at certain drug traffic rendezvous. And all of them resent the all-night noise levels that entertain the drug salespeople and their friends as they work the streets. This activity lowers property values even more and creates more embarrassment for them when they entertain guests at their homes.

The middle-class residents have two churches on North Lang Avenue (see pictures, Williams 1981b:86–87) where I lived and conducted my studies. These churches, the community college branch, the library, and community agencies are usually the only organizations in which middle-class residents participate. They seldom shop in Belmar but in the adjacent white neighborhoods, the suburban malls, and downtown area. I often engaged them as they cleaned their cars, yards, sidewalks, and streets. I talked with them as they trimmed their grass and shrubbery or painted and repaired their property. Because I lived on North Lang Avenue in an abandoned commercial zone and not in a middle-class enclave, many of them were reluctant to associate with me until they were convinced that I was "clean," "educated," "decent," "professional," and from a "good" family background. Very early, they wanted to know if I knew the "right people." My wife was helpful here because her family had no Southern roots, had a unique German surname, and was well known among the city's middle class. Once I assured them that I was "respectable," they were anxious to talk with me. They then assured others that I was "all right."

Notwithstanding the special circumstances of the social context that embattles these middle-class residents, many of their attitudes and values are similar to other African Americans who think of themselves as among the Black middle class. That class is a worldwide phenomenon of the peasants' trek to the city to acquire the resources to be urbane, suburban, sophisticated, and "Western." Samples of these values and attitudes are supplied here.

MRS. HOFFMAN

Mrs. Hoffman, sixty-seven, has lived in her corner house for forty-five years. She reared one son, who has left home and is a great disappointment to her and her husband because of his lack of ambition. She blames much of her son's failure on the changes in the neighborhood and the "bad crowd" he associated with in Belmar. But today she has as much disgust for him as she does for the teenagers and young adults that parade her neighborhood streets. She releases much of this anger by her self-appointed duty of cleaning the four corners of her intersection as well as a large grassy area (former site of demolished houses) across the street from her house and on one of the corners.

Mrs. Hoffman is an example of the members of the Black middle class whose main epistemology of class is cleanliness (see Hoy 1995). She is fanatical about dirt of any kind anywhere. Her home is spotless, and she burns incense and uses pine-scented cleaners so her rooms smell clean. She has a lifelong habit of smelling clothes to determine how clean they are. Her prize possessions are her laundry room and its equipment, and she spends many of her hours there even though laundry loads have decreased considerably since her son has moved away. When you enter her house, you are struck by the order, sanitary smell, and cleanliness. Yet she never misses an opportunity to tell you how clean she is and how "filthy" her neighbors are. As she frequently expresses it, "They live like animals."

Every day Mrs. Hoffman surveys the four corners of her intersection and her park. And every day that the weather permits she carries her battery of brooms and shovels out to clean the area. Even at her age she uses a fine bristle hand brush that requires her to bend to the ground to clean it "so clean that you can eat off it." Cleaning all four corners of the intersection takes Mrs. Hoffman onto other people's property. These neighbors ward off the embarrassment of having an elderly woman do their cleaning by reporting that she is "touched" (emotionally disturbed or senile).

Mrs. Hoffman enjoys cleaning and conversation about cleaning. She spends hours with relatives and friends discussing cleaning, clean people, and those who live and behave "like animals." These conversations are rich and lively because she is talking with people who are "clean." Her intersection is the cleanest in Belmar, and we will miss her when she is gone.

JOSHUA CAMPBELL

Campbell, sixty-two, has worked for the same corporation for thirty-three years. He has "moved up" from the sales force to an assistant vice president's position in product distribution, which he calls the "glass ceiling for Blacks in my company." As Campbell approaches retirement, he feels "cheated" by his corporation and his society. In his opinion he is more qualified than his white superiors, but he cannot expect to be promoted any further because of his race. He takes some satisfaction in the fact that he is the first Black to reach his position, and he has mentored three others into similar ones.

He explains:

I have a nice title, a nice office and a good salary. I like my work and I know my job. There is no one here better than me at this work. And I walk around the office looking important. But I have no real power! My decisions are really made for me by the white bosses upstairs. Some people may think they're my decisions but they're all cleared upstairs before I announce them. My bosses like me, so they try to make me think that I have some input. As they say, "We just need to get consensus." That means that I don't do anything unless they know about it.

Blacks in jobs like mine must be liked by all the whites that work around you and that's a whole 'nother job. Any white that does not like you can poison it for you by spreading what I call race rumors. They can say you date white women and talk about them. They can say you disguise the fact that you are a radical Black militant that resents white supervision. They can say you play favoritism with the Black employees; anything that says you don't know your place. None of these may be true, but you have to work at proving that they aren't true. This doubles your work without added pay, cuts down on your productivity and keeps you watching your back when you should be watching your responsibilities. It makes you especially aware of how you must treat your white subordinates. I persuade them to work. I don't tell them.

Even worse, I have to fire Blacks who are victims of these conspiracies. The white bosses say that they're "too uppity, not the right people for our company." I feel bad about the job performance reports that I have to file on them because I know the real reasons that they have to go. But it is part of my job—getting rid of Blacks that the whites don't like. It looks better if Blacks do it to Blacks, especially if a grievance is filed.

Sometimes I feel the guilt for days. But then I tell myself that it is not my fault. I didn't make this world. And in my company if you are Black, being liked is part of your job no matter how good your work is.

Campbell seems somewhat broken by the years of loyalty he has given a corporation that has always considered him and his people inferior, regardless of their abilities. He is convinced that he could even accept their condescending attitudes toward his race if they would just admit that his work was superior to his colleagues. Many days he contemplates moving to a different corporation, but his associations with Blacks in them reveal that the patterns are very similar. African Americans at his level are like mascots. Everyone thinks they are there because of affirmative action, and most question their abilities and their loyalties. That means they must work at convincing others of both. Convincing others of one's loyalty continually puts one at risk of being obsequious.

JAMES BOND

Bond, thirty-eight, has a B.S. degree in economics and has worked for the United States Postal Service for eighteen years. He worked his way through college, and ever since he has been dreaming of resigning and establishing his own business and becoming a millionaire.

Bond has attempted several business enterprises, struggling to continue his employment until his ventures appear to have a successful future. He has solicited joint ventures with his middle-class neighbors, and he has convinced many of them to participate in his visions. But he and his visions have always failed. Bond is a small man (5' 4" and 140 pounds.) He appears very intelligent, well read, and sincere. But today he is a broken man. He no longer believes in his own ventures, and none of the neighbors takes him seriously now.

Bond inherited a large house in Belmar when his parents died and attempted to convert that into an apartment building when he was establishing his real estate business. With little capital, he attempted most of the remodeling himself. When his capital was depleted, the house was torn apart and most of the remodeling was incomplete. The building was useless. It was in such a state that he had to move for shelter. That was his last business venture. He had created the visible evidence that he was a disastrous businessman. No one took his ideas seriously after that. This financial failure resulted in an emotional illness, and Bond had to take disability from his employment.

During his healthy period, Bond enjoyed delivering the mail in Belmar. He knows most of the residents and cultivated the respect of most of the middle class. He would spend hours talking to members of the "respected" middle class. Some poor neighbors were often angry with him because he was frequently off schedule on their "check days." He attempted to compensate for his procrastination and their anger by illegally delivering checks to people on the streets rather than waiting to place them in their mailboxes.

I often wondered how Bond could keep his job and routinely engage in lengthy conversations with his middle-class neighbors along his postal route. He never seemed to be aware of the time as long as he had an attentive middle-class listener. He would boast about his property, his ventures, his college education, his "respectable" family, and his ultimate aspirations. He always disassociated himself from the poor in Belmar, and he was ever ready to complain about them and condemn them. But he was friendly with everybody.

Bond has a difficult burden. His parents and his extended family were middle class and provided him with a middle-class home. When his parents died, they left him a house to live in and one to lease. He married a middle-class woman who had a middle-class income as an elementary school teacher. Together they appeared to have a bright future, so bright that Bond began to make unreasonable plans to become rich. His wife was the first to discover his folly, and she divorced him, reducing his capital considerably. This divorce prodded him to prove to his former wife and others that he was a business genius. He failed. Now he avoids all the middle-class neighbors who know him. He has nothing to support his claim to superiority.

JONATHAN SWIFT

Swift is "permanent" associate professor at a major research university. He refers to his rank as "permanent" because his publishing productivity is never likely to provide a basis for his promotion to full professor. He attempts to appear resigned to this, but his bitterness frequently surfaces. He often rails against the university administration and the university's lack of respect for "good" teaching. He, his colleagues, and his students consider Swift an able teacher.

Swift's university position provides him high rank among the middle class in Belmar. His rank is so high that he can afford to dress shabbily. He can be more familiar with the lower class in Belmar without earning the disapproval of his middle-class neighbors and associates. He can neglect his house and its grounds and be excused as an intellectual eccentric. Swift enjoys this freedom, rank, and privilege. He also enjoys the status of his wife, who is a middle manager in a large corporation. She earns more than he since his salary increases have been small because of his poor productivity. Together they have an income that allows him to pretend he has little interest in money or materials. His clothes, car, office, and habits confirm this.

Nothing is more entertaining to Swift than to listen to himself talk, and his favorite subject is his university. Notwithstanding the characteristics I have ascribed to him, he is a keen and reliable observer of university life. Much of what he describes at his university can be found in most large research universities. For the African-American middle class and the aspirants thereto, these descriptions are disheartening.

Swift is convinced that "inferior" people do not escape punishment by being a part of the university community. But that reality appears more harsh in a community of scholars where truth, beauty, and merit are supposed to reign over emotion and prejudice. Swift has observed the narrow entrances for "inferior" people into his "superior" university. Not only are their entrances few, but they are also "inferior": women's, Black, Asian, Latin American, and other studies (for administrators it is supportive staff—the assistant to . . . , assistant . . . , associate . . . , associate vice. . . , or vice). The "superior" traditional departmental faculty are contemptuous of the people in these programs and often of the programs themselves. The young scholars may not realize their plight until they attempt to gain tenure in or retreat to the departments of their respective disciplines.

Once in the university, the Black scholars discover that there are white experts on African Americans who control their entrance, support, and success there. Only "collaborating" Blacks have a role in this process. These "collaborating" African Americans are selected for all of the "critical" committees because they can detect the moods of their white experts and powerful white colleagues and they are unfailing in their support (which is often disguised in garbled rhetoric and evasive rationales). Such African Americans are promoted and supported at Swift's university. But they are sparse in number and must spend long years in service to be trusted for strategic positions.

Swift cites the case of the Black woman who directed the Office of Affirmative "Inaction" for almost twenty years before it was discovered that, in spite of the inspiring statistics she released every year, minority participation was worse when she left than when she began. But she was "good" at working with the handicapped and attending all of the national conferences. When she left, she was promoted to a better position because of her loyalty. Swift tells the story of the rare Black provost of a major research university who has worked his way to the "top." But the official Black student organization of the provost's university is campaigning to warn African-American students not to matriculate there because of the rare Black faculty, the few African-American cultural programs, and the "disastrous" attrition rate for Black students. For Swift these Black "collaborators" are the real "New Black Middle Class."

He explains the trials and tribulations of the rare African-American faculty person who is hired at his university.

I often attend large meetings with colleagues where we discuss the racial climate on campus. These colleagues expend hours discussing strategies to improve the racial atmosphere in order to recruit and retain underrepresented groups for faculty, staff, and students. I often tell my colleagues that it is they that create the climate, not the university and not other people. I relate to them the experience of a young female assistant professor who was recently recruited to the university. She was warmly greeted at the reception for new faculty. Colleagues inquired about her personal and professional interests. She met many friendly colleagues and felt warmly received that day. But in the following weeks she was continuously embarrassed and hurt as she greeted those same colleagues individually at various campus locations. They often ignored her, seemed not to recognize her, seemed too busy to say hello, or seemed reluctant for their companion to know that they had a Black faculty acquaintance. Some just raised their eyebrows in silence to acknowledge her. Some spoke with their lips and no vocal sound. Some ignored her completely. At occasional subsequent meetings these same colleagues seemed to prefer talking to administrators or prestigious senior faculty but never to her.

I tried to reassure her that this was not behavior that was directed at her personally. I told her that colleagues are busy, absent-minded, preoccupied, etc. They often treat me and even their white colleagues the same way. Unfortunately, she was not convinced. She remained unsure about her welcome here. She is not as young and perhaps as sensitive as Black students or insecure Black staff. Can you imagine how they must feel?

I will not take the time to discuss the very few white students who took her classes or came to visit her during office hours, or the department colleagues who seemed afraid to come in her office. But I will conclude by suggesting that the efforts to recruit and retain abstract populations of minorities on predominantly majority campuses can only be humanized by individual efforts to treat those minorities with respect and human dignity on a one-to-one basis when and if they get there.

Some socially desperate young women proceed during their probationary periods to confuse colleagueship with friendship and "love" with career commitments and tenure votes for them.

Swift complains of the "corporate mentality" of the increasing university administration. He questions the ranking system that allocates more prestige to high-ranking administrators than to outstanding teachers. He asks that you compare their salaries, office space, and expense accounts. He decries the university atmosphere in which the time that is used to be creative, to recreate, and to think is considered unproductive time and in which the madness of back-to-back committee meetings is a badge of productivity. He asserts that most people in his university do not expect that he or his African-American colleagues will produce anything of great and lasting merit, and they treat them that way. This is not very inspiring. As a consequence, their superiors conspire to "rob" them of as much of their time as possible. They even require them to file annual reports describing their time expenditures. All of this is compounded for the Black faculty and staff, who are few in number and already the objects of racial discrimination and exclusion.

Swift believes that faculty governance is almost a sham at his "community of scholars." If you are not a "star" grantsperson or a celebrated scholar that the administration is reluctant to lose, you have very few decision-making roles. Like students, faculty have power when they act in unison, but those are rare occasions, and the administration is aware of that fact. Many faculty are groomed to be in awe of high-ranking administrators by means of continual exposure to academic ritual and ceremony that places such administrators in the most prestigious circumstances. So even when they are on strategic committees, these faculty are reluctant to differ with administrative decisions. Administrators enjoy "docile, eccentric, and nonactivist faculty who leave all the big decisions to them."

Swift also believes that faculty are groomed to be excessively critical of one another. This prevents them from unifying to protect their community of scholars and their community of interests. It prevents many young creative and talented scholars from ever being permanent members of that community. He gives an example:

Our libraries are overflowing with "scholarly" treatises that no one reads (especially without coercion) and no one will probably read in the future. Yet the same people who wrote these volumes of academic jargon are the gatekeepers for other young talented scholars who cannot get their ideas published unless they conform to the tortuous conceptual norms of these referees. These old guard referees prevent new ideas, new frames of reference, and new conceptual paradigms from ever seeing the light of day. They reproduce themselves as well as social inequality.

This brief visit with Jonathan Swift illustrates the uneasy predicament of the Black middle class in a white university.

Social scientists are aware that their categories and classifications do not always match the real world. There are some members of the African-American middle class who are downwardly mobile or who are struggling to keep up appearances after they have fallen from their former economic levels. Their struggles often demonstrate the values and attitudes of the middle class as well. Two such contiguous households are in Belmar. They at least have the company and solace of each other. I will describe one of them.

MRS. CECILIA BROWN

Mrs. Brown is fifty-one. She is a small woman at 5' 3" and 102 pounds. She comes from a "respectable" middle-class family and has well-known and highly visible relatives in the city who run a large business enterprise. But Mrs. Brown has married "beneath" her family's expectations, and her husband has forced her below the economic lifestyle to which she was accustomed.

Mr. Brown is a disabled veteran, a very attractive man who has retained his handsome Native American looks even into old age. But his war injuries have left him alcohol-dependent, and he has periodic emotional failures that cause him to behave violently. Belmar, like most African-American ghettos, is tolerant of such behavior. The Browns can live here and not be objects of scorn, derision, or pity, notwithstanding Mr. Brown's strange behavior. Both of them are very private people who speak to their middle-class neighbors but have nothing to do with the others. They rent a modest house with four rooms and a small kitchen, and they house and care for Mr. Brown's ill and bedridden mother.

Mrs. Brown is responsible for the house, her mother-in-law, and her disabled husband. She has a difficult life and often relies on alcohol herself to sustain her healthy outlook. An example of her plight is the night she was forced to climb out of her second floor window, onto her porch roof, run along the roof to her neighbor's second floor window and bang loudly to awaken them. When they opened the window, she explained that her husband was in a violent rage and was threatening her with his rifle. She called the police from the neighbor's house and returned home to her mother-in-law as soon as her husband had been removed. But she is usually cheerful and proud of her family background.

Because of her economic and social problems, her siblings do not associate with her and she has few friends. But she lavishes her attention on some "promising" lower-class children in the neighborhood. She takes them to museums, concerts, chamber music, and dramatic plays. She takes them to events they would never see or experience without her. She acts as their guardian, demanding that they behave properly in the streets, not associate with "bad" children, correcting their speech, and giving them money for doing errands for her. She has partially adopted them. She is a delicate and sophisticated Black woman whose vulnerability seems out of place in this inner city neighborhood.

DISCUSSION

Most of the middle class in Belmar compete with one another in the maintenance and remodeling of their houses and grounds, in the purchases of clothes and cars, in their church, community, and party visibility, and in their exposure in the Black city newspaper. These are important measures of their middle-class success. The Black city newspaper appears to depend more on the pictures of the aspiring Black middle class for its success than on advertising revenues. Each week the residents of Belmar buy the newspaper to see themselves and their associates at one affair or another. They recognize each other as the "pillars of the community" without much embarrassment for what they seem to be supporting.

The shopkeepers, the self-employed, the landlords, local politicians, community "leaders," librarians, the school teachers, and the school traffic guards seem to support the aspirations of one another to be firm members of Belmar's middle class. Perhaps if their numbers were larger, their impact on the neighborhood would be more visible.

Some middle-class residents overdecorate, remodel, and plant. Their stockade fences dominate and overshadow their houses. They plant large bushes at the street curb that obstruct the sidewalks and the street. They cement concrete blocks at the curb to prevent automobiles from parking on the sidewalks in front of their houses. They overload their porches with so many plants that the view is unsightly. Others remove their small lawns and replace them with cement to park and secure their cars. All of them are plagued by the residents who do not care or cannot afford to maintain their property.

It is a pleasure to walk through the neighborhood and see the variety of houses and lawns that are in various states of maintenance and repair. The external appearances give vital clues as to who lives beyond the outside walls. Most residents are "house-proud" and spend as much as their incomes will allow to decorate their homes. As you view the different properties, you receive a rapid education about the disparities and misfortunes that afflict the people of this neighborhood. You begin to understand the hostile DDDAV (denial, defiance, and defilement of American values) of those who have so little to keep up appearances and yet must live so close to those who do. And you can also comprehend the hostility of those who work so hard (on their jobs and on their property) only to have their assets and their largest investments hopelessly depreciated by neighbors who do not have access to such middle-class interests.

This variety gives an excitement to Belmar (see Williams 1992a) that most homogeneous middle-class communities lack. As an anthropologist I can appreciate this diversity and vitality, and I look forward to a time—the Ecological Revolution—when most people can enjoy other people as neighbors and friends regardless of their material destinies and their designated classes.

The Ecological Revolution will bring a new vitality to places like Belmar. Feelings of inferiority will be vanquished by the knowledge and ecological necessity that all humans are equal members in the Earth's web-of-life. A heightened sense of respect for life and the social communities that nourish that life will give neighborhoods a new spiritual mission and social responsibility. The Ecological Revolution is as much a human spiritual transformation as it is a change in human values.

Part III

Social Transformations

Chapter 8

Human Insecurity and Urban Ethnography

Ethnography in America is flawed by hegemony (see Rose, 1990). It is culture-bound. We have third world regions in the United States (e.g., Black inner cities) where imperialism and colonialism are international. We sell the finished industrial products there and increasingly deny the people who reside there the opportunities to participate in the rewards of production. The dilemmas of race and ethnic relations know few boundaries.

The frequent themes of ethnography in cities—sexism, racism, classism, colonialism and imperialism—are human adaptive strategies that have evolved during cultural evolution (e.g., the Agricultural and Industrial Revolutions and the impending Ecological Revolution). Those strategies will become obsolete after the Ecological Revolution. The new ethnography will consider these social transformations and eschew its traditional participation in the reproduction of social inequality. The new ethnography will compensate for the old, which documented the "traditional" lives of the people as they and their way of life were being systematically destroyed.

A new theoretical approach to urban ethnography is one that ceases to treat oppression and discrimination as abnormal human behavior. It is one that takes a realistic look at the needs and possibilities of behavior modification in this area. It is one that discusses the prospects and possibilities based on this new perspective.

Social scientists examining the cities of the world and the racial relations therein have failed to discover the common denominators of oppression and discrimination. I suggest that there are basic panhuman characteristics of these practices.

In this chapter I outline the basic character of humans that underlies racial, ethnic, religious, and class oppression and discrimination, treating the problem as a worldwide phenomenon. I then describe some of the dilemmas and predicaments of urban oppression and discrimination. I present some of the contributions of African Americans, despite the lack of access to many of the institutional resources. Finally, I discuss avenues of ending poverty, oppression, and discrimination throughout the world. The discussion includes brief examinations of the Black middle class, the Black underclass, women, and the power elite who oppress all of them.

INTRODUCTION

This new examination of race relations analyzes those relationships as another human design for the reproduction of social inequality. It abandons the Marxist model for an evolutionary one that focuses particular attention on the development of human culture. This paradigm is broad, simple, and general. It attempts a metatheory that organizes the reproduction of social inequality, including artificially defined human populations, as another abuse of the Earth and its resources. I attempt to offer a hypothesis for this abuse and its ravages and use race relations as a simple test of that hypothesis. The test, if successful, promises a different human relationship with and perception of the poisoned planet and all of its resources, including its people and other forms of life. The history and the study of race relationships demonstrate how difficult the problems are to ameliorate. But this situation must be transformed if humans are to survive into and through the next century.

In my earlier examinations of Black people and their relationships (Williams 1981a, 1982, 1984, 1991, 1992a, 1992b), I have followed them into their institutional arrangements and questioned both the values and attitudes that constitute the ideology of racial superiority and the people who sacrifice so much to reach for racial supremacy and attempt to maintain it. I am convinced that such examinations and the insights that derive from them can tell us far more about human behavior than we learn from the drive and tenacity in racial supremacy. The drive to separate ourselves into artificial groups and populations for invidious comparisons, discrimination, oppression, and genocide (e.g., of African Americans, Native Americans, Jews, Armenians, Kurds, Iraqis, and Kuwaitis) is closely related to that which is compelling us to destroy indiscriminately the Earth's ecosystems. That human inferiority complex (after Alfred Adler, the Austrian psychiatrist) cannot be assuaged by achievements wrought in our cultural evolution— the Agricultural and Industrial Revolutions. It must be socialized out of us in the Ecological Revolution. Otherwise it is like pouring ocean water over a man dying of thirst. It may give the illusion of help, but it does not treat the malady.

With this new theoretical approach to urban ethnography, we must also train ethnographers who resist the traditional research paths of studying the victims, their social contexts, and social networks. Instead we must study the perpetrators and the collaborators. Most oppressed racial and ethnic groups have members who collaborate with the oppressing group (see discussion below). Who are they, and why and how do they function? We must abandon the dead-end research pathways that focus on the symptoms and behaviors of oppression and discrimination. Many of the researchers themselves enjoy privileges of status, prestige, income, and class that are structurally supported by the racial and ethnic relations they continue to study and fail to transform. Such privilege creates vested interests in the structures and influences the nature and conduct of the researchers. Ethnography has its problems (recall the Margaret Mead controversy and the reflexive ethnography debate), as does any research design that studies human behavior, but an able ethnographer can identify and communicate the values and attitudes of "his people." He/she must be accepted as a member of the population. Thus we need to train members of the "power elite" to study, understand, and explain the needs, designs, and ramifications of the oppressors' behavior. This will be possible once we convince ourselves of the bases for racial oppression and the present maladaptive nature of the behavior.

CONTRASTS OF OPPRESSION

Almost a hundred years ago (1903), W.E.B. Du Bois said: "We feel and know that there are many delicate differences in race psychology, numberless changes that our crude social measurements are not yet able to follow minutely, which explain much of history and social development" (Du Bois 1961:123).

Du Bois was expressing a sentiment that has continued until today. That sentiment is that African people from sub-Saharan Africa have a distinctive psychological temperament. Léopold S. Senghor described it as Négritude; Asante (1987) has described it as Afrocentric; and recently Leonard Jeffries, at the City College of the City University of New York, has called it humanistic, communal, and caring. Of course, Michael Levin, at the same university, persists in claiming that the difference is lower intelligence for African Americans (Blum 1990).

My own suggestions about DDDAK are motivated by the resistance to modernity in sub-Saharan Africa. We can yet find hunters and gatherers among the Bushman, Pigmy, Sandawe, Hatsa, and Dorobo. The African-American endurance during slavery, the Civil War, and Reconstruction is noted. My explanations are that the quality and intensity of the human inferiority complex may vary among human populations. These variations determine the extent to which people perceive themselves as a part of the web-of-life, a component of the biosphere rather than as a separate species designed to control the planet and other species. Certain populations, such as those in sub-Saharan Africa and women generally, may have less of a drive to manipulate, control, and exploit the environment. A popular American perspective on some individual ramifications that may result from the intense human inferiority complex are discussed by Kinder (1990) in his book *Going Nowhere Fast,* as well as by Baritz (1988) in *The Good Life.* Thorstein Veblen (1987) discussed some of these same behavioral dynamics almost seventy-five years ago.

If my suggestions have some validity, humans will have some exemplary selective populations to examine when it finally becomes evident that we can no longer survive with the quality and intensity of inferiority complexes that have created modern society.

I have observed oppressive human environments among the Straits Salish indigenous people of Vancouver Island, British Columbia (Williams 1979b, 1989a), and among the Black ghettos of Pittsburgh, Pennsylvania (Williams 1984, 1992a, 1992b). The contrasts are noteworthy. African Americans are often robust, ribald, and vividly expressive in their poverty and economic oppression. Such responses have often created the mythology that they are "happy" by nature. But the Native Canadians seem desolate, despairing, abandoned and hopeless. Even when in groups that were drinking to become intoxicated and to forget life for a while, my Indian informants were sullen and forlorn. Both populations are oppressed and the recipients of social and economic discrimination, but the African Americans appear to endure these conditions so well that the myth of the poor, happy Black has been perpetuated for centuries. This is not so on the Native Canadian reserves.

This phenomenon was also recorded on the American slave plantations. The Native Americans were decimated in slavery and ultimately rejected as not suitable. Meanwhile African Americans survived and propagated to make slavery in the New World a profitable enterprise. Blacks adopted the master's religion. It is often described as a "slave religion" for Blacks because it preaches that the slave should love his masters notwithstanding his servitude. African Americans not only adopted the master's religion, but they adopted it with a passion. They may be the most religious population in the United States. I argue that this adoption of Christianity is the result of a lack of intensity of DDDAK. Such a constitution allows them to endure hardship in the hegemony of America. Such a constitution is an African survival. It has prompted those more endowed with DDDAK to call Africans and African Americans lazy, shiftless, happy, and irresponsible for four hundred years.

It would seem that the oppressed African American would have high levels and more intense qualities of inferior feelings as a result of the socialization in this society. But that logic is at a lower level of abstraction. DDDAK is a constitutional emotion that determines the relational identity with life forms within ecosystems. Such identity tends to control inferior feelings generally. So in spite of oppression in America, this suspected lower level of DDDAK in the general population of African Americans may allow them constitutionally to endure and tolerate better the hardships of living. This tolerance and level may be a factor in the global discrimination against dark-skinned people. In any case, a technique to measure and calculate the intensity of DDDAK will further clarify the usefulness of the concept. And further, we need to study the landlords of Blacks, the Black middle class, the merchants in African-American neighborhoods, and the power elite to understand why they tolerate, perpetuate, and collaborate in these conditions for the Black and the poor.

Much of the biological basis for the concept of race and ethnicity has lost its credibility, especially after the racial determinism scholarship of Stewart Houston Chamberlain, the Comte de Gobineau, Dinesh D'Souza, Richard Herrnstein, Charles Murray, and Friedrich Nietzsche. So the examination of human culture will require us to return to the discussions of Leslie White (culture is autonomous) and Alfred Kroeber (culture is superorganic) to determine the possibilities of social transformations that contemporary society may require to ban these forms of human distinctions, discriminations, and intraspecies hostilities.

RESEARCH PROBLEMS

Innercity ethnography must focus on the sources of innercity problems, not on the symptoms of those problems. Like the slaves throughout recorded history, the serfs of Europe, the peasants of the world, the workers in early industrial England, and the proletariat in the U.S.S.R., the underclass in American cities are not the source of the problems there. So why do we continue to study them? Perhaps it is to avoid identifying the source of the problems. Black scholars, particularly, must make the difficult transition from their historically limited roles in scholarship to the study of the white, rich, power elite who determine life in the inner cities. There is a critical need for welfare reform, education reform, housing programs, employment training, child care, child support, medical access, and equal opportunity. Studying the Black and the poor will never provide these.

As Hylan Lewis (1971:358) has advised, we need to study the rich and the oppressors:

My own view is that the most important research into this area now should focus not on the culture of poverty but on the culture of affluence—the culture that matters more and that is far more dangerous than the culture of poverty. Jean Mayer has put the thrust and the focus succinctly:

"There is a strong case to be made for a stringent population policy on exactly the reverse of the basis Malthus expounded. Malthus was concerned with the steadily more widespread poverty that indefinite population growth would inevitably create. I am concerned about the areas of the globe where people are rapidly becoming richer. For rich people occupy much more space, consume more of each natural resource, disturb the ecology more and create more land, air, water, chemical, thermal and radioactive pollution than poor people. So it can be argued that from many viewpoints it is even more urgent to control the numbers of the rich than it is to control the numbers of the poor."

In the postindustrial age when service employment will supersede industrial employment, we must learn to understand the values and attitudes that abandon the people who operated the industrial plants after the closing of the factories of the rust belt. Just as we should not abandon the retired elderly, we should not abandon the closed-mill unemployed. We must study the human processes that allow such abandonments and resocialize our children to prevent them. This is the task of the new research in urban ethnography. Arbitrarily defined and identified populations must be included within the human community, not only rhetorically and ideally but also in terms of social policy and human values. I argue that these are values and attitudes that are not only desirable but obligatory in the twenty-first century. Our research must show us the pivotal institutions that have created this cultural lag in our social and political skills in an era when our technological sophistication is threatening life on Earth.

Hegemonic groups expend great efforts and resources to maintain their hegemony. What are the pervasive natures and resources of these efforts, and how are they executed, operationalized, and perpetuated in cities? What drives people to maintain exclusive power from generation to generation even at considerable human cost to themselves, their families, and those they exploit? How can we examine these discourses in power?

The poor do not suffer in silence. They rob, kidnap, and assassinate their oppressors. They deprive their oppressors of privacy. The poor support the media that expose them and their families to lies and distortions. The oppressed punish the power elite again and again, but their actions are often not recorded. Like the "great man" histories of the past, our ethnographies have not escaped their colonial and historical origins. The new urban ethnography must break with these old conceptual models and examine the nature and character of the oppressors. It must fully explore how racial groups and their perpetuation serve the purposes of the oppressors. We must study the nature and character of a social system that constructs "racial relations" and then directs all the attention of the problems created by such concepts on the victims. Such traditional ethnographic research is not designed to ameliorate the plight of these victims, for we know that as long as these social systems persist "the poor will always be with us"; it is analogous to studying pornography and vividly describing the artifacts and the illustrations, a process that reinforces the abuse of women and children and pornography's other victims.

ETHNOGRAPHIC DISTORTIONS

This process of blaming and debating about the victims diverts attention from the problem—"inferior" people created by those who require "inferior" people to sustain their own mythical superiority. That problem has reached gigantic proportions—infant mortality, the AIDS epidemic, the homeless, the "underclass," the health care debacle, environmental disaster, and irrational economic greed—that can no longer be ignored. There are no superior people or other less important forms of life. We are all in this web together, and together we must begin the Ecological Revolution.

The human inferiority complex created by DDDAK has forced us into a mythical superior status and role on Earth. But we humans are animals that perspire, and perspiration has its odor. We secrete mucous from the eyes, lungs, bronchial tubes, skin, sexual organs, and the colon. We salivate, masticate, expectorate, regurgitate, urinate, defecate, masturbate, fornicate, gestate, exudate, suppurate, lacrimate, lactate, fight, kill, sleep, hemorrhage, die, and decay. Yet we reject our animal kinship and even subordinate other arbitrarily defined humans to prove our superiority. This is the problem, and it has become so severe that it threatens an endangered Earth as well as Belmar. Shakespeare illustrates the problem: "What a piece of work is man! How noble in reason! How infinite in faculties! In form, in moving, how express and admirable! In action how like a god! the beauty of the world! the paragon of animals!" (*Hamlet,* Act 2, Scene 2).

As long as humans use artificial categories to conceptualize arbitrarily identified human populations and place other forms of nonhuman life outside the human community and inferior to humans, then there is little to prevent circumstances that allow human populations to be shifted about in terms of significance and even to be regarded as nonhuman (e.g., Jews in Nazi Germany) and thus outside the concentric circles of the human community. This concentric circle conception of the human community is an abiding threat to all humans. At any time genocide, homelessness, war, or some other human circumstance may place any of us on the margins or outside the human community along with other "lower" forms of life.

It is not easy to communicate the values of one population to another population with different values. The translation attempts are distorted, despite precautions. My approach here is to illustrate by the analogy of an invading army. The analogy is only suggestive.

It is difficult to occupy a people's territory for long without their own complicity and corruption. Approximately thirty million African Americans experience discrimination as a result of American values that posit all African Americans as inferior and deprive many of them economically.

The "genuine" (some lower-class) African Americans can be depicted as cultural resistance fighters who attempt to demoralize the occupying army. In their sabotage they have many casualties, take great risks, and are the objects of the enemy's relentless roundups, hostage taking, firing squads and other persecutions. But these "freedom fighters" never allow the enemy to forget they are occupying another people's territory. The sufferings of the "genuine" keep the truth before us and benefit all African Americans when the propaganda of the enemy would have us believe that his rule and control will create a better world for African Americans. The enemy teaches us that his values are best for everybody, notwithstanding that those values create the perception that African Americans are inferior. The enemy selects only the cultural traitors as his collaborators and gives them limited economic opportunities. But he does not share power with them. The enemy "props up" these collaborators as "leaders," role models, scholars, businessmen, and politicians. He gives them a dubious status and the illusion of power and pretends that they are important, allowing them limited association among the enemy as long as they provide useful information and perform activities vital in the control of their own people. Like the accused "Vichy French," these collaborators court power. They have sex, friendship, and conspiracies with their enemy, the occupying army. They do the enemy's bidding in scholarship, business, education, and politics. In this analogy the "spurious" (those with "white" values) and mainstream (most middle-class) Blacks are the collaborators. Every occupying army depends upon collaborators to oppress and control the conquered peoples. The collaborators rationalize that if you have no power or courage, then you must live by the myths of those who do. The resistance fighters say that the will and courage to resist is power. We have heard the stories of the enemy burning the books of the conquered people, but there is no need to burn books that you have never allowed to be published and if published, are not distributed, promoted, and used in the schools. You do not have to be concerned with the truth if you control most of the means of communication.

The "freedom fighters" prefer to die in the resistance movement rather than acquiesce to perpetual "inferiority" and servitude. Like Harriet Tubman, they come from a long line of African-American resistance fighters. They are being labeled as "gangs," "crack dealers," "roving packs" (note the animal imagery), and the "underclass." They are not only victims but "inferior" devils as well. But perhaps many of them are just members of the resistance movement who are saying in their own subcultural way, "Give me liberty or give me death."

We must cease to discover diversionary devils in the inner city and instead attempt to locate the evils that rob these neighborhoods of community, family, education, and churches. Proposing idealistic social and economic policies without the value and attitude transformations that must accompany them is mere ivory tower "scholarship." It is economic mythmaking. It will require a revolution—the Ecological Revolution—to halt this reproduction of social inequality.

I argue that this revolution, an aftermath of the Agricultural and Industrial Revolutions, will come as a result of a series of ecological disasters (e.g., the Persian Gulf oil spills, the desertification of California, and nuclear accidents) that force global transformations for human survival. These transformations will require the appropriate ethnographies of cities (where most people live) to understand the policies and procedures that will allow humans to endure and manage such changes.

CULTURAL EVOLUTION

As the brain in the nonhuman primate developed into the Rubicon of self-reflection, the ability to objectify oneself, to stand apart from oneself, and to consider the kind of being one is and "what it is that" one "wants to do and to become" (Bidney 1964:3), man began to separate himself from the "lower" animals. This panhuman characteristic or universal cultural pattern is coterminous with the human mind that is conscious of awareness, experiences the self as an object, and conceptualizes changes in that object. That mind compared other species of animals with its self and created "consciousness of kind." It conceptualized that the other animals were "lower" animals and began an unconscious process of creating inferiority complexes in human groups, complexes that have influenced human behavior ever since.

In the beginning the conceptualization of other species as "lower" animals facilitated the creation and development of culture. Culture allowed man to adapt successfully throughout the world. This success has reached a point at which man now dominates and manipulates the world without the necessary respect for the delicate web-of-life that includes man himself. This success has also resulted in the conceptualization of artificially distinct human populations as "lower" or "inferior" people. Collective inferiority complexes have been exacerbated by this process.

In a book that remains one of the definitive statements on collective inferiority complexes, E. Franklin Frazier (1968) describes the behavior of middle-class African Americans who are socialized to be "inferior" and are desperately attempting to legitimate their upward mobility. Frazier's critics (1968:13) asserted that the behavior he describes and discusses can be observed among middle-class Jews in particular and among all middle-class populations in general. Frazier agrees with his critics and explains that he had merely limited his account to middle-class African Americans. He concludes: "Some of my Jewish friends, including some young sociologists, went so far as to say that the book was the best account that they had ever read concerning middle-class Jews."

Much of this work by Frazier (e.g., 1927) has not been well received because it strikes to the heart of human nature and human mythology. Not only all middle-class groups, but all human beings, regardless of race, class, and ethnicity, are victims of a collective inferiority complex. That is my thesis. I explain this complex on the basis of a theory called complex theory.

As Rogers (1988:819) states: "Most social scientists would agree that the capacity for human culture was probably fashioned by natural selection, but they disagree on the implications of this supposition. Some scientists believe that natural selection imposes important constraints on the ways in which culture can vary, while others believe that any such constraints must be negligible." At a certain period in human evolution, increased brain capacity, self-consciousness, and fear caused man to distinguish and to divorce himself psychologically from "lower" animals. The fear was created by the unknown, the unknowable, and the meaninglessness of the animal cycle of birth, struggle, and death. This transition to a unique pattern of human social learning constrained the ways in which culture can vary. The extent of those constraints I leave, for now, to the sociobiologists and their critics. My efforts in this chapter are to examine, describe, and explore the constraints themselves and some of their effects on human behavior.

Freud, Jung, other psychologists, and Lévi-Strauss have attempted to give us some insights into the psychology of human origins and evolution. The transition to human social learning or culture must have occurred with severe traumas, as the biblical story of Eden demonstrates. Man's response was to perceive himself as superior to the other animals and to select his companions on the basis of these perceptions. These perceptions of qualitative distinction and superiority had severe impacts on the psyche of humans forced to survive in similar ecological niches with the "lower" animals, especially as these other animals possessed so many physical characteristics that were similar to man's own. The response of human beings was an ever stronger effort to distinguish themselves from animals, a strength that I characterize as a denying, defying, and defiling of their animal kinship (DDDAK). This effort may help to explain the development of primate traits that biological anthropologists cannot adequately trace, such as upright posture, language, skin color, and bipedalism.

DDDAK was critical in the origin of man, in the formation of a permanent component of his constitutional character. That character, discussed below, helps explain certain behaviors in human societies. Man's three million years as a hunter and gatherer, in competition with "lower" animals and other humans, reinforced DDDAK in human character and transferred it by psychological displacement into an important component of human perception, a perceptual dichotomy and deep structure binary opposition: inferior-superior. During this entire period and in the present, "lower" animals are vivid perceptual images and models for man's codified standard of the "inferior."

During the three million years man roamed the Earth as a hunter and gatherer, he stood upright to stretch as tall above the "lower" animals as possible and to free his hands to make tools and weapons. With these he killed animals for food and for their habitats. This was a further expression of DDDAK for this omnivore. It was manifested by ranking human populations (even fossil man was once described in terms of the hunted *(Zinjanthropus)* and the hunter *(Homo habilis)*. Status was conferred on the basis of knowledge of ritual, tradition, game movements, terrain, healing, articulate speech, and other critical aspects of social life. But power continued to elude man. DDDAK took the form of elaborate kinship relationships among humans themselves and their intricate regulations against indiscriminate sexuality. It encouraged cooperation for hunting, for protection from "lower" animals, for social solidarity that contrasted with its perceived absence among the "lower" animals, and for survival as a "higher" form of animal life that maintained relationships with the supernatural.

Approximately fifteen thousand years ago, hunters and gatherers began to domesticate plants and "lower" animals. On the fertile banks of certain rivers, more food was grown than the populations growing it could consume. The nonhuman primate that stood and freed his hands perhaps had increased his brain capacity by using them. That brain capacity had created culture, which continued to increase brain capacity. All of this culminated in the Agricultural Revolution, which brought man economic surplus. The convergence of economic surplus and DDDAK was the equivalent of an explosion in culture. And man's brief history after this period has been dominated by DDDAK-inspired attempts to utilize the economic surplus to prove his superiority. The human inferiority complex has dominated man's efforts to distribute and utilize the economic surplus. Thus the surplus changed the character of human societies, which became characterized by social stratification, slavery, human exploitation, oppression, warfare, and tyranny. The events of the next fifteen thousand years have been dominated by questions of who gets the surplus and how to control the "inferiors" who are deprived of it.

Another major event in the cultural history of man, the Industrial Revolution, occurred about two hundred years ago with the scientific discoveries that led to modern machine technology, which in turn created surplus even more rapidly. For two hundred years human populations have waged warfare and economic intrigue to determine who would control the vast surplus created by modern science and machine technology. Ingenious distinctions have been created in the world's populations to rationalize the distribution of that surplus. Some of these distinctions are regional, racial, religious, ethnic, national, class-specific, or a combination of them. All these distinctions are manipulated by man's DDDAK and the resulting human inferiority complex. Humans have used the surpluses from the Agricultural Revolution and the Industrial Revolution to surround and clothe themselves in elaborate wealth, sophisticated technology, meaningless leisure (see Veblen 1987), a complexity of titles, and systems of social stratification to document their superiority to "lower" animals and fellow humans.

This brings us to the present era of modern society. Technology, communication, and the military-industrial complex of the present have created a global society that is completely interdependent. The competitive race for human superiority has raped the planet's resources, polluted the planet's elements, eliminated many of the planet's species, threatened the existence of all forms of life, and reduced the lives of many humans and "lower" animal populations to despair and desperation. Ironically, however, our human solution to all this is to become even more "superior." With our superior intellects we propose to solve the problems the intellect has created. We propose to save our "Endangered Earth" (see *Time* 1989).

Humans evaluate their own activities as intricate, complex, and modern. We create and validate our own "progress" and its resulting "civilization." But as Lowie (1922:161) said years ago:

Voilà! L'ennemi! In the insidious influence of group opinions, whether countenanced by Church, State or a scientific hierarchy, lies the basic peril. The philosophic habit of unremitting criticism of one's basic assumptions is naturally repugnant to a young and naive culture and it cannot be expected to spring up spontaneously and flower luxuriantly in science while other departments of life fail to yield it nurture. Every phase of our civilization must be saturated with that spirit of positive skepticism which Goethe and Huxley taught before science can reap a full harvest in her field.

My thesis is a simple effort to reexamine a basic assumption—that man is the "highest" form of animal and that this preconception exalts his existence. My position suggests several propositions:

1. that the denial, defiance, and defilement of the animal kinship is an important component of contemporary human behavior;
2. that culture is designed to disguise and destroy the animal character of man;
3. that man, the animal, is unique but no "higher" or "lower" than the other animals and that his cultural design for this hierarchy permeates our social systems and creates, supports, and reinforces racial, religious, ecological, and nationalistic prejudices;
4. that much of the world population is disdained because it lacks the resources to pretend that it is "higher" than the other animals or its fellow men;
5. that all these propositions have impeded the scientific study of primates and of prehistoric and "primitive" man;
6. that considerable confusion can be avoided if we substitute the word "animal" for the word "nature" in the discussion of "Nature, Culture and Gender" (see Ortner 1974);
7. that we are the primate animal with the big brains, "and we are not saved."

The analysis is in the tradition of structural thought. The unconscious component of it began with Boas' (1911) distinction between the conscious and the unconscious. As Lévi-Strauss (1967) states, Boas was the first to argue that a structural interpretation is easier when the population has not attempted to explain a category of facts. Lévi-Strauss says that conscious structural models are usually known as "norms" and are "very poor ones, since they are not intended to explain the phenomena but to perpetuate them" (1967:273). So it is with man's hierarchical position in the animal kingdom.

The discussion presented here does not follow that aspect of structural anthropology that examines the relationships of items as contrasted to the content of items. Rather, in this work I attempt to discover the structural character of social phenomena. Like Lévi-Strauss (1967), I attempt to look for universals, the basic social and mental processes of which cultural institutions are the concrete external projections or manifestations. If anthropology is a science of general principles, the ones I adopt here are general and purposefully simple. They are applicable to all societies and valid for all possible observers. They underlie the various manifestations of social life cross-culturally.

Genesis (1:26) states that God decided to make man in the image of God, in his "likeness." And then God (1:28) gave man "dominion" over all the animals of the Earth. God created Eve as Adam's companion, "and they were both naked, the man and his wife and were not ashamed" (2:25). But when they ate the forbidden fruit, "the eyes of them both were opened and they knew that they were naked; and they sewed fig leaves together and made themselves aprons" (3:7). In this account we have an early written record of man's obsession with and concern for his animal appearance and character. An ecological anthropologist observed that:

An enormous amount of intellectual effort and not a little emotion has been expended by men on distinguishing themselves from the other creatures with which they share the Earth and it may be that some fundamental characteristic of human psychology lies beneath this enterprise, for it seems to manifest itself in both science and religion as well as in everyday thought. Be this as it may, the notion that through culture man has transcended nature is perhaps reminiscent of certain religious notions. It can be argued that in its attempt to view man naturalistically, anthropology unwittingly produced a conceptualization of man's position in nature not unlike that of the theology with which it took issue. (Rappaport 1971:248)

As long as man was not self-conscious, he, as other animals, was not ashamed of his anatomy. But when his brain developed the capacity for self-consciousness, he began the long trek to disguise himself, re-create himself, and create a world in which he controlled the other animals. These efforts manifested themselves in culture.

Sexual "inferiority" is only a small component of the human inferiority complex that is created by DDDAK. Race is another. Human beings compensate for perceived animal deficiencies by releasing aggression on suitable scapegoats. DDDAK and our ever-present animal bodies create an appropriate framework for legitimating the practice of racial discrimination. As we struggle to prove that we are not "lower" animals, we are constantly made aware that we cannot escape our own animal-based feelings of inferiority by projecting and displacing that "inferiority" onto others. These projections and displacements are a part of the human condition, but they do not resolve the human dilemma. We have the mark of the beast (an animal body) and a mind that contemplates God.

Such a powerful obsession with our animal kin requires a reevaluation and reanalysis of human behavior to consider the overarching effects of this obsession and our exaltation of the human position in the animal kingdom. Man may have acquired language and upright posture in distinguishing himself from the other animals, but he heralds these as characteristics of a "higher" being. Race, class, gender, and poverty must be reexamined in terms of the stresses and tensions of DDDAK and of the use of available resources to behave and appear different from the "lower" animals. Some of the earlier examinations are confused by the use of the general term "nature" where the specific term "animal" would be better. Darwin, Freud, Jung, and Rousseau struggled with these ideas, but all were reluctant to treat man as the animal he is. They lacked the key insight—DDDAK.

The inferiority complex of humans has motivated them to achieve and to be "superior." That motivation has provided us with three million years of survival and dominion over most of the animals of the Earth. But that motivation has also been very costly in terms of racism, classism, sexism, and warfare.

The human inferiority complex urges us constantly to provide things and people that will allow us to evaluate ourselves up from the "lower" animals and the "lower" people. To reinforce that end, we have allocated privileges and surplus resources to the "elites." But to create the concept and the working categories of "elite" people requires "inferior" people for conceptualization. The "elites" spend countless hours and fortunes surrounding themselves with expensive things and wealthy people in their efforts to constantly reinforce the myths of superiority.

We have created human categories and multiplied them since the Agricultural Revolution. For instance, one of the unique inventions in the New World was the creation of the category of race. Race, which is almost meaningless outside political designs, has become pregnant with political interpretations and beliefs (see Montagu 1952). We attempt to assign all humans to a race, to give all races a rank, and to deny the depravity of this process. Notwithstanding the denial of their existence, racial classification and ranking persist. And most nations of the world reflect this persistence in their respective minority problems. The Ibo of Nigeria; the Luo of Kenya; the Blacks (note the bellicose situation between the Xhosa and the Zulu), Colored, Boers, British, and Hindus of South Africa; the Tamil of Sri Lanka; the Hutu of Ruanda; the Kurds of Iraq; the Ukrainians of the former U.S.S.R.; the Armenians of Turkey and the Soviet Union; the Jews of Nazi Germany; the Eta and Ainu of Japan; the Indians of the Americas; the barbarians in China; the Catholic Irish in Britain; the African Americans and Hispanics in the United States, and the Indians of Canada are all examples of the use of race (or similar categories) by people to separate other people, often for oppressive ends (see Berreman 1972).

CONCLUSION

I have attempted to discuss an approach to racial relations that ceases to treat discrimination as abnormal human behavior. To discriminate, to rank, and to iden-tify "inferior" people is part of the nature of man/woman (see Hobson 1947). If we choose to transform this modern malady, with all of its technological threats to life on Earth, then we must alter the socialization of our children. Fortunately, these changes—the Ecological Revolution—must come if humans are to survive our modern ecological crises.

The future focus of urban ethnography must be on the structures and the people within them that create and perpetuate "inferior" people and neighbors. For ex-ample, the city police departments are very effective in identifying, creating, and maintaining "inferior" neighborhoods. They are among the first to know when political patronage is distributed in the form of permissive illegal commerce in designated districts. This permissiveness in one crime area attracts other criminal elements. It is similar to legal gambling and the criminal elements that are at-tracted by it. Such criminal trade sets the stage for the deterioration of communi-ties in utility services, zoning, housing, street and sewer maintenance, refuse col-lection, code enforcement, condemnations, and demolitions. Other city agencies follow the lead of the police by benign neglect, and then real estate interests con-form as well. These are the processes we must study, not the Black and the poor.

I have attempted to point out that the basic characteristics of humans create racial, ethnic, religious, class, and gender discrimination and oppression, a world-wide phenomenon. What follows from these practices are social systems in which the power elite and their collaborators systematically socialize the poor and the oppressed to be "inferior" societal "failures." This allows the oppressors to en-force the myths of superiority and to distribute the limited resources unequally. It allows, in hegemonic fashion, some of the wretched lives of the rich to be per-ceived as "happiness" by the prevailing values and attitudes. I have described some of the dilemmas and predicaments of urban discrimination and oppression. Some of the contributions of African Americans (see Williams 1990:144) to Ameri-can culture and society have been crucial, despite the denial to African Americans of access to many of the institutional resources and opportunities considered nec-essary rungs in success. And I have suggested the mechanism—the Ecological Revolution—for ending racial strife, poverty, oppression, and discrimination throughout the world. The new cooperation between the United States and Russia in the United Nations Security Council may facilitate the Ecological Revolution—the real "new world order."

The Earth has become analogous to a closed system. We cannot transform rac-ism in an artificially isolated culture and society. The brief discussions of the Black middle class, the Black underclass, women, and the power elite who op-press them all put in bold relief the urgent need for major transformations in human social and political skills. Such changes will compensate for the cultural lag relative to human technological expertise. That cultural lag renders humans impotent to control the massive destruction of the Earth, its resources, its people, and its life-forms in their ecosystems. Race and ethnic relations cannot be divorced from these phenomena.

Finally, race and ethnic relations are only one component of a massive problem, and we cannot control racism in isolation from the total transformation—the Ecological Revolution—that will end social inequality and its reproduction.

Chapter 9

Social Transformations and the Ecological Revolution

Early in the next century we humans will discover that the Earth can no longer support human life if we continue to behave as we presently do (e.g., turning the Persian Gulf into a dead sea, darkening the Kuwaiti skies with oil well fires, and the desertification of California). We will be forced to alter our behavior, lifestyles, attitudes, and values. I believe that these changes will be easier if we learn how to solve the problems facing our endangered Earth. This book attempts to contribute to that understanding.

Since 1970 we have been bombarded with information about global pollution and the ravages of Earth's resources. "Earth Day" is recognized throughout the world. Many nations and communities within them are working to reduce the threats to the environment. On June 3, 1992, the United Nations Conference on Environment and Development—the Earth Summit—convened. But these are cosmetic efforts to address a human dilemma by treating the environmental symptoms rather than the problem. We must recycle (transform the culture of) people as well as their products. Our recycled people will think and behave as members of the global ecosystems.

The discipline of anthropology has informed us that human culture is malleable. Thus, after we learn how maladaptive human culture has become and how dangerous this maladaptation is to all life on the Earth, we humans may transform human culture to an adaptive mode. Culture is integrated (Murdock 1965). Any significant change in a social institution is accompanied by profound transformations in the other institutions of a society. Witness how changes in the institution of religion in the United States have affected other institutions during the twentieth century. The abandonment of the churches by the 1970s caused Carl Dudley (1979) to title his book *Where Have All Our People Gone?* They went to sports, drugs, and consumerism. The Catholic Church has found it difficult to recruit nuns, priests, and members. It began to abandon churches and schools that it could no longer afford. Other denominations suffered as well.

This decline in religious activity was accompanied by changes in the family. The extended and nuclear family traditions were radically altered. Gay and lesbian households began to be formed and legitimated. During this same period, education was undergoing profound changes. Public education lost its traditional support, and universities were also at risk. School discipline began to occupy more and more instructional time. Students graduated without the expected skills in reading, writing, history, geography, mathematics, and critical thinking. During this same period, our political institutions were impacted by the Vietnam War, the Nixon and Reagan constitutional crises, and the plethora of scandals in national, state, and local governments. Our economic institutions did not escape. The value of the dollar continued to decline. Our children found it impossible to buy homes as their parents had done before them. Those who owned homes discovered rising taxes that they could not afford. Salaries in sports, movies, and corporations became spectacular. Consumer, business, and government debts became overwhelming. Savings and loan associations failed in record numbers, and our banking system was threatened. The Japanese bought our land, industry, corporations, farms, and the paper for our national debt. Junk bonds heralded a period of earning profits on paper rather than through productivity. This failed, too, as Michael Milken, the junk-bond king, was sentenced to ten years in prison (November 1990).

All these events give us a recent view of cultural change. They show us that if we can make effective changes in one of our social institutions, then those transformations will impact on the others. This knowledge will be vital for us during the Ecological Revolution.

The Ecological Revolution will occur early in the next century as a result of leadership and as a result of a series of serious global warnings that the nations of the Earth can no longer ignore. Countries such as Japan, which is just beginning to reap the full "benefits" of industrialism, will be the most difficult to persuade to abandon the exploitation of the Earth. That persuasion may involve military coercion as well as education.

HUMAN ADAPTATIONS

Nonhuman primates compete for food, sex, safety, and territory. They have endured their positions in the food chain. But as the transition from nonhuman to human primate occurred, brainpower was a crucial component of humans' increasingly selective adaptation. We became more self-conscious and self-aware. We began to perceive ourselves as separate, superior, and distinct from the other animal species. Eventually we denied, defied, and defiled our animal kinship. This process of perception was the beginning of human culture, and it continued to develop until the present. The process has been successful. Humans have spread throughout the Earth, and they dominate its animals and other resources.

But perhaps like the dinosaurs before us, we have become too successful. We are overwhelming Earth's resources. We are undermining the global web-of-life. But unlike the dinosaurs, we have culture and the capacity to change rapidly (the

Ecological Revolution). Our global ecosystems must be protected, and we are now aware of that need. What we must learn quickly is that such protection requires a major transformation in human values and attitudes. DDDAK must be discarded. Humans must accept their humble places in the biosphere. We must change people in order to protect the environments. These are some of the issues this book has attempted to examine.

The painful sacrifices of social change and the dynamics of social interaction will never allow a utopian human existence. The Ecological Revolution will not usher in an earthly utopia, but it may allow the continued existence of human life on Earth and revolutionize the nature and character of human relationships. The myriad of artificial categories of human populations will be eliminated, and the human species will work, play, and disagree together in the common enterprise of protecting their Earth and respecting the universe.

THE ECOLOGICAL REVOLUTION

As I have stated above, biophobia is as old as humans. It is a component of human cognition. Children are born with an intuitive cognitive map that is systematically structured to incorporate the external environment (E. Margaret Evans, *Personal Communication*, March 10, 1998). That intuitive map facilitates the learning of language, the distinction between animate and inanimate objects, responses to gravity, identifications with arbitrary individuals and groups, and the ranking of individuals, groups and species, among other facilities. Humans develop their proclivity for "superiority" and power. Some societies promote the proclivity while others discourage it. As a response to human insecurity (especially about their physical bodies) humans create and perpetuate conflict and violence to seek and to secure power (superiority).

The human quest (often appearing irrational) for power and the exploitation and misappropriation of natural and human resources in that quest are the seeds of human extinction or of a new cultural revolution. Power seems a pervasive human addiction and the exploitation of the resources support the habit. The global transformations in world technology, communications, transportation, information systems, weapon systems and commerce are being diverted to the quest for power in a world in which the natural and human resources are limited. The global waste and abuse of those resources are symptomatic of a species gone amuck. The waste and abuse of the resources are also a result of a continuing contempt for nature. We still perceive women as inferior to men because they process more water (e.g., menstruation, gestation, lactation and labor).

A rational reconstruction of the human relationship with Earth's resources will ultimately readjust the intuitive systems of babies. Some aspects of the old intuitive paradigm are obsolete. The new models will repair the water, air, forests and soils of Earth. It will repair consumerism, weapon mania and power addiction. It will equate the welfare of Earth with the well-being of people, other species and life on the Planet. Humans are reaching a species maturity.

They are becoming caretakers of Earth rather than expropriators. They are arriving at a social responsibility commensurate with their space and other technologies, information systems and weapon systems. In this century alone we have witnessed the demise of the British, Nazi and U.S.S.R. Empires. We have learned the way of power. We embark on the way of peace on Earth and goodwill to life thereon.

INSTITUTIONAL HYPOCRISY

Like prisons and jails, many social agencies and organizations—hospitals, universities, colleges, public schools, churches (e.g., the Catholic priests' sexual abuse of children), fraternities, sororities, corporations, gangs, sports organizations, industries, and military organizations—conceal the abuse, humiliation, and destructive control of the powerless people within them. These agencies and organizations are often managed and controlled by people with severe feelings of inferiority who cherish their positions as symbols of superiority and power. The agency or organization becomes a brotherhood and sisterhood that protects their abusive behavior, and all of the benefactors guard the agency as team players to disguise their images of themselves as well as of their jobs. They merge their identity with the organization. Their crimes and abuses are concealed by members who are afraid to divulge them or who believe that the organization is more important than the abuse and destruction of individuals.

The corridors of power in these organizations corrupt the people who walk in them. They begin to believe they are the organizations. They become larger than life, more important than other people, paranoid about the appearance of disrespect (lack of homage), and ruthless about the maintenance of the structural arrangements that keep them within the corridors of power. These people create institutional "devils" (e.g., Willie Horton, inner-city gangs and drug enterprises, ghetto, national, and democratic enemies) as diversionary evils to direct attention away from the evil within their own ranks. Much of this behavior is the result of humans trying to be as powerful as gods in futile attempts to escape their fate as tiny specks of animate stardust among cotillions of billion-year-old constellations.

Much of college and university "education" is designed to prepare our young people for such organizations and agencies. The decades of complaints about college fraternities have gone uncorrected because they are crucial to the socialization of young men in our society. It is here as elsewhere (in gangs, reformatories, and prisons) that young men learn to be generic males. They learn to endure pain and punishment for the organization. They inflict pain and punishment on individuals for the identity of the group. They rape and abuse women, discriminate against Blacks and gays, and destroy the resources of others to establish the superiority of males and the power they wield in groups (see Sanday 1973, 1981, 1990).

People who work within social agencies and organizations learn very quickly that they are subject to colleagues who have been socialized in fraternities or similar groups. One must be prepared to sacrifice (even one's principles) for membership. The uncooperative are dismissed, tortured, or killed. Whistle-blowers are tracked for life. Some of these agencies and organizations have a high concentration of high achievers, people who have severe feelings of inferiority. They spend endless hours discovering ways to be superior to others. They tolerate only abject humility and deference. They cause years of stress and anxiety to their colleagues, and they camouflage their behavior with rules, regulations, and evaluations. Many of our workplaces will be pleasant places in which to produce after we transform these people in the Ecological Revolution.

A PEOPLE AND PLANETARY PEACE

The Ecological Revolution will usher in a people and planetary peace. At Christmas we will say "peace on Earth, goodwill to life," and we will mean it and believe it. Many "successful" people in our society suffer from a severe neurosis (see Frazier 1927). They have intense feelings of inferiority. Our society selects and rewards them because they support and promote the kind of society we revere—one built upon success, status, prestige, fame, money, materialism, competition, recognition, and greed. But they are sick. They are forced from within and without to spend their lives proving they are not inferior. They ask the mirror on the wall daily, "Who is the fairest of us all?" It will never matter what they accomplish and achieve because the disease is internal and their achievements are external. They learn and manipulate the rhetoric of "helping people" and the gracious styles of human interaction and subordination to superiors, but their real purposes are helping and becoming the superiors themselves. They are similar to sick populations that develop sophisticated propaganda about how they have and are suffering at the hands of others to disguise the suffering they are perpetrating on other peoples. Much of "white" America seems more chagrined by the alleged two murders of O. J. Simpson than of those (160 dead and 500 wounded) by Timothy McVeigh.

There cannot be peace on Earth until these people have peace within themselves. In the Ecological Revolution they will be resocialized so that they no longer feel inferior or need to oppress others to assuage those painful feelings. The rich and the powerful must finally learn and understand that what (abuse) they have inflicted upon the poor and powerless for almost fifteen thousand years, the Earth can no longer abide.

THE BLACK MIDDLE CLASS IN THE
ECOLOGICAL REVOLUTION

I, like many middle-class African Americans, have been attempting to escape "inferiority" most of my life (see Chapter 2). Notwithstanding my efforts to achieve and my successes, I continue to fail in my escape. I have finally discovered that it was my society that ascribed "inferiority" to me and that I could escape only by changing that society and not by achieving. This is my message to the Black middle class. So I welcome the Ecological Revolution because I realize that my society could not change insularly without the transformation of the people of the world.

Lately I have asked, why does my society need me to be "inferior?" And I have begun to attempt to understand this social pathology. Others have examined this issue (e.g., Clark 1965) in terms of the fragility of the ego and the resultant quest for power, the inferiority complex of humans, or a biologically based protection of ego-esteem (Allport 1958). But few have simplified the issues for the average person, and until that is done a great transformation—the Ecological Revolution—will be delayed.

THE CRADLE OF HUMANKIND

The populations of the world reflect the diversity of Africa's contribution to America and the world. That diversity has an infinite character when one is discovering those contributions. In this chapter I focus on a major contribution from the African continent—mythological symbols of social inferiority—that has been rarely conceptualized and described as a contribution to Americans and to the world.

There is evidence that race consciousness and other social and political devices that artificially distinguish and separate human populations from one another are central factors in the development of the United States and indeed of social life among most human populations (see Williams 1990,1992b). Africa has served as a significant symbol of that human divisiveness. As the Dark Continent of "backward," "irrational," "savage," "barbarian," and "primitive" people and third world nations, Africa contaminated African Americans with these stigmas. Such a perception of Africa provided a justification and rationalization for colonialism, slavery, and capitalism; and it had significant ingredients for a perception of human inferiority. Not only did Africa supply people, but it also furnished a rationale for the exploitation of Native Americans. "Inferior" people had few human rights and privileges. Thus Africa helped to fuel the Industrial Revolution with resources that included people. (Africa was also at the eye of the Agricultural Revolution and will be a major impetus for the next cultural revolution—the Ecological Revolution.) This dehumanization of Africans and their descendants that has depersonalized a large portion of the human race is an important component of the heritage of African Americans. But the significance does not stop there. This process of the production and reproduction of social inferiority is universal, and Africa and African Americans, as primary mythological symbols of this process, can assist in its explication. I argue that an understanding of this process is necessary for human survival. Africa, its people, and its heritage will point humanity toward the Ecological Revolution. That revolution will end the reproduction of social inferiority and witness the evolution of colonialism, socialism, communism, capitalism, and environmentalism into universalism.

Race consciousness has been a fundamental instrument in the reproduction of social inequality in America and in the world. Indeed, that may be its only conceptual value. I argue that it is only one component of a panhuman process of producing and reproducing social inferiority—classism, racism, ethnocentrism, sectarianism, sexism, ageism nationalism, and speciesism (CRESSANS). Most social institutions participate in regulating social inequality (e.g., the physical locations of ghettos, barrios, waste dumps, prisons, crime, pollution, junkyards, cigarette ads, liquor ads, lottery ads, and other sites of dehumanization). This pervasive component of universal culture accounts for the little success achieved during the last 150 years of combating racism in America. African Americans are still socially "inferior" in America in the final decade of the twentieth century. (Women are socially "inferior" worldwide after three million years.)

Chattel slavery was an institution in the United States. During that period, racism was institutionalized. There was a codified decree that all Caucasoids in America were superior to African Americans. The whites in the United States were guaranteed that their inferiority complexes would be assuaged by the Black population. "Up from Slavery" and through Reconstruction, Booker T. Washington continued to advise and admonish us of the structural nature of racism. An "inferior" population could not expect to mingle with whites, only to serve them. That service contract was heralded as the best this "inferior" population could negotiate. W.E.B. Du Bois was run out of Atlanta because he did not agree.

Marcus Garvey confronted the wall of racism by accepting it. He advised African Americans not to be influenced by racism. Because someone thinks and says that you are inferior does not mean that you are. He told Blacks to "rise up" and recognize their own intrinsic values. Such teachings and ethos would have undermined the mythologies of racism if allowed to continue. They were not, and Garvey was stopped by the American government. The mythologies of Black inferiority would continue to support white America.

During the 1930s, Hortense Powdermaker, John Dollard, Allison Davis, and St. Clair Drake, among others, studied and documented the institutional nature of racism in the South. In the North, Lloyd Warner, St. Clair Drake, Horace Cayton, and Robert and Helen Lynd, among others, studied classism and racism up to the 1940s. World War II documented the international epidemic of racism, ethnocentrism, and sectarianism. Yet after the war the nation created the myth that racism was the result of the denial of civil rights and with the guarantee of these rights racism would disappear. Later the nation would attempt the same strategy for sexism by attributing it to equal rights. Laws were enacted to guarantee the civil rights of minorities, and social and psychological theories guaranteed that attitudinal changes would follow. Industrialization, urbanization, and education were heralded as social changes that would assist in these attitudinal transformations in a society where such attitudes were un-American and against the American creed (Myrdal 1944). Racism was explained as a historical accident of slavery and its aftermath.

But the deep sense of African-American oppression and powerlessness erupted in the 1960s, and all the myths of social change exploded into the Civil Rights Movement, ghetto revolts, Black power skirmishes, and a renewed political and social oppression of African Americans (e.g., the Rodney King beating, trial, and revolts). The continuing cycles of racial hatred (on university campuses, in police policies, in housing, education, and employment policies) in the 1970s, 1980s, and 1990s leave little doubt that American racism is as intractable as worldwide CRESSANS. The solutions are more fundamental to human nature than previously understood. That is why I have called the problem of the twenty-first century the problem of the human line, which requires a revolution in human behavior—the Ecological Revolution.

Since the Agricultural Revolution, humans have not been able to cooperate without frequent eruptions of unmanageable conflicts. CRESSANS and environmental abuse are pervasive human problems that we have failed to solve notwithstanding the resources in scholarship, conferences, wars, and weapons that have been expended to confront such problems. Humans have sought solutions everywhere except in themselves where the solutions lie. These devious searches can no longer be tolerated. The conflicts must be managed with people, plants, animals, and Earth. It can be accomplished only with the cessation of the search for social superiority and the end of the reproduction of social inferiority.

We have lived in the most violent century in human history. We have had two world wars, numerous regional ones, and a forty-five-year cold war that has destroyed the societies of the main adversaries (the U.S.S.R. and the United States) with their trillion-dollar defense budgets. The Nazis, the Soviets, the Serbs, the Burundis, the Rwandans, the Turks, and the Khmer Rouge in Cambodia have practiced genocide on a grand scale. Television has destroyed the myths of honesty and integrity for our citizens. For them, corruption and violence are replacing family, religion, education, and community. The corruption is created in the process of humans trying to be equal or superior, and they cannot become equal or superior by such efforts. Some humans say and often think that they are made in the image of God and spend their entire time on Earth trying to prove it. This quest for superiority is no longer required for survival; it is an attempt to control the human inferiority complex. It corrupts our political leaders. It induces political consultants to sell secrets, influence, and national interests. It undermines leadership with careerism. The quest for superiority encourages the media to debunk and shred our public heroes into flawed people.

CRESSANS, like other human problems—prostitution, rape, child abuse, sexual deviancy, cruel and unreasonable punishment, cruel and unreasonable entertainment, murder and other crimes, war, political prisoners, torture, starvation, grinding poverty, and environmental abuse—have not been solved because humans have not been prepared to transform their behavior. Social science scholars have conspired with the power elite to build their own paper industries and academic empires by analyzing the symptoms of social problems rather than by attacking their causes. The Earth's time has come. Its message is clear, "You clean up your act or I will clean you out." Environmental abuse can no longer be tolerated, and with its cessation in the Ecological Revolution the other social problems will end. Human behavior will be transformed. The Pandora's box of Greek myth will begin to close.

The Ecological Revolution will usher in a rapprochement between the biological determinists and the nurture-oriented social scientists. The sociobiologists and the humanists will no longer require the manufacture and perpetuation of competing academic turfs to assuage their inferiority complexes. The invidious and artificial contrast between "scientists" and humanists will cease, and scholars will work together to understand global citizens in the global village (see Anderson 1992).

The analysis of DDDAK is an attempt to understand metaculture, to examine the transcultural nature of humans, and to permeate the human conscious and unconscious resistance to knowing human nature. As Pfeiffer (1972:498) stated more than twenty years ago:

In all areas a realistic picture of human behavior is only beginning to emerge and nothing discovered to date is more remarkable than our long resistance to such studies. The resistance has been so intense and so effective that it must have been of special value to the species, serving some vital adaptive need. Perhaps it was a matter of survival for early man to feel supremely confident and all-powerful, most of all at times when the wilderness seemed most alien and daily routines most futile. Feelings of superiority are not easy to maintain in the face of too much self-knowledge.

In any case, if insight once threatened man's security, today ignorance is an even greater threat.

The sociobiologist can assist in explaining the premature sexuality of humans. The nurture social scientist can help us understand the long period of childhood. But only DDDAK suggests that the long period of childhood and parenthood is a cultural design to prevent humans from reverting to prehuman behavioral patterns. Myth and propaganda require a long childhood. And even after that long period, humans often remain in or revert to behavior that is "uncivilized." This constant struggle to live superior to animals and simultaneously to be one is the human dilemma. Being an animal and being a "superior" spectator of animals is indeed a struggle that results in the human inferiority complex. Humans must come to terms with that struggle in order to understand the problems that humans have created on Earth.

The people who have come to terms with their animal selves and have determined that there is no basis for being superior to other forms of life have dealt a lethal blow to their inferiority complexes. They recognize their animal nature and character without any diminution of their ego structure or self-esteem. They are global citizens in the global village. They play their little parts on life's stage and never feel inferior. Maslow (1954) called them "self-actualizing people." Whatever you call them, they are not "superior" people. They are merely in tune and in touch within the connected circle of life on Earth.

Capitalism and the consumerism associated with it feed effectively off the inferiority complexes of DDDAK. When one is surrounded by masses of humans who are poor, miserable, and "inferior," the motivation is keen to accumulate unreasonable wealth by investing capital and conspiring to exploit government and labor. A capitalistic system encourages the members of its society to collect wealth and materials to demonstrate their status. The system preys upon the inferior feelings that are created by DDDAK by reproducing social inferiority. Not only does capitalism reproduce social inferiority, but it also codifies and institutionalizes it. People spend all the days of their lives attempting to accumulate enough money, material, and property to wipe out their inferiority complexes. They die with their inferiority complexes. Equating superiority with money, material, and property invites desperate attempts to accumulate them without regard for law or ethics. Capitalism operates on the basis of DDDAK. Without DDDAK after the Ecological Revolution, capitalism will be defunct.

As an Africanist colleague wrote to me, sub-Saharan Africans do not possess enough reserve of energy to create ecologically threatening waste. They live in a climate that demands the conservation even of human energy. They have a perspective of the world we may need to reexamine for the Ecological Revolution. There are remnants of forager groups—Bushman, Pigmy, Sandawe, Hatsa, and Dorobo—in Africa whose anthropological records and oral historians may assist us in learning, adjusting, and adapting to universalism in the Ecological Revolution. Thus it will come to pass that Africa, the cradle of humankind, will have made major contributions to the Agricultural, Industrial and Ecological Revolutions. (The only cultural revolution in which it did not participate is what I term the Potential Revolution. That era created the power and energy to destroy humankind.) The land where humans began may play a significant role in human survival during a period when there is an imminent threat of human extinction.

There has been a history of scholarship that has attempted to examine, analyze, and explain the animal nature, character, and evolution of human behavior. Darwin studied the animal and its evolution. Freud analyzed the tension between the human animal and human society. Jung, Joseph Campbell (1973), and Erving Goffman explained the dominant role of myth and drama in the lives and nature of human function and communication. Freud attempted to show the paradigms of equilibrium for individuals. The social contract, the animal nature, the myths, and the tensions between all of them must be understood and managed if humans are to survive the next century. Humans can no longer pursue material "progress with abandon and selfishness under one or another banner of mythology. The Earth will no longer tolerate this human "folly" (see Gore 1992). Just as children who survive long enough must become adults to succeed in society, so humans have survived long enough that they must now become socially and ecologically responsible. The days of planet play for three-million-year-old humans is over. Humans have acquired technology (especially weapons), habits, and population sizes that threaten their own survival. Playing material "progress" with such tools, behavior patterns, and population numbers is no longer tolerable. The social contract must now include the Earth.

The concentration of Earth's resources in a few human hands where they are used with abandon for destruction and for individual profiteering must cease. The writers of the twenty-first century, like those of the eighteenth and nineteenth centuries (e.g., Victor Hugo, Dickens, Rousseau, Marx, and others) must inspire the middle class and the upper middle class to transform their societies.

An understanding of the production and reproduction of social inferiority, of which sub-Saharan Africa is a major symbol, will help lead humanity to the Ecological Revolution and universalism.

The contributions of African Americans to America in materials, resources, creative innovations, styles, and military service are well known. Less recognized are the spiritual and psychological contributions. The DDDAK archetype of human behavior and the accompanying inferiority complexes of humans have required there to be "inferior" populations to drive dominant populations toward material and military "progress." It is difficult to measure the tremendous motivation, solidarity, and feelings of well-being that African Americans have provided to white Americans in the Black roles of "inferior" Americans. Hour after hour, day after day, year after year, and generation after generation, white Americans have had the rights and privileges of acting and feeling superior to African Americans and treating them accordingly. That social and psychological capital has yielded great personal profits for white America. Not the least among such profits has been the Reconstruction of the South on the backs of Blacks after the Civil War, not to mention the prior growth and development of the South to a level before the war that enabled the secessionists to challenge the industrial North. I would argue that the "inferiority" of the African American has been a major social and psychological factor in every military and material victory that the United States has enjoyed. As the time has come for us to recognize the psychological damage to Native Americans that persists to the present as a result of the United States' "winning of the West," so it is time to understand the similar destruction and the same exploitation that has been and is the heritage of Africa and African America.

I use the occasion of the grand ball to illustrate my argument. Imagine a "beautiful" young woman at the ball who is receiving most of the attention of most of the young men and women there. She is enjoying her popularity. She is also being observed by an "unattractive" female "friend" whom she and her admirers have abandoned. The abandoned woman languishes in a corner of the grand hall. She and all of the other "ugly" women must suffer to provide the social and psychological capital for female "beauty" in America (see Ball 1991). In just this way is the African American forced to attend such parties every day as the "inferior" American who provides the psychological capital for white supremacy (Young 1989). Like the "beautiful" young woman, the majority population expropriates social and psychological capital from us, invests it in themselves, and then claims and pretends that all of us have a level playing field.

For many years I have observed, in my most insecure colleagues, the amount of deference they demanded and required of me because of my race (African American). I was required to bolster their defensive feelings of superiority by being treated as an inferior. I had to speak first. It was my responsibility to get and try to maintain their attention. I had to visit their offices. I had to telephone them repeatedly until I could find them. They were so busy and important they could not see, hear, or find me. I had to learn to behave as an inferior in order to be a "good" colleague and not "disruptive," "aggressive," "radical," "bellicose," "uppity," or "unfriendly." In a highly competitive society, they had and must have a permanent and pervasive "failure" around them with which to compare and contrast themselves. It is no surprise that they and other dominant populations have produced and reproduced social inferiority. It is unfortunate for Africans and African Americans that they have been exploited for such production. But the future requires a new world order—the Ecological Revolution—in which all life will have its appropriate opportunity and respect. Universalism, naturism, and ecosophy must replace the human devastation and divisiveness of the past.

This book provides a vision for the future. For approximately three million years, human divisiveness (CRESSANS) has sustained the psychic and physical competitiveness among people that enabled them to adapt and survive. This divisiveness has exploited an endless range of human perceptions: beauty, intelligence, eye color, hair texture, lip shape and size, skin color, sex, height, physical strength, muscularity, athletic ability, linguistic ability, professional activities, occupation, education, social rank, and even geography, for if people associate and identify with a certain part of town, that may categorize them by class, race, ethnicity, and religion. If that association and identification are with a certain part of the globe, the people may be classified by race, ethnicity, and nationality. This geography of identity and its accompanying human divisiveness are obsolete. The population, communication, weaponry, ecosystems, and pollutions of Earth have eliminated the adaptiveness of these former strategies. The new strategies will create identity, self-esteem,and association without the deprecation of other people or other forms of life.

People are born on the Earth. They will identify with it. They are members of one species among many. They will associate themselves with all of Earth's life-forms and ecosystems. They will consider themselves neither superior nor inferior to any of them.

I have chosen the acronym CRESS to express human divisiveness because the term is applied to any of numerous crucifers with pungent leaves. Eaten alone, these leaves are not palatable; consumed in a salad or garnish, they are. This seems analogous to human diversity. Attitudes and values of different cultures can be alien to one another. But if they are understood and mixed appropriately, they become a human salad.

Different cultures, customs, lifestyles, and human adjustments add interest, variety, and innovation to existence. Human diversity can be stimulating and rich in people's lives. But people must be mature enough to appreciate rather than deprecate diversity. They must be secure enough not to require or practice what Thackery described as the human pleasure of associating with one's inferiors.

The treatment of CRESSANS has been cosmetic to date. Humans have been reluctant to probe such revealing human behavior. They have been handicapped by preconceptions that obstructed their vision. Today circumstances require that they probe deep into the human psyche and cut the cords of human insecurity that have "conquered" people and planet for three million years. They have not adequately understood themselves or their adaptive strategies of divisiveness, but now they must.

It is not productive to criticize the practice of CRESSANS because those who engage in such behavior require it for their own fragile identity and personal security. Criticism merely compounds their feelings of vulnerability. People must be rendered reasonably safe in themselves, for themselves, and about themselves in order for them to relinquish the production and reproduction of social inferiority. Such productions and reproductions are the present strategies for humans to be comfortable with themselves. There must be new strategies for adaptive life on Earth.

The production and reproduction of social inferiority will cease, and the geography of identity will have a global character. Humans will identify with their species and their planet. The Ecological Revolution will arrive on Earth.

HUMAN ORIGINS AND PERCEPTIONS

In 1981 (Williams 1981b:140) I concluded my description of an African-American neighborhood with the following words:

Humankind is on the threshold of new experiments in human societies. The old models have run their course and appear inadequate to deal with the social problems they have inherited and created (see Nisbet 1975). My material may suggest new lifestyles and new orientations toward living once we destroy old preconceptions about material excesses and obsessions with possessions, property, prestige, power, fame, money, wealth and competition. We are beginning to appreciate the nature of our limited world and the potential of human satisfaction without the waste of manpower and materials (see Dubos 1976; McHarg 1972). The crisis of our times is such that we begin to think the unthinkable and attempt to achieve the impossible. The alternative is to end it all in human folly—the present petty goals and successes that fill our daily lives.

Here in this book, almost two decades later, I attempt to explain to my readers what new lifestyles and new orientations toward living my studies have suggested.

Human history is a history of myth and power. Mythmaking and his/her increasing power over the environment is the story of humankind. One of the earliest myths (archetypal) was the denial, defiance, and defilement of man's animal kinship (DDDAK). This animal phobia, like homophobia, resulted in part from the similarity humans perceived in themselves and in the others whom they chose to distinguish from themselves. In the beginning, sexual dimorphism (see Bordo 1991, Hunt 1991, Laqueur 1991) was one of the few bases of power available to humans. As a result, sexism is probably the oldest human oppression. Significant human power over the environment began with the Agricultural Revolution. There is a great truth in the biblical creation story and in the creation story of every human society that ever was. That truth is that the creation of man (including woman) is based upon myth, just as his history, present and future, is. For myth is the nature of man. Myth and increasing power have insured his survival until now when his power threatens the planet's ecosystems and life on Earth. Only an understanding of our primary myths will allow us to challenge and change them and thus change our pathway to extinction.

One of the manifestations of DDDAK is the *idée fixée* on the human body (Bordo

1991, Hunt 1991, Laqueur 1991). Pregnancy, birth, genitals ("indecent exposure"), body functions, body cleanliness, race, phenotype, color, and death occupy an inordinate amount of human interest and anxiety. "The dark, the naked, the breasted and the feathered" (Raymond 1991:A5) have been a central focus of an entire twentieth-century science—anthropology.

DDDAK causes the mind to misunderstand the human body and misinterpret its needs and signals. The body strives to live today. The mind attempts to have everlasting life. The body strives to survive all present dangers. The mind attempts to protect against imagined ones. The body asserts its importance over all others for survival. The mind creates superiority for status and power (see Midgley 1995).

The social science mission today (Williams 1981b:141) is to explain the myths of our present trajectory and to demonstrate that the accumulations of planet-specific power over a planet that is not separate and isolated from the universe has allowed man to put the Earth in danger for all living things (Gore 1992). Until man can control the universe, he must respect it. We live in a universe community, and we cannot pretend with impunity that our home is our property only and that we can exploit it as we choose. The community will not tolerate such abandon and irresponsibility. We must humble ourselves to the realization that our scientific knowledge and technological exploitation are relative and Earth-specific and that we cannot continue to ignore the universal community of which Earth is but a minute part. We know only 10 percent of the universal content. We are even humbled by our powerlessness on Earth (i.e., comets, earthquakes, global climate changes, volcanoes, forest fires, genetic mutations, incurable diseases, epidemics and pandemics [see Garrett 1994], birth defects, the limitations on all life, natural resource depletions, locust swarms, and weather). With all our power and understanding of the Earth, we seem powerless to protect it from ourselves. We cling to our mythology even to our own demise. The conditions (myth and power) that created humans contain within them the dynamics of our extinction.

This is my central thesis. I use the Black middle class to illustrate it. It is important that the reader understand this thesis because much of what I have written can be used to support various political agendas in which I have no vested interest and for which this book is not designed. My discussions here are designed to demonstrate and support my thesis; any other perceptions are purely coincidental.

DDDAK (animal phobia) is an archetypal myth that was as crucial in the creation of man as language, upright posture, bipedalism, incest rules, self-perception, and belief in the supernatural. But like the fitness of the dinosaur, the development of human power has undermined the usufruct of the DDDAK myth. We have overpopulated the Earth. Those populations live too close to one another to continue to survive with a binary opposite deep structure (superior-inferior) that categorizes and perceives "others" as "inferior" or "lower" animals. DDDAK requires that the poor, the homeless, the Black, the Jew (see Hobson 1947), the mentally ill, the "primitive," and the people of the third world be perceived as inferior. Our conception of and need for an inferior are based on the primal necessity of separating ourselves from "others" (animals). That characteristic remains with us and allows us to participate in the destruction of "inferior" people because we can effectively separate ourselves from them. As long as we have DDDAK, we cannot conceive of ourselves as one species, and our commitment to other populations and other life will be largely rhetoric. Willie Horton could be your son or mine, your brother or mine, any sick human being, but in the presidential campaign of 1988 he was a Black depraved animal. And most of America believed. The political strategist knew you would believe because they had tested that "inferior" animal image in focus groups. It works.

THE ECOLOGICAL REVOLUTION:
SOCIAL TRANSFORMATIONS AND HUMAN VALUES
(GLOBAL CITIZENS IN A GLOBAL VILLAGE)

In an increasingly interdependent world, where relations with real others pose urgent problems and on a poisoned and overpopulated planet where respect for the web-of-life and ecosystems demand immediate attention, a study of alternate human values in the new global village may be a worthwhile endeavor.

The origin and evolution of human culture appear to be accompanied by some persistent values and attitudes that have allowed humans to dominate and ultimately endanger the Earth. These adaptive propensities have become maladaptive in modern society. Various societies have responded by attempting to regulate and change human behaviors that threaten life on Earth, but the near future will witness doomsday demands that humans transform the human values and attitudes that are the basis for the behaviors that create the window of species-extinctions.

Scholars in the humanities must ask how humans arrived at the end of the twentieth century and what they must do to survive the next one. Those scholars must understand the myths that have allowed humans to reach the present. They must know how those myths must be transformed for the future, and they must comprehend the socializing strategies that will accomplish these goals. My effort here is to begin this study. It seeks to discover new value systems that will place humans in the web-of-life, make them components of the Earth's ecosystems, allow them to perceive other forms of life as vital parts of the living community of the global village, and rid them of the need to reproduce social inequality in any form. My long-term endeavor is an examination of this complex process and the production of a picture of a new world order—Post Civilization—after the arrival of the Ecological Revolution.

Ultimately this journey will require a revisit of researchers in a variety of disciplines. There must be a reexamination of Erving Goffman to appreciate the importance of performance in human behavior. Both Freud and Alfred Adler will confirm such inquiries. If a million years of adaptable human behavior is to be altered, there must be a suitable costume, stage, and script for the future human performers. If the anthropologist Leslie White is accurate and human culture is significantly autonomous, there must be a detailed description of the global conditions that will precede the cultural explosion—the Ecological Revolution. That description will be facilitated by the historical records of the other three cultural revolutions—the Agricultural, the Industrial, and the Potential. Darwin will provide the raw material to launch our investigation, and psychological anthropologists such as Richard Shweder will guide our efforts in the socialization of children for a new world order—the transformation of society.

Environment, education, and human culture must be examined holistically if we are to socialize and educate humans for the next century, for the next stage in social development in a global village. Humans must begin to perceive themselves as being a part of the Earth rather than living on it. This will require our next cultural revolution—the Ecological Revolution—or the "coming of age" in the global village. During this period, "ecosophy" may become one of our most important disciplines (versus the winner-take-all value system; see Frank and Cook 1995).

Human efforts to control their environments (including identifiable populations) and to control most forms of life within those environments have allowed humans to adapt, multiply, and spread over the Earth. Now as we approach the twenty-first century, our scientific and technological sophistication demand that we transform our attitudes and values about our environments—those same attitudes and values that have been the basis for human "progress and successes" in the past. We have devoted many of our resources to attempt to change human habits that are harmful to the environment, but I argue that we must also change the nature of human culture itself. That culture, which has allowed us to master our environments, must be transformed into one that protects them.

A social science approach that creates an understanding of the social dimension of renewable natural resource management problems and of the dissemination of research findings and that creates efforts for the promotion of a conservation ethic and the idea of sustainable development at global, regional, national, and local levels, my efforts will develop a vision of human attitudes and values that are essential to protect global, national, regional, and local ecosystems—a new moral order. A major component of that vision will be to identify attitudes and values that enable people to understand and accept the necessity for conserving and protecting the world's biological diversity (including that phenotypic diversity within the human species itself) and to create the technology and policies that will support these efforts.

Policy studies, conservation ethics, human rights, and new technology for effective biological diversity and conservation require a certain "recycling" of our present attitudes and values to meet the ever increasing demands of and threats to global, national, regional, and local ecosystems. Those threats include the ones that result from conceptions of race, class, gender, ethnicity, and religion. Other efforts will not be sufficient without an educated world population that understands the threats to and demands on our ecosystems. These educated people (global citizens) must be committed to the protection of these ecosystems, including our children, our aged, our poor and our ill. The social commitment must be one that combines the education of parents, educators, policymakers, and industrial and military managers with the socialization of children to view the world's ecosystems and its biological diversity as crucial parts of human life and health itself.

The appropriate social science approach will explain how humans have arrived at their present ecological dilemma through the Agricultural Revolution, the Industrial Revolution, the Potential Revolution, and modernity—adaptive cultural evolution that now emerges with a dangerous cultural lag and with attitudes and values that are no longer appropriate with present levels of science and technology (see Count 1958, 1972). It will examine value and attitude transformations and will determine how new worldviews about ecology and human populations can be formulated and channeled into action:global change, curriculum development, interdisciplinary courses and state, local, regional, national, and global leadership training.

These social science endeavors (global change research) will eventually create a catalyst to reintegrate the four fields of anthropology (archaeological, biological, cultural, and linguistics) of which our department at the University of Michigan has been a traditionally strong advocate. Such a catalyst will offer a desirable balance to the positivistic and deconstructionist trends in the discipline. This development will be parallelled by common research interests and new working relationships among the humanities and the social and natural sciences.

INSTITUTIONAL INTEGRATION

Culture is malleable. Society can socialize and resocialize humans. Black Americans must seek cultural expressions of a negotiated symbolic understanding. The concern is widespread about educational quality, family stability, moral order, and economic growth. Such concern is generated by the fear that our social institutions continue to change without clear directions and goals for such transformations. The specific needs for minority participation in industrial production and commercial services in the twenty-first century require that Black communities devise strategies and techniques for attitudinal and behavioral modifications for educational quality, family stability, moral order, and economic growth. The socialization efforts must reach into the families, churches, schools, communities, and workplaces of African Americans. Note that you cannot omit the churches. You cannot transform educational attitudes and values in isolation from family, religious, economic, and community discourses. Cultural change must be holistic. We hear much rhetoric about the twenty-first century and the new world order that must accompany it. But we neglect to state that none of this can occur without a new moral order and new ethics that work. Black churches can be a starting place.

As stated above, humans have not been free since they were foragers fifteen thousand years ago. The Agricultural Revolution was the result of the captivity of plants, nonhuman animals, and humans themselves. Peasants were bound to the land. Warriors were confined to the armies. Slaves were constrained by their masters. Priests, scribes, nobles, and royalty were circumscribed by ritual-ceremony, bureaucracy, war, fealty, and fear. In the Industrial Revolution, plants, nonhuman animals, and humans were further enslaved to machines. In the Potential (world destructive power) Revolution, they were further enslaved to the awesome destructive potentials of modern weapons. The Earth and all of its living forms await the freedom of the Ecological Revolution.

Humans have never understood that when they put plants and nonhuman animals into captivity during the Agricultural Revolution, they were also enslaving themselves. For fifteen thousand years, captivity has been a ritualized human ceremony that is most celebrated today in the international rituals surrounding the hostages in Lebanon and Israel. Amnesty International has worldwide recognition. Most humans live in one form of captivity or another: prisons, inner cities, public housing, corporate bureaucracies, transportation regimes, educational regimens, assembly line occupations, and career routines. Thus it is that when we conceptualize our animal kin in zoos, circuses, rodeos, husbandries, pet stores, entertainment industries, occupations, wars, home confinements, and the hunt, we actually see our "superior" selves. We are enslaved to the clock, the calendar, and the company. We thank God for Fridays, weekends, vacations, and holidays. We try to escape to oceans, parks, movies, television, drugs, and alcohol. We overuse our national parks, yet we fail to recognize how we abuse one another.

In the Ecological Revolution we will learn to understand human relationships to the nonhuman animals, and thus we will comprehend humans, animals, and, most important, humans' abuse of Earth and all forms of life on it.

CONCLUSION

The course of human history has come full circle. The human animal that became bipedal, cultural, and "superior" discovers today that the selection advantages of three million years of DDDAK have been nullified by the "sophistication" of human technology in postmodernity. The culturally operated "advances" have raced ahead of any further genetic ones in a human animal that is taught by parents as no other animal, ever. So human genes lag behind, and despite all the environmental-molding "achievements," humans are threatened today and tomorrow by their own nature (see Weisz 1970:37,45).

Humans that want "more" are less for not having it, and the few that control the "more" have corrupted our cultural systems as they became overwhelmed by anxiety, ambition, and avarice. Postmodernity is the end of innocence as human mythology is exposed and ridiculed. Humans before and after Prometheus cannot share the same Earth. Modernity has brought us from the promise of "progress" to that of extinction. Only the Ecological Revolution will save us.

Human divisiveness that is created by human insecurity must be domesticated in the Ecological Revolution. Multiperspects, multifocals, and multicultural systems must be incorporated into human socialization. Human "inferiority" must be eradicated by the embracing of human sex, death, and digestion. The denial of sex, death, and digestion has culminated to some of the leading human problems of our time—nonnutritional feeding, nonprocreational sex and death from unnatural causes. The human body is not inferior, and the divisive stratagems to produce and reproduce social inferiority must be exposed and destroyed. Human insecurity will be replaced in the Ecological Revolution by an acceptance of the human body, social diversity, and the human capacity for genius. Human sex, death, and digestion will be transformed into the "beauty" that it is. Children will finally learn that sex creates life, death defines it, and digestion deconstructs it.

Chapter 10

Biophobia and Social Boundaries

This book is written for the student and for the general reader. It attempts to share, in a simple manner, the thoughts of an aging anthropologist with a public that needs to understand the "human dilemma" (see Williams 1992b). Many of the social problems that threaten human extinction may be understood without "intricate analysis, tightly woven arguments or methodological rigors." The dangers that face humankind demand unusual efforts to communicate with people in the global village (see Fox 1992). In my profession such efforts are infrequent. Many spurious intellectual pursuits (e.g., "discourse theory"; see Watts 1992) that pose as scholarship (see Baritz 1960, Rydell 1993:109) are designed merely to produce and reproduce the social inferiority that originated fifteen thousand years ago and has continued since, with kings, nobles, priests, scribes, and warriors who placed themselves "above" and "beyond" the primary producers (peasants) in human societies (see "hegemonic discourses," Handler 1993:994). Social hierarchy permeates the entire fabric of our society, including the roles of African-American anthropologists.

The thesis here is simple. The origin and development of the human animal were very traumatic for the species. The coping devices shaped the nature of being human and created persistent archetypes of human culture. Those devices have outlived their usefulness and have become maladaptive (see Gore 1992). They help to produce and reproduce social inferiority—the basis of most of the global social problems. They are the source of human divisiveness.

The African-American material in this book is primarily for illustrative purposes, making use of data available to the author from interviews and participant observations over a period of twenty years. But the thematic discourse is about all classes and all people. Class itself is only one approach to understanding human divisiveness (e.g., CRESSANS). Why have scholars conducted such a history of research on caste, gender, and religion rather than on generic human divisiveness? Like colonial anthropology, it reminds one of a situation in which "beautiful" (a gender-connoted term) women research, organize, and publish data on "beauty" among females for a period of a century. It raises the specter and suspicion of conflict-of-interest or at least of vested interests.

The reader will not find the traditional analyses or race solutions here. Those analyses and solutions are widespread in the social science literature, "and we are not saved." This is my preliminary effort at "the reparation of cultural critique."

As Chief Seattle said (in a script written by Ted Perry) to the president of the United States in 1855:

We know that the White Man does not understand our way of life. To him, one piece of land is much like another. He is a stranger who comes in the night and takes from the land whatever he needs. The Earth is not his friend but his enemy and when he has conquered it, he moves on. He cares nothing for the land. He forgets his parents' graves and his children's heritage. He kidnaps the Earth from his children. He treats his Mother the Earth and his Brother the Sky like merchandise. His hunger will eat the Earth bare and leave only a desert.

... What are human beings without animals? If all animals cease to exist, human beings would die of a great loneliness of the spirit. For whatever happens to the animals will happen soon to all human beings. Continue to soil your bed and one night you will suffocate in your own waste.

Humankind has not woven the web-of-life. We are but one thread within it. Whatever we do to the web, we do to ourselves. All things are bound together. All things connect. Whatever befalls the Earth befalls also the children of the Earth (Nabokov 1978:107). Or as the Yarralin, an aboriginal people of the Victoria River in Australia's Northern Territory, say, "Dingo makes us human" (Rose 1992).

The Earth's resources are distributed, accumulated, and exploited to separate people into ranks (Lewis 1993). The denial of those resources forces the poor to live as if and with "animals" (e.g., cats for the rodents, dogs for the neighbors, fleas, flies, lice, mice; parasitic worms, bacteria, and viruses; rats and roaches). The use of wealth enables its owners to disguise and conceal their animal character and behavior. The lack of subsistence resources exposes these features among the poor. Economic systems are designed to produce and reproduce social inferiority by such unequal distribution of the Earth's resources and the subsequent exposures among the Earth's poor.

In this book I continue my efforts to combine personal experience with professional writing (see Heller 1992:A7) as well as my attempts at visionary anthropology (Bohannan 1992:309).

The twenty-first century will require humans to understand themselves in order to save the Earth. Western scholars can no longer avoid the truth by studying "others." They must heed the advice of Polonius to Laertes: "This above all, to thine own self be true and it must follow as the night the day Thou canst not then be false to any man. Farewell. My blessing season this in thee!"(Hamlet 1.3)

Human divisiveness (e.g., CRESSANS) is a result of human nature. In a shrinking world and a global village, that divisiveness constitutes a human dilemma (Williams 1992b). Humans must become ecologically correct (see Psalms 24:1 and

Martin 1992) to survive in the twenty-first century. Comprehending human behavior requires considerable attention to the origins and development of human psychological experiences. The production and use of tools, the development of upright posture and the hand, and the increasing brain capacity in human origins has been and continues to be investigated and debated rigorously, notwithstanding the sparsity of evidence. Yet the ramifications in human perceptions from increased brain capacity during the transition from prehuman primates to humans has been neglected (Donald 1991). This human experience of increasing self-consciousness is as much the origin and nature of man (woman) as tools, brain capacity, the hand, and bipedalism. The trauma of that perceptual experience in the origin and development of humans enables us to explain modern human behavior and the social problems of contemporary human conflicts. These conflicts are human, not just American.

Such human conflicts require global and panhuman solutions from global citizens with recycled human natures. The Black middle class represents two dimensions of this global crisis—classism and racism. In this book, I have examined race and class within the context of global transformation—the Ecological Revolution.

Madame de Sévigné was not a vicious woman by the standards of the late seventeenth century. She, like other aristocrats of her circle, could view hangings with disinterested fascination because the person being killed was a creature whose inner nature had little relation to her own. As good Christians, the highborn had of course to believe that all men were equal in the sight of God, but fortunately he had not gone to the extreme of demanding that they look at things among themselves in quite the same way. When the word "caste" is applied to the ancien régime in Europe, it refers, beyond all barriers of custom and hereditary right, to the notion that people of different social stations belong to different species, that the humanity or worthiness of a duchess has little relationship to the kind of humanity accessible to the common peasant. The corollary—explicitly stated in another letter of Madame de Sévigné's—is that *the "humbling" of inferiors is necessary to the maintenance of social order.* (Sennett and Cobb 1973) (added emphasis is mine)

This book attempts to place a discussion of human divisiveness into the context of postmodernity and world transformations. It attempts to respond to the culture-bound scholarship on humans that neglects to contextualize their struggles within the nature of humanity and the structure of social inequality that pervades most societies. My brief and simple discussions cannot explicate all of the dimensions that impact upon human insecurity, but they have been approached with an effort to be sensitive to these dimensions.

The discourse of human insecurity is influenced by:

1. the formation of gender inequality;
2. the origin of hegemony;
3. the deconstruction of deities;

4. the nature of humans in postmodernity;
5. the reproduction of social inequality;
6. the hegemony of scholarship on the dispossessed;
7. the cultural transformations of a postmodernity that is a menace to all humankind;
8. the precondition that (wo)man must adapt to himself before he can adapt to his environment;
9. the inferiority complex (after Alfred Adler, 1870–1937, Austrian psychiatrist and founder of individual psychology) that dominates the character of human culture (see Becker 1962:35);
10. the myth, ritual, and ceremony that allow humans to disguise themselves in rank, privilege, and power relationships;
11. the myth that freedom and democracy are linked with bourgeois values; and
12. power relationships that delegitimize arbitrary populations and exploit them (i.e., the construction and deconstruction of race).

A brief discussion of these follows.

The formation of gender inequality and the origin of hegemony, like racism and classism, are the result of the human inferiority complex that originated in the transition from prehuman primates to humans by means of the acquisition of culture. That transition and acquisition are crucial to the comprehension of gender inequality. The deconstruction of deities is required in order to question the images we create for humans. Those images determine the nature of humans in postmodernity and reproduce social inequality.

Deities are supernatural mirrors with which to see ourselves. Our quest for omnipresence drives us to master ocean, land, sky, and space. All are our highways to everywhere, and travel is a pervasive human value. If we are able, we attempt to live everywhere with our beach, country, summer, and mountain houses. Our apartments on both coasts, our winter retreats, and European "getaways" facilitate our travel and insure that we are omnipresent. We also strive for the energy and technology to be omniscient. Our computers, libraries, universities, research facilities, information systems and networks represent these pioneer efforts. We have created the power to destroy the Earth in our quest to be omnipotent, and even the wastes from these creations and from our other manifestations of power threaten to destroy us.

The Hebrews expressed it when they said that we were made in God's image (Genesis 1:27, 5:1–2). The Christians went further and explained that God's son and partner walked in our midst and was born of woman. But the menaces of postmodernity demand that we cease attempts to be godlike and be reasonable and fair partners in the biosphere and in the web-of-life. Such transformations would redetermine the nature of humans in postmodernity and cease the reproduction of social inequality in postmodern societies. They would also disarm the myth, ritual, and ceremony that disguise us in rank, privilege, and power relationships. We can learn to adapt to ourselves without such false images and thereby provide the basis for adapting intelligently to our ecology.

Scholarship on the dispossessed validates the hegemony of the scholars themselves and to that extent contaminates the scholarship. The study of social inequality must envision the kind of structural deformation that ceases to validate the rank, status, and privilege of the scholars themselves. The anthropologist can study social inequality by studying the "power elite" in postmodern society. There is no need to continue to research the dispossessed and the "inferior" and thereby provide therapy for the inferiority complexes of the anthropologists themselves. As Scott Malcomson (1989) has expressed it: "If anthropology was once part of a grand therapy session in which white civilization acted as analyst for the uncivilized other—pretending to treat the dark patient while actually treating itself—anthropologists are now mired in a miserable auto-therapy, at once self-mutilating and precious."

Culture-bound scholars have attempted arbitrarily and artificially to separate racism, classism, and sexism (the triad). African-American scholars, "the ex-primitives themselves, or rather their indigenous, post-anthropological representatives, the 'evolved,' educated natives who now speak on behalf of their dark brothers and sisters" (Malcomson 1989), continue that scholarly tradition. They have "taken up, by themselves, their own monologues. The Savage speaks . . . and what does he say? He recites books of ethnography. Oof! The anthropologists let out their breath! The Savage has learned his lesson well" (Rognon 1986). Some of these scholarly efforts appear to be designed to create hegemony from these distinguished forms of oppression as arbitrarily defined groups declare that racism, classism, or sexism should receive the most vindication and proceed to compete for affirmative action advantages. But racism, classism, and sexism are the results of the same panhuman inferiority complexes. One of this triad cannot be eliminated as long as the others exist.

The women's movement, encouraged especially in the 1970s and 1980s by the Civil Rights Movement, has enlightened us about sexism without realizing that much of that enlightenment was relevant to the entire triad. The male quest for superiority (power, status, recognition, and prestige) has always oppressed women. Women (before they joined the competition) have attempted to advise men that they are the same babies that women fed and washed clean of their urine, feces, and perspiration. The men are only older and larger. The women loved us then, and they love us now. Men do not need to be strong, powerful, rich, and superior, just lovable (see Gilmore 1990). Men can cry, cook, and clean (houses and children) and still be men. Men can be weak, innocent, and fragile. Any woman who loves a man can endure that; just as any man who loves a woman does so exclusive of her sexual organs and appetite.

Women have attempted to counsel men not to allow romance and "love" to disguise male lust and sexual design. Women have mocked men's duplicity. As one female informant stated it: "He loved her so much that he stole her virginity, violated her chastity, impregnated her out of wedlock and lost her the respect of her family and her community. She thought that he loved her, not her sexual organs. She believed that he wanted to satisfy her needs for security, not his sexual and property appetites." Women have asked for three million years, "Love me for myself." They have told us that we do not have to be gods to be loved. They loved us since we were babies. The "basic human rights" espoused by Eleanor Roosevelt (the most famous uncredentialed anthropologist) and Malcolm X recognized the relationships of the triad; these rights remain today the avenue for their elimination. Men and women are both merely human (Gilmore 1990).

The quest for consumerism (as is now occurring in Eastern Europe and the former U.S.S.R.) must not be confused with the quest for freedom and democracy. The former quest often leaves arbitrarily defined populations (e.g., African Americans) without freedom or democracy because of materialistic power relationships that delegitimize them in racism and classism. The myths of "the good life" (Baritz 1988) collapse all of the American values that we prize into a pudding of confusing ingredients called the middle class.

What is the actual good life? Popular images indicate that it is fertilizing, watering, and mowing the lawn; it is the trimming of shrubbery, the shoveling of snow, and the annual planting, painting, and cleaning of house and yard. The middle class paint and repair their houses. They clean their windows and refurbish their rooms. They buy themselves and their children the latest fashions, boats, toys, appliances, furnishings, and automobiles. All of this is enforced by their real or imagined neighbors and "friends." They take their savings and pay taxes, tuition, mortgages, and interest on loans (for cars, boats, appliances, cabins, beach houses, and so on), vacation costs, cleaning bills, entertainment costs, and repair bills (on extensive material possessions).

Not surprisingly, the tensions, stresses, and anxieties of success threaten the health of the middle class. The small failures in every life are magnified or made more threatening by their fear of failure. These pressures require continual reassurances that their "good life" is worth the pain and suffering. The reassurances are provided, in part, by the contrived glamour of the lifestyles of the upper class and the awareness of the real or imagined sufferings of the poor, lower class, and underclass, as well as the failures of their families, friends, and neighbors. The costs of their heightened sense of well-being—health, teeth, grooming—and their sensitivity to obsolescence keep many of them near bankruptcy, notwithstanding the frequent two-earner incomes. But the media entertain them with "horrors" about the plights of the lower and underclasses, which validate the efforts and fears of the middle class. Meanwhile, despite their numbers and poor prospects for upward mobility, we refuse to legitimize (give equal social status to) the poor in this society. On the contrary, we barrage them with ceaseless propaganda about the well-being of "the good life."

Selfish, materialistic greed leaves its devastation everywhere, but most will concede those ill effects among African Americans. Such a quest requires the mythological, ritual, and ceremonial creation and maintenance of humans who are "inferior." My own interest in African Americans for many years has resulted from an abiding concern for the generally corrosive effects of social inequality and the irrational ability of humans to perpetuate it. My thesis is that we must comprehend the basis, structure, and reproduction of social inequality to liberate the oppressed of the world, including African Americans, as well as to maintain an Earth where humans can continue to survive.

Class is relative. The middle class requires a lower, upper, and perhaps underclass. That requirement creates "superior" and "inferior" people, as well as people who are "superior" to the Earth rather than a part of it. (Wo)man is the only animal that does not live by bread alone, but he has accumulated too much power to continue to live by myth. Social hierarchy, social leveling, upward mobility, and human oppression are part of the same process. The limited resources of the Earth can no longer tolerate this human folly with the present technology of modernity. The dilemma of the Black middle class is an example of this folly.

We need a bold effort to begin to formulate a unified theory of race, gender, and class distinctions (see Sacks 1989) as well as to understand the human destruction of the Earth's environment. The reproduction of social inequality and the abuse of the Earth's environment are the problems of the twenty-first century. My discussions of the Black middle class in America have attempted to address these larger issues in preliminary fashion.

MYTH AND POWER:
THE CULTURE OF EXTINCTION

As I have written elsewhere (Williams 1992b), the human superiority myth (DDDAK) helped to create culture and the human species. Humans have guarded and reinforced (with available power) that myth for three million years. The myth is a part of the nature of man (including woman). Humans throughout the Earth for as long as we have available records have believed and protected the myth.

But for most of that period, man has had very limited power to enforce the myth (see White 1949, 1973). Whenever he acquired more power (e.g., the Agricultural and Industrial Revolutions) he enslaved more animals and more people. This process reinforced the myth. Voilà, modernity arrived, and the technological achievements of the last fifty years have provided man the power to enforce the myth to the extent that the ecological homeostasis that supports all of life on Earth is threatened. The myth and man have come full circle. The myth created man, and now it will eliminate him. Are humans malleable enough to change the myth and save the world?

The oppression of human populations is endemic to man. He need only acquire the power. Thus genetic engineering is humanity's ultimate Frankenstein. Our prior efforts to understand oppression have focused on the symptoms and not the causes. Our solutions have depended on the exposure and goodwill of those who were powerful enough to cause change. These are not solutions. The solution is to destroy the myth. Man is a unique animal, but he is no higher or lower than any other animal or form of life. Thus no man is superior to any other man, regardless of his characteristics. We must protect life on Earth, all life, or as part of the web-of-life, we must perish with it.

We must develop an ethic that includes the entire biosphere. We must develop humans that are strong enough to live life without the myth that they are superior to other people or other forms of life. We must respect life and demand that life have its dignity in order that we will continue to have our own. When this time appears, then racism and oppression will disappear, but not until then.

In this book I have discussed the Black middle class within the context of a suggested human nature. One of my assumptions is that such an artificial category of the human population will have more meaning from this perspective.

Humans are defensive about their animal nature, and that defensiveness renders them insecure about themselves (see Williams 1991). This human insecurity has helped to determine human attitudes and behaviors toward nonhuman animals and humans themselves. An understanding of humans and their history will help one to comprehend the African-American middle class and their plight in the final decade of the twentieth century.

My perspective on human history is that humans probably became human by their abilities and intensive efforts to distinguish themselves from the other animals. These embellished and adaptive contrasts (e.g., culture) enable humans to achieve an ambivalent (the animal in humans is ever present) sense of superiority at the expense of "inferior" animal characteristics that extended to even their own human females. Such attitudes continued until the Agricultural Revolution when they were transformed into a hostage mentality. "Inferiority" now had to be captured and confined. So humans not only domesticated plants and "lower" animals but also other humans (peasants and slaves). The captured forms of life were the basis for social ranks among humans. Those people perceived to be most free (from labor confinement and land) were the most "superior."

The hostage mentality has continued into contemporary times: the Nazis imprisoned the Gypsies and the Jews to document their "inferiority," the Iranians took American hostages, and the Lebanese took western ones. The Industrial Revolution allowed humans to become hostages to machines, and the Potential Revolution made life on the Earth hostage to potential annihilation. The myths of human superiority have required continual increases in human power to document them. That power now threatens to overwhelm humans and the Earth that sustains them. In the next era—the Ecological Revolution—humans will abandon the hostage mentality, the myths of superiority, and the obsessive need to capture and confine plants, nonhuman animals, and other humans. African Americans will be released from prisons, grinding poverty, welfare, slums, ghettos, inner cities, public housing, menial labor, and the permanent stamp of inferiority. Middle-class Blacks will no longer have to escape themselves, their communities, and their people to avoid being "inferior."

The dilemmas of the African-American middle class are based on the human dilemmas discussed in this book. In the Ecological Revolution, humans will discover that only respect for all forms of life on Earth will permit the survival of any.

"The need is not really for more brains, the need is now for a gentler, a more tolerant people than those who won for us against the ice, the tiger and the bear."

—Loren Eiseley, 1946

This section is an attempt to continue to search for human nature within the Italian intellectual tradition in social thought (see Degler 1991). The Italian tradition (Jonas 1969) did not emphasize society as an objective reality with discernible laws of its own. (The philosopher and jurist Giovanni Vico was a notable exception in this tradition.) Beginning with Machiavelli, humans were not depicted as socialized (see also Wrong 1961) in a web of social relations and social institutions but as shaped by fundamental human nature. Human conduct might vary in different circumstances, but it was perceived as being essentially determined by human nature. Machiavelli describes human nature in *The Prince* as "ungrateful, fickle, lying, hypocritical, fearful, and grasping." These fundamental human characteristics must be understood by social theorists as the raw materials of human behavior. Machiavelli and his successors sought to analyze the components of human nature rather than to identify the social laws that determine human stability and change—the social order. Social order does not have its own laws but is imposed on society and unruly people by "superior" (elite) leaders. These elites were the major theoretical focus of Italian social thought from Machiavelli to Vilfredo Pareto (1848–1923).

This book does not subscribe to the Italian tradition's ideas of elites. My own view is that people with inferior feelings can be easily seduced by the myths, rituals, values, and ceremonies that create "superior" people. "Superior" people can induce "inferior" people to live and die (in wars and other human sacrifices) by such seductions. This is especially true if the "inferior" people are allowed to identify but not associate with the "superior" people. The ranking power of social distance is to the belittling power of intimacy as biophobia (fear of the body and of full membership in the animal kingdom) is to sex, death, and digestion. My point of departure is that of searching for human nature (Degler 1991). I argue that socially constructed boundaries were fundamental perceptions in the origin of humans. As Geertz (1973b:52) has stated, "the concept of culture has its impact on the concept of man." Thus, in my view, social boundaries and biophobia define and determine much of culture.

BIOPHOBIA AND CULTURE

Where did culture come from? Why did it occur? For what kind of animal did it appear? Social scientists have often given culture a *sui generis*, self-generating character as well as a definitional mystique (see Kroeber and Kluckhohn 1952). This leaves much of the fundamental origin and character of culture unexplained. I argue that human biophobia was a primary ingredient in the creation of culture and that it continues to dominate it today. Biophobic animals invented superior "gods" and superior people, some of whom were claimed to be directly connected with gods. The biophobic nature of culture determines the social boundary character of humans. That character allows us to understand the history of human "superiority" and the human sacrifices—wars, slaves, offerings, misery ("And mourn the miseries of human life," Dryden, Sowerby 1986:213)—required to produce and reproduce it. Human biophobia also helps us understand why most scholars and thinkers have ignored it in their treatises on human behavior and continue to do so even today (see Tiger 1969, 1979b, Tiger and Fox 1971).

As a student of social boundaries (race, class, and gender) and a product of those boundaries (African American), I bring my own experiences and perceptions to the discussion of human behavior. I aspire to understand culture by means of comprehending social boundaries. It is one approach to examining, probing, and searching for human nature, and it provides some basis for analysis of human behavior from its origin to the present. I have studied social boundaries for twenty-five years (see Williams 1974, 1981a, 1992a, 1992b), and here I collect those experiences into a statement about social boundaries and culture as they derive from human biophobia. The social construction of biophobia has created biopower and biopolitics on race, class, and gender (see Foucault 1978).

As evolving animals, prehuman primates had developed many of the traits common to other primates: patterns of dominance, territoriality, hunting proclivities (food chain sensibilities), sex (Friedl 1994), death, and digestion. The transition from prehuman primates to human primates was dependent upon changes in the brain and the resulting transformations in self-consciousness (Parker, Mitchell, and Boccia 1994). I argue that many of the existing primate traits were superimposed with meaningful social constructions for humans. Both the preexisting traits and the new social constructions had similar benefits: they aided adaptation.

One of the most significant social constructions was the identification of one's human group as distinct, superior, and connected to supernatural powers as was no other form of life, plant or animal. This social construction rationalized for humans much of the drive for survival that existed in other primates and other animals. This successful (adaptive—we would still be flaking Mousterian points and eating cave-bears' leftovers) rationalization provided humans the basis for eventually overwhelming the Earth and its other inhabitants. Such a rationalization appears to possess the seeds of human extinction, if Alfred Kroeber (the superorganic) and Leslie White (culture as autonomous) are correct. But if humans can influence culture and thus human nature, they can socialize their children to alter the drive for survival. Humans no longer require the impetus to dominate and control the Earth and all of its life-forms.

The perception of a distinct, superior, and supernatural-related human has become obsolete. Notwithstanding its success (adaptiveness), this perception has become the basis for many intractable social problems—health crises, poverty, war, and CRESSANS. Thus by transforming their perception of the "imperial animal," not only could humans eliminate the threat of their own extinction, but they could also improve the quality of life for their children.

Increasing self-consciousness also made humans aware that "lower" animals lived in a meaningless world, a world that humans could not endure. So the social construction of humans, or "higher" animals, provided a world of meaning, of "God," of "lower" animals, and of "others." Today that meaningful world requires a different social construction, one in which humans are able to value themselves and all forms of life, including Earth itself, without ranking any of them (see Cuzzort and King 1989 and Kellart 1980, 1985, 1989, 1991, 1993a, 1993b). Of course, that new social construction must channel the animal traits mentioned above into culturalized pursuits other than the old quests for superiority (e.g., power, fame, gender, wealth, and immortality).

As an animal that created socially constructed boundaries to become human, humans became obsessed with those boundaries in most phases of their lives. The obsession is caused by the fragile and artificial character of the boundaries. The human animal must constantly repair these boundaries with myth, ritual, ceremony, and other activities. These repair processes dominate human life and proliferate that life with more artificial social boundaries. Today socially constructed boundaries pervade human existence.

I attempt to develop a general hypothesis. A fundamental characteristic of human nature is the fear of its animal component. Human behavior results from the fusion of that animal body and the social constructions that eliminate some of the dread about it. The persistent insecurities of such ambiguities create divisive social boundaries (see Gamson 1995, Keller 1985, Roy 1995)—race, class, and gender—and biopower and biopolitics. Fear of ourselves is assuaged by contempt for "others"—untouchables, burakumin, homeless, Jews, and all the social lepers of the world. That contempt is institutionalized by depriving its objects of the necessary resources to hide, disguise, or otherwise socially construct their animal needs, activities, characteristics, and nature. The deprived human is ranked near "low" animalization, while those with resources to waste are ranked near "high" deification-civilization. We can test our identity dependence on "lower" animals and "inferior" people.

As humans perceive and conceive the world by means of cognitive categories and classifications, they also conceptualize their own existence in terms of socially constructed boundaries. That process of conceptualization makes humans captives within the social boundaries they have generated. But if humans can change culture, then they can reconceptualize themselves without such boundaries, as a part of the web-of-life

THE TWENTY-FIRST CENTURY

Many of the old social boundaries in the global society are being dismantled by such "cultural" exchanges as tourism, the information highway, cartels, blocs, industrial-commercial markets, financial conspiracies, migrants, migrant workers, refugees, and other forms of transnationalism. The cultural lag in social relations reflects the human fear of uncertainty and transformations. It results, in part, from the self-serving bias of human self-esteem. Consciousness of kind (Giddings 1896) leads to a destructive process of attribution and bolsters the socially constructed boundaries that produce and reproduce class, race, ethnicity, sex, sect, age, nation, and species. But those social boundaries will change (see Baker 1994, Stanfield 1985, Williams 1993a) in the twenty-first century. They have already become obsolete.

Population conflicts were perceived as crucial components of social relationships in such conceptions as fission and fusion, but now, after the technological revolutions and the development of modern warfare and smart weapons, the bases for such perceptions have been eroded. The old social boundaries are frayed and obsolete. Some of the ceremonies, rituals, myths, and values that produce and reproduce those old social boundaries are under siege by dispossessed populations and the global media. The elimination of the human fear about themselves will enable the global society to replace the social boundaries with a web-of-life conception of global populations that will be embued with new themes, symbols, myths, rituals, ceremonies, values, and celebrations.

Most efforts to confront the pain and suffering of racism (see Kaus 1992, Shanklin 1994) have been confined to the symptoms rather than to the malady. Humans must remove biophobia from human culture. It has been adaptive for three million years, but in postmodernity biophobic human culture is destined for extinction (see Babbie 1994). The advent of biocentrism (Gross and Levitt 1994) will remove and replace Eurocentrism (Herzfeld 1992), feminocentrism, and Afrocentrism (Asante 1987).

Postmodernity is ushering in the Ecological Revolution in which humans are devising new social constructions that are reclaiming the body, eliminating biophobia, and creating social boundaries that are adaptive for the twenty-first century and beyond (Levine 1988).

Bibliography

Aceves, Joseph B. 1974. *Identity, Survival and Change: Exploring Social/Cultural Anthropology.* Morristown, N.J.: General Learning.

Adler, Alfred. 1964. *Social Interest: A Challenge to Mankind.* New York: Capricorn Books.

Agar, Michael H. 1986. *Speaking of Ethnography.* Beverly Hills, Calif.: Sage.

Alland, Alexander. 1971. *Human Diversity.* New York: Columbia University Press.

Allport, Floyd H. 1967. "A Theory of Enestuence (Event-Structure Theory): Report of Progress." *American Psychologist* 22:24.

Altman, Irwin, and Setha M. Low. 1992. *Place Attachment.* New York: Plenum.

Alway, Joan. 1995. "The Trouble with Gender: Tales of the Still-Missing Feminist Revolution in Sociological Theory." *Social Theory* 13(3):209–28.

Anderson, C. H. 1976. *The Sociology of Survival: Social Problems of Growth.* Homewood Ill.: Dorsey Press.

Anderson, Elijah. 1978. *A Place on the Corner.* Chicago: University of Chicago Press.

———. 1990. *Street Wise: Race, Class and Change in an Urban Community.* Chicago: University of Chicago Press.

Anderson, Martin. 1992. *Impostors in the Temple.* New York: Simon & Schuster.

Aron, Raymond. 1970. *Main Currents in Sociological Thought, II: Durkheim, Pareto, Weber.* New York: Anchor Books.

Asante, Molefi K. 1987. *The Afrocentric Idea.* Philadelphia: Temple University Press.

———. 1988. *Afrocentricity.* Trenton, N.J.: Africa World.

Babbie, Earl R. 1994. *What Is Society: Reflections on Freedom, Order and Change.* Thousand Oaks, Calif.: Pine Forge Press.

Baer, H. A. 1984. *The Black Spiritual Movement: A Religious Response to Racism.* Knoxville: University of Tennessee Press.

Bailey, B. L. 1965. "Toward a New Perspective in Negro English Dialectology." *American Speech* 40:171–77.

Baker, Lee D. 1994. "The Role of Anthropology in the Social Construction of Race." Ph.D. dissertation in Anthropology. Philadelphia: Temple University.

Ball, Aimee Lee. 1991. "Hate Them Because They're Beautiful." *Mademoiselle* (April):186.

Baritz, Loren. 1960. *The Servants of Power: A History of the Use of Social Science in American Industry.* Middletown, Conn.: Wesleyan University Press.

————. 1988. *The Good Life: The Meaning of Success for the American Middle Class.* New York: Knopf.

Barkow, Jerome H. 1989. *Darwin, Sex and Status: Biological Approaches to Mind and Culture.* Toronto: University of Toronto Press.

Barkow, Jerome H., L. Comides, and J. Tooby, eds. 1992. *The Adapted Mind: Evolutionary Psychology and the Generation of Culture.* New York: Oxford University Press.

Baumeister, Roy F., ed. 1993. *Self-Esteem: The Puzzle of Low Self-Regard.* New York: Plenum.

Beauvoir, Simone de. 1953. *The Second Sex.* New York: Knopf. Originally published in French in 1949.

Beck, Brenda E. F. 1975. "The Anthropology of the Body." *Current Anthropology* 16(3):486.

Becker, Ernest. 1962. *The Birth and Death of Meaning.* Glencoe, Ill.: Free Press.

————. 1973. *The Denial of Death.* New York: Free Press.

Benjamin, Lois. 1991. *The Black Elite.* Chicago: Nelson-Hall.

Bennett, J. 1976. "Anticipation, Adaptation and the Concept of Culture in Anthropology." *Science* 192:847–53.

Berdie, R. F. 1947. "Playing the Dozens." *Journal of Abnormal and Social Psychology* 42:120–21.

Berreman, Gerald D. 1972. "Race, Caste and Other Invidious Distinctions in Social Stratification." *Race* 13(4):385–414.

Beuf, Ann Hill. 1990. *Beauty Is the Beast: Appearance-Impaired Children in America.* Philadelphia: University of Pennsylvania Press.

Bidney, David. 1964. *Theoretical Anthropology.* New York: Columbia University Press.

Blackwell, J. E., and M. Janowitz, eds. 1974. *Black Sociologists: Historical and Contemporary Perspectives.* Chicago: University of Chicago Press.

Blalock, H. M., Jr. 1989. "Race versus Class: Distinguishing Reality from Artifacts." *National Journal of Sociology* 3:127–42.

Blauner, R., and D. Wellman. 1973. "Toward the Decolonization of Social Research." In J. Ladner, ed., *The Death of White Sociology.* New York: Vintage.

Bloom, Allan. 1987. *The Closing of the American Mind.* New York: Simon & Schuster.

————. 1993. "Requiem for Romance." *Detroit Free Press Magazine* (June 27):14–16.

Blum, Debra E. 1990. "Inquiry Prompts Professor to Sue College and Panel." *Chronicle of Higher Education* (Oct. 10):17.

Blumer, Herbert. 1958. "Race Prejudice as a Sense of Group Position." *Pacific Sociological Review* 1(Spring):3–6.

Boas, Franz. 1911. *The Mind of Primative Man.* New York: Macmillan

————. 1920. "The Method of Ethnology." *American Anthropologist* 22:311–21.

————. 1966. *Race, Language and Culture.* New York: Free Press.

Bohannan, Paul. 1992. *We, the Alien.* Prospects Heights, Ill.: Waveland Press.

Bonacich, E. 1972. "A Theory of Ethnic Antagonism: The Split Labor Market." *American Sociological Review* 37:547–59.

Bonacich, E., and J. Modell. 1980. *The Economic Basis of Ethnic Solidarity: Small Business in the Japanese-American Community.* Berkeley: University of California Press.

Bonner, John Tyler. 1988. *The Evolution of Complexity by Means of Natural Selection.* Princeton: Princeton University Press.

Bordo, Susan Rand. 1991. *Gender/Body/Knowledge: Feminist Reconstruction of Being and Knowing.* New Brunswick, N.J.: Rutgers University Press.

Bowker, John. 1993. *The Meaning of Death*. New York: Cambridge University Press.

Boyarin, Daniel. 1993. *Carnal Israel: Reading Sex in Talmudic Culture*. Berkeley: University of California Press.

Brace, Loren C. 1964. "On the Current Anthropology Concept." *Current Anthropology* 5:313–14.

Brachfeld, Oliver. 1951. *Inferiority Feelings*. New York: Grune & Stratton.

Branch, Taylor. 1988. *Parting the Waters: America in the King Years, 1954–63*. New York: Simon & Schuster.

Branzei, Sylvia. 1995. *Grossology*. Reading, Mass.: Addison-Wesley.

Breton, Raymond, et al. 1990. *Ethnic Identity and Equality: Varieties of Experiences in a Canadian City*. Toronto: University of Toronto Press.

Bronowski, Jacob. 1973. *The Ascent of Man*. Boston: Little, Brown.

Brown, Donald E. 1991. *Human Universals*. New York: McGraw-Hill.

Brown, Peter. 1988. *The Body and Society: Men, Women and Sexual Renunciation in Early Christianity*. New York: Columbia University Press.

Brown, Peter J. 1997. "Culture and the Evolution of Obesity." In A. Podolefsky and P. J. Brown, eds., *Applying Cultural Anthropology*. Mountain View, Calif.: Mayfield Publishing.

Browning, Christopher R. 1996. "Human Nature, Culture and the Holocaust." *Chronicle of Higher Education* 43(8):A72.

Burghardt, G. M., and H. A. Heryog, Jr. 1989. "Animals, Evolution and Ethics." In R. J. Hoage, ed., *Perceptions of Animals in American Culture*. Washington, D.C.: Smithsonian Institution Press, pp. 129–51.

Buss, D. 1995. "Evolutionary Psychology: A New Paradigm for Psychological Science." *Psychological Inquiry* 6(1):1–30.

Bynum, Caroline Walker. 1995. *The Resurrection of the Body in Western Christianity, 200–1336*. New York: Columbia University Press.

Campbell, A., and H. Schuman. 1968. *Racial Attitudes in Fifteen American Cities: A Report Prepared for the National Advisory Commission on Civil Disorders*. Ann Arbor, Mich.: Institute for Social Research.

Campbell, Joseph. 1959–67. *The Masks of God*. Princeton: Princeton University Press.

———. 1968. *The Hero with a Thousand Faces*. Princeton: Princeton University Press.

Cannon, L. W., E. Higginbotham, and M. A. Leung. 1988. "Race and Class in Qualitative Research on Women." *Gender & Society* 2:449–662.

Carmichael, Dan. 1991. "White House Accused of Scuttling Civil Rights Negotiations." *Pittsburgh Courier* 82(33):1(April 24).

Carter, Stephen L. 1993. *The Culture of Disbelief: How American Law and Politics Trivialize Religion*. New York: Basic Books.

Cartmill, Matt. 1993. *A View to Death in the Morning: Hunting and Nature through History*. Cambridge, Mass.: Harvard University Press.

Chamberlain, Houston Stewart. 1910. *The Foundations of the Nineteenth Century*. New York: J. Lane.

Chronicle of Higher Education. 1978. "John Hope Franklin: 'I Try To Wear It with Some Grace.'" (Jan.9):6–7.

Clark, Kenneth B. 1965. "What Motivates American Whites?" *Ebony* 20(10):69–74.

———. 1967. *Dark Ghetto: Dilemmas of Social Power*. New York: Harper Torchbooks.

———. 1978. "No. No. Race, Not Class Is Still at the Wheel." *New York Times* (March 22):25

Cohn, Norman. 1961. *Pursuit of the Millennium*. New York: Oxford University Press.

Coles, R. 1977. *Privileged Ones: The Well-Off and the Rich in America*. Boston: Little, Brown.

Collins, Randall. 1975. *Conflict Sociology: Toward an Explanatory Model*. New York: Academic Press.

Commoner, B. 1971. *The Closing Circle: Nature, Man and Technology*. New York: Knopf.

Comte, Auguste. 1858. *A Catechism of Positive Religion*. London: J. Chapman.

Cooley, C. H. 1922. *Human Nature and the Social Order*. New York: Charles Scribner's Sons.

Cooper, Eugene. 1986. "Chinese Table Manners: You Are How You Eat." *Human Organization* 45:179–84(Summer).

Coser, Lewis A. 1971. *Masters of Sociological Thought*. New York: Harcourt Brace Jovanovich.

Count, Earl W. 1958. "The Biological Basis of Human Sociality." *American Anthropologist* 60:1049–66.

———. 1972. "Beyond Anthropology: Toward a Man-Science." *American Anthropologist* 74:1358.

Crook, J. H. 1980. *The Evolution of Human Consciousness*. Oxford: Clarendon Press.

Csordas, Thomas J., ed. 1994. *Embodiment and Experience: The Existential Grounds of Culture and Self*. New York: Cambridge University Press.

Cuzzort, R. P., and E. W. King. 1989. "The American Pet: An Exercise in Social Theory." In *Twentieth Century Social Thought*, 4th ed. Fort Worth: Holt Rinehart and Winston, pp. 314–23.

Daly, Martin, and Margo Wilson. 1988. *Homicide*. New York: Aldine De Gruyter.

Darwin, Charles. 1975. "The Descent of Man." In John F. Henshal, ed., *The Ascent of Man*. Boston: Little, Brown, pp. xiv–4.

Davis, A., and J. Dollard. 1940. *Children of Bondage: The Personality Development of Youth in the Urban South*. Washington, D.C.: American Council on Education.

Davis, A., B. Gardner, and M. Gardner. 1941. *Deep South: A Social Anthropological Study of Caste and Class*. Chicago: University of Chicago Press.

Degler, Carl N. 1991. *In Search of Human Nature*. New York: Oxford University Press.

Demott, Benjamin. 1990. *The Imperial Middle*. New York: Morrow.

Dennis, R. 1988. "The Use of Participant Observation in Race Relations Research." In Cora B. Marrett and Cheryl Leggon, eds., *Research in Race and Ethnic Relations*, vol. 5. Greenwich, Conn.: JAI, pp. 25–46.

———. 1991. "Dual Marginality and Discontent among Black Middletown Youth." In R. Dennis, ed., *Research in Race and Ethnic Relations*, vol. 6. Greenwich, Conn.: JAI, pp. 3–25.

Diamond, Jared M. 1987. "The Worst Mistake in the History of the Human Race." *Discover* 8:64–66(May).

Dillard, J. L. 1972. *Black English:Its History and Usage in the United States*. New York: Random House.

Dimen-Schein, Muriel. 1977. *The Anthropological Imagination*. New York: McGraw-Hill.

Divale, W. T., and Marvin Harris. 1976. "Population, Warfare and the Male Supremacist Complex." *American Anthropologist* 78:521–38.

Dobzhansky, T. 1966. *Mankind Evolving: The Evolution of the Human Species*. New Haven, Conn.: Yale University Press.

Dollard, J. 1937. *Caste and Class in a Southern Town*. New Haven, Conn.: Yale University Press.

Donald, Merlin. 1991. *Origins of the Modern Mind: Three Stages in the Evolution of Culture and Cognition*. Cambridge, Mass.: Harvard University Press.

Douglas, Mary. 1966. *Purity and Danger*. London: Routledge and Kegan Paul.

————. 1972. "Pollution." In W. A. Lessa and E. Z. Vogt, eds., *Reader in Comparative Religion: An Anthropological Approach*, 3rd ed. New York: Harper & Row, pp. 196–202.

Douglas, Mary, and Baron Isherwood. 1979. *The World of Goods: Toward an Anthropology of Consumption*. New York: Basic Books.

Drake, St. Clair. 1965. "The Social and Economic Status of the Negro in the United States." *Daedalus* 94:771–814.

————. 1987. *Black Folk Here and There*, vol. 1. Los Angeles: Center for Afro-American Studies.

Du Bois, William E. B. 1896. *The Philadelphia Negro: A Social Study*. New York: Benjamin Blom.

————. 1961. *The Souls of Black Folk*. Greenwich, Conn.: Fawcett.

————. 1968. *The Autobiography of W. E. B. Du Bois*. New York: International.

Dubos, René. 1968. *So Human an Animal*. New York: Scribner.

————. 1976. "Symbiosis between the Earth and Humankind." *Science* 193:459.

————. 1980. *The Wooing of Earth: New Perspective on Man's Use of Nature*. New York: Charles Scribner's Sons.

Dudley, Carl S. 1979. *Where Have All Our People Gone?* New York: Pilgrim.

Dumont, Louis. 1970. *Homo Hierarchicus*. London: Weidenfeld and Nicolson.

Durant, T., and J. Louden. 1986. "The Black Middle Class in America: Historical and Contemporary Perspectives." *Phylon* 47:253–63.

Ebony. 1965. "The White Problem in America." Special Issue 20 (August 10).

Ehrenreich, Barbara. 1989. *Fear of Falling: The Inner Life of the Middle Class*. New York: Pantheon.

Eiseley, Loren. 1946. *The Immense Journey*. New York: Random House.

Ellison, R. 1952. *Invisible Man*. New York: Random House.

Essed, Philomena. 1991. *Understanding Everyday Racism: An Interdisciplinary Theory*. Newbury Park, Calif.: Sage.

Featherstone, Mike. 1991. *The Body: Social Process and Cultural Theory*. Thousand Oaks, Calif.: Sage.

Ferguson, Marjorie. 1992. "The Mythology about Globalization." *European Journal of Communication* 7(1):69–94.

Finkler, Kaja. 1994. *Spiritual Healers in Mexico: Successes and Failures of Alternative Therapies*. Salem, Wisc.: Sheffield Publishing Co.

Foster, Patricia. 1994. *Minding the Body: Women Writers on Body and Soul*. New York: Doubleday.

Foucault, Michel. 1978. *The History of Sexuality*. New York: Pantheon.

Fox, Richard G., ed. 1992. *Recapturing Anthropology: Working in the Present*. Santa Fe: SAR Press.

Frank, Robert H., and Philip J. Cook. 1995. *The Winner-Take-All Society: How More and More Americans Compete for Even Fewer and Bigger Prizes, Encouraging Economic Waste, Income Inequality and Impoverished Cultural Life*. New York: Free Press.

Frazier, E. Franklin. 1927. "The Pathology of Race Prejudice." *The Forum* 77(6):856–62.

————. 1964. "Black Bourgeoisie: Public and Academic Reactions." In A. J. Vidich, J. Bensman, and M. R. Stein, eds., *Reflections on Community Studies*. London: John Wiley, pp.305–311.

————. 1968. *Black Bourgeoisie*. New York: Collier Books.

Freud, Sigmund. 1949. *Civilization and Its Discontents*. London: Hogarth Press.

Fried, Morton H. 1968. *The Study of Anthropology*. New York: Crowell.

Friedl, Ernestine. 1994. "Sex the Invisible." *American Anthropologist* 96(4):833–44.

Fuchsberg, G. 1990. "Blessed Are They Who Sit by Thrones of Corporate Gods." *Wall Street Journal* (April 27):1.

Game, Ann. 1991. *Undoing the Social: Toward a Deconstructive Sociology*. Toronto: University of Toronto Press.

Gamson, Joshua. 1994. *Claims to Fame: Celebrity in Contemporary America*. Berkeley: University of California Press.

Gamson, William A. 1995. "Hiroshima, the Holocaust, and the Politics of Exclusion." *American Sociological Review* 60 (Feb.):1–20.

Gans, Herbert. 1962. *The Urban Villagers*. New York: Free Press.

Garrett, Laurie. 1994. *The Coming Plague: Newly Emerging Diseases in a World out of Balance*. New York: Farrar, Straus & Giroux.

Gatewood, Willard B. 1991. *Aristocrats of Color: The Black Elite, 1880–1920*. Bloomington: Indiana University Press.

Geertz, Clifford. 1965. "Impact of the Concept of Culture on the Concept of Man." In J. R. Platt, ed., *New Views of Man*. Chicago: University of Chicago Press.

————. 1973a."The Impact of the Concept of Culture on the Concept of Man." In Clifford Geertz, ed., *The Interpretation of Culture*. New York: Basic Books pp. 33–54.

————. 1973b. *The Interpretation of Culture*. New York: Basic Books.

Giddings, Franklin H. 1896. *Principles of Sociology*. New York: Macmillan.

Gilmore, David D. 1990. *Manhood in the Making*: Cultural Concepts of Masculinity. New Haven, Conn.: Yale University Press.

Gimbutas, Marija. 1974. *The Goddesses and Gods of Old Europe*. New York: Harper & Row.

Gluckman, Max. 1949. *An Analysis of the Sociological Theories of Bronislaw Malinowski*. Rhodes-Livingstone Papers 16. London: Oxford University Press.

Gobineau, Arthur Comte de. 1984. *The Moral and Intellectual Diversity of Races*. New York: Garland.

Goffman, Erving. 1967. *The Presentation of Self in Everyday Life*. New York: Penguin.

Goldberg, David Theo. 1993. *Racist Culture: Philosophy and the Politics of Meaning*. London: Blackwell.

Goldsmith, Edward, et al. 1990. *Imperiled Planet: Restoring Our Endangered Ecosystems*. Cambridge, Mass.: MIT Press.

Goode, Judith. 1992. "Food." In Richard Bauman, ed., *Folklore, Cultural Performances and Popular Entertainments*. New York: Oxford University Press, pp. 233–45.

Gore, Albert. 1992. *Earth in the Balance: Ecology and the Human Spirit*. Boston: Houghton Mifflin.

Greenberg, Joseph H. 1968. "Language and Evolution." In R. O. Manners and D. Kaplan, eds., *Theory in Anthropology*. Chicago: Aldine Publishing Co., pp. 260–68.

Greer, Colin. 1973. *The Solution as Part of the Problem: Urban Education Reform in the 1960's*. New York: Harper & Row.

Griot, The. 1990. "Black and Old in an Anthropology Department." 9(1):15–19.

Gross, Paul R., and Norman Levitt. 1994. *Higher Superstition: The Academic Left and Its Quarrels with Science*. Baltimore: Johns Hopkins University Press.

Guthrie, R. V. 1976. *Even the Rat Was White*. New York: Harper & Row.

Gwaltney, J. 1980. *Drylongso: A Self Portrait of Black America*. New York: Random House.

Hallowell, Irving A. 1959. "Behavioral Evolution and the Emergence of the Self." In Betty Meggers, ed., *Evolution and Anthropology: A Centennial Appraisal*. Washington, D.C.: Anthropological Society of Washington, pp. 36–60.

Handler, Richard. 1993. "Anthropology Is Dead! Long Live Anthropology!" *American Anthropologist* 95(4):991–99.

Haraway, Donna. 1989. *Gender, Race and Nature in the World of Modern Science*. New York: Routledge.

Harbage, Alfred, ed. 1969. *William Shakespeare: The Complete Works*. Baltimore: Penguin.

Hare, Nathan. 1970. *The Black Anglo-Saxons*. New York: Macmillan.

Harrington, Michael. 1976. *The Twilight of Capitalism*. New York: Simon & Schuster.

Harrison, Ruth. 1964. *Animal Factories*. London: Vincent Stuart.

Hartmann, P., and C. Husband. 1974. *Racism and the Mass Media*. London: Davis-Poynter.

Heilbroner, Robert. L. 1976. *Business Civilization in Decline*. New York: Norton.

Heller, Scott. 1992. "Experience and Expertise Meet in New Brand of Scholarship." *Chronicle of Higher Education* (May 6)38:A7.

Herzfeld, Michael. 1992. *Anthropology through the Looking Glass: Critical Ethnography in the Margins of Europe*. New York: Cambridge University Press.

Hinsley, Curtis, and Bill Holm. 1976. "A Cannibal in the National Museum: The Early Career of Franz Boas in America." *American Anthropologist* 78:306.

Hirschfeld, Lawrence A. 1988. "On Acquiring Social Categories: Cognitive Development and Anthropological Wisdom." *Man* 23:611–38.

———. 1996. *Race In the Making: Cognition, Culture and the Child's Construction of Human Kinds*. Cambridge, Mass.: MIT Press.

Hoage, Robert J. 1989. *Perceptions of Animals in American Culture*. Washington, D.C.: Smithsonian Institution Press.

Hobson, Laura Z. 1947. *Gentleman's Agreement: A Novel*. New York: Simon & Schuster.

Hockett, Charles. 1960. "The Origin of Speech." *Scientific American* 203(3):88–96.

Hollander, Anne. 1995. *Sex and Suits*. New York: Knopf.

Honigmann, John J. 1963. *Understanding Culture*. New York: Harper & Row.

Hopewell, John F. 1980. "The World View of a Congregation." Mimeograph. Candler School of Theology. Atlanta: Emory University.

Hopkins, Ellen. 1987. "Blacks at the Top: Torn between Two Worlds." *New Yorker* 20 (Jan. 19):20–31.

Horwitz, Tony, 1990. "The Right to Roam Is Protected by Law in the English Moors." *Wall Street Journal* 71(142):1 (May 7, Midwest edition).

Horwitz, Tony, and Forman, Craig. 1990. "Clashing Cultures: Immigrants to Europe from the Third World Face Racial Animosity." *Wall Street Journal* 71:1 (no. 211):1(Aug. 14).

Hoy, Suellen. 1995. *Chasing Dirt: The American Pursuit of Cleanliness*. New York: Oxford University Press.

Hunt, Lynn. 1991. *Eroticism and the Body Politic*. Baltimore: Johns Hopkins University Press.

Hunter, Albert. 1974. *Symbolic Communities: The Persistence and Change of Chicago's Local Communities*. Chicago: University of Chicago Press.

Hymes, D. H. 1972. *Reinventing Anthropology*. New York: Pantheon.

Jacobson, David. 1991. *Reading Ethnographies*. New York: State University of New York Press.

Jankowiak, William J. 1993. *Sex, Death and Hierarchy in a Chinese City: An Anthropological Account*. New York: Columbia University Press.

Jargowsky, Paul A. 1996. *Poverty and Place: Ghettos, Barrios and the American City*. New York: Russell Sage Foundation.

Jencks, Christopher. 1988. "Deadly Neighborhoods." *New Republic* 198:22.

———. 1992. *Rethinking Social Policy: Race, Poverty and the Underclass*. Cambridge, Mass.: Harvard University Press.

Jenkins, R. 1986. *Racism and Recruitment: Managers, Organizations and Equal Opportunity in the Labour Market*. Cambridge: Cambridge University Press.

Johnson, Diane. 1995. "Sex and Suits." *New York Review of Books* 42(3):19–21.

Jonas, Friedrich. 1969. *Geschichte der Soziologie*. Reinbeck bei Hamburg: Rowohlt.

Jordon, Winthrop D. 1974. *The White Man's Burden: Historical Origins of Racism in the United States*. New York: Oxford University Press.

Jung, Carl G. 1933. *Modern Man in Search of a Soul*. New York: Harcourt Brace Jovanovich.

Kagan, Donald. 1995. *On the Origins of War*. New York: Doubleday.

Kardinar, Abram, and Lionel Ovesey. 1962. *The Mark of Oppressions: A Psychological Study of the American Negro*. New York: World Publishing Co.

Katz, P. A., and D. A. Taylor, eds. 1988. *Eliminating Racism: Profiles in Controversy*. New York: Plenum.

Kaus, Mickey. 1992. *The End of Equality*. New York: Basic Books.

Keller, Evelyn Fox. 1985. *Reflections on Gender and Science*. New Haven, Conn.: Yale University Press.

Kellert, Stephen. R. 1980. "Contemporary Values of Wildlife in American Society." In W.W. Shaw and E.H.. Zube, eds., *Wildlife Values*. Fort Collins, Colo.: U.S. Forest Service, Report #1.

———. 1985. "American Attitudes toward and Knowledge of Animals." In M. Fox and L. Mickley, eds., *Advances in Animal Welfare Science*. Washington, D.C.: Humane Society of the United States.

———. 1989. "Perceptions of Animals in America." In R. J. Hoage, ed., *Perceptions of Animals in American Culture*. Washington, D.C.: Smithsonian Institution Press, pp. 5–24.

———. 1991. "Japanese Perceptions of Wildlife." *Conservation Biology* 5:297–308.

———. 1993a. "Attitudes toward Wildlife among the Industrial Superpowers: United States, Japan, and Germany." *Journal of Social Issues* 42:53-69.

———. 1993b. "The Biological Basis for Human Values of Nature: A Typology." In S. R. Kellert and E. O. Wilson, eds., *The Biophilia Hypothesis*. Washington, D.C.: Island Press, pp. 42–69.

Kellert, S. R., and E. O. Wilson, eds. 1993. *The Biophilia Hypothesis*. Washington, D.C.: Island Press.

Kidd, Benjamin. 1908. *Individualism and After*. Oxford: Clarendon.

Kinder, Melvyn. 1990. *Going Nowhere Fast*. New York: Prentice-Hall.

Koestler, Arthur. 1978. *Janus: A Summing Up*. New York: Random House.

Kornblum, William. 1974. *Blue Collar Community*. Chicago: University of Chicago Press.

Kozol, Jonathan. 1988. *Rachel and Her Children: Homeless Families in America*. New York: Ballantine.

Kroeber, Alfred Louis. 1917. "The Superorganic." *American Anthropologist* 19:163–213.

———. 1923. *Anthropology*. New York: Harcourt, Brace.

———. 1948. *Anthropology*. New Edition Revised. New York: Harcourt, Brace.

Kroeber, Alfred Louis, and Clyde Kluckhohn. 1952. *Culture: A Critical Review of Concepts and Definitions*. Papers of the Peabody Museum of American Archaeology and Ethnology, Harvard University, vol. 47(1). Cambridge, Mass.

Kübler-Ross, Elisabeth. 1970. *On Death and Dying*. New York: Macmillan.

La Barre, Weston. 1955. *The Human Animal*. Chicago: University of Chicago Press.

Landry, Bart. 1987. *The New Black Middle Class*. Berkeley: University of California Press.

Laqueur, Thomas W. 1990. *Making Sex: Body and Gender from the Greeks to Freud*. Cambridge, Mass.: Harvard University Press.

Leach, Edmund. 1970. *Claude Lévi-Strauss*. New York: Viking Press.

———. 1972. "Anthropological Aspects of Language: Animal Categories and Verbal Abuse." In W. A. Lessa and E. Z. Vogt, eds., *Reader in Comparative Religion: An Anthropological Approach*. 3rd ed. New York: Harper & Row, pp. 206–20.

Leeds, Anthony, and A. P. Vayda, eds. 1965. *Man, Culture and Animals: The Role of Animals in Human Ecological Adjustments*. Washington, D.C.: American Society for the Advance of Science.

Lekachman, R. 1976. *Economists at Bay: Why the Experts Will Never Solve Your Problems*. New York: McGraw-Hill.

Lemann, Nicholas. 1991. *The Promised Land*. New York: Knopf.

Lessa, W. A., and E. Z. Vogt, eds. 1972. *Reader in Comparative Religion: An Anthropological Approach*. 3rd ed. New York: Harper & Row.

Levine, Lawrence W. 1988. *High Brow/Low Brow*. Cambridge, Mass.: Harvard University Press.

Lévi-Strauss, Claude. 1963. *Totemism*. Boston: Beacon Press.

———. 1966. *The Savage Mind*. Chicago: University of Chicago Press.

———. 1967. *Structural Anthropology*. New York: Doubleday Anchor Books.

———. 1969. *The Raw and the Cooked: Introduction to a Science of Mythology*. New York: Viking.

———. 1979a. *Myth and Meaning*. New York: Schocken Books.

———. 1979b. *The Origin of Table Manners*. New York: Harper & Row.

Lévi-Strauss, Claude, and Didier Eribon. 1991. *Conversations with Claude Lévi-Strauss*. Chicago: University of Chicago Press.

Lewis, Bernard. 1990a. *Race and Slavery in the Middle East: On Historical Enquiry*. New York: Oxford University Press.

———. 1990b. "The Roots of Muslim Rage." *The Atlantic* (Sept.) 266(3):47–69.

Lewis, Hylan. 1971. "Culture of Poverty? What Does It Matter?" In E. B. Leacock, ed., *The Culture of Poverty: A Critique*. New York: Simon & Schuster, pp. 345–63.

Lewis, Michael. 1993. *The Culture of Inequality*. Amherst: University of Massachusetts Press.

Liebow, Elliott. 1967. *Tally's Corner: A Study of Negro Streetcorner Men*. Boston: Little, Brown.

Linden, Eugene. 1992. "A Curious Kinship: Apes and Humans." *National Geographic* (March):2–45.

Linton, Ralph. 1943. "Nativistic Movements." *American Anthropologist* 45:230–40.

Lorant, Stefan. 1975. *Pittsburgh: The Story of an American City*. Lenox, Mass.: Published by the author.

Loudon, Joseph Buist. 1977. "On Body Products." In John Blacking, ed., *The Anthropology of the Body*. New York: Academic Press, pp. 161–78.

Lowie, Robert H. 1922. "Science." In H. E. Stearns, ed., *Civilization in the United States*. New York: Harcourt Brace, pp. 151–61.

MacCormack, Carol P., and Marilyn Strathern, eds. 1980. *Nature, Culture and Gender*. New York: Cambridge University Press.

Maher, Vanessa, ed. 1992. *The Anthropology of Breastfeeding*. Oxford: Berg.

Majors, Gerri. 1976. *Black Society.* Chicago: Johnson Publishing Company.

Malcomson, Scott L. 1989. "How the West Was Lost: Writing at the End of the World." *The Voice Literary Supplement* (March 7)34:9–13.

Malinowski, Bronislaw. 1954. *Magic, Science and Religion.* New York: Anchor.

Manners, R. O., and D. Kaplan, eds. 1968. *Theory in Anthropology.* Chicago: Aldine Publishing Co.

Mannheim, Karl. 1952. "On the Interpretation of 'Weltanschauung.'" In Paul Kecskemeti, ed., *Essays on the Sociology of Knowledge.* London: Routledge & Kegan Paul.

Marshall, Eliot, and Joseph Palca. 1992. "Cracks in the Ivory Tower." *Science* (Aug. 28) 257:1196–1201.

Martin, Calvin Luther. 1992. *In the Spirit of the Earth: Rethinking History and Time.* Baltimore: Johns Hopkins University Press.

Martin, Emily. 1987. *The Woman in the Body: A Cultural Analysis of Reproduction.* Boston: Beacon Press.

Martindale, Don. 1982. *Personality and Milieu: The Shaping of Social Science Culture.* Houston: Cap and Gown Press.

Maslow, A. H. 1954. *Motivation and Personality.* New York: Harper & Row.

Mays, B. E., and J. W. Nicholson. 1969. *The Negroes' Church.* New York: Russell and Russell.

McDavid, R. I., Jr., and V. G. McDavid. 1951. "The Relationship of the Speech of American Negros to the Speech of American Whites." *American Speech* 26:2–17.

McHarg, Ian L. 1972. "Man: Planetary Disease." In R. V. Guthrie and E. J. Barnes, eds., *Man and Society: Focus on Reality.* Palo Alto, Calif.: James E. Freel and Associates.

Mead, Margaret. 1948. "World Culture." In Quincy Wright, ed., *The World Community.* Chicago: University of Chicago Press, pp. 47–55.

———. 1960a. "Anthropology among the Sciences." *American Anthropologist* 63(3):1961.

———. 1960b. "The Modern Study of Mankind." In Lyman Bryson, ed., *An Outline of Man's Knowledge of the Modern World.* New York: McGraw-Hill, pp. 322–41.

———. 1975. *World Enough: Rethinking the Future.* Boston: Little, Brown.

Meadows, D. H., et al. 1974. *The Limits to Growth.* New York: Universe Books.

Messenger, John C. 1971. "Sex and Repression in an Irish Folk Community." In D. S. Marshall and R. C. Suggs, eds., *Human Sexual Behavior: Variations in The Ethnographic Spectrum.* New York: Basic Books.

Metcalf, Peter, and Richard Huntington. 1992. *Celebrations of Death: The Anthropology of Mortuary Ritual.* New York: Cambridge University Press.

Midgley, Mary. 1995. *Beast and Man: The Roots of Human Nature.* New York: Routledge.

Milgram, Morris. 1976. *Good Neighborhood.* New York: Norton.

Miller, William Ian. 1993. *Humiliation: And Other Essays on Honor, Social Discomfort and Violence.* Ithaca, N.Y.: Cornell University Press.

Mills, C. Wright. 1956. *The Power Elite.* New York: Oxford University Press.

Mincy, R. B., I. V. Sawhill, and W. A. Douglas. 1990. "The Underclass: Definition and Measurement." *Science* 248:450–53.

Mintz, Sidney W. 1987. *Sweetness and Power: The Place of Sugar in Modern History.* New York: Penguin.

Montagu, M. F. Ashley. 1952. *Man's Most Dangerous Myth: The Fallacy of Race.* New York: Harper & Brothers.

———1968a. Man and Aggression. New York: Oxford University Press.

————1968b. "The New Litany of 'Innate Depravity,' or Original Sin Revisited." In M. F. A. Montagu, ed., *Man and Aggression*. New York: Oxford University Press, pp. 3–17.

Moore, J. Howard. 1908. *The Universal Kinship*. Chicago: Charles H. Kerr.

Murdock, George P. 1945. "Common Denominator of Cultures." In Ralph Linton, ed., *The Science of Man in the World Crisis*. New York: Columbia University Press, pp. 123–42.

————. 1965. "Fundamental Characteristics of Culture." In G. P. Murdock, ed., *Culture and Society*. Pittsburgh: University of Pittsburgh Press, pp. 80–86.

Myrdal, Gunnar. 1944. *An American Dilemma: The Negro Problem and Modern Democracy*. New York: Harper & Row.

————. 1969. *An American Dilemma: The Negro Problem and Modern Democracy*. New York: Harper Torchbooks.

Nabokov, Peter, ed., 1978. *Native American Testimony*. New York: Harper & Row.

Nelkin, Dorothy, and Laurence Tancredi. 1994. *Dangerous Diagnostics: The Social Power of Biological Information*. 2nd ed. Chicago: University of Chicago Press.

New York Times. 1977. "Chinese Report Success in Effort to Turn Deserts into Vineyards." Aug.31:A12.

Nisbet, Robert A. 1975. *Twilight of Authority: The Redecline of the West*. New York: Oxford University Press.

Noske, Barbara. 1989. *Humans and Other Animals: Beyond the Boundaries of Anthropology*. London: Pluto Press.

Novak, Michael. 1972a. "The Nordic Jungle: Inferiority in America." In Michael Novak, *The Rise of the Unmeltable Ethnics*. New York: Macmillan, pp. 72–115.

————. 1972b. "Nordic Prejudices: Race and History." In Michael Novak, *The Rise of the Unmeltable Ethnics*. New York: Macmillan, pp. 78–87.

————. 1972c. *The Rise of the Unmeltable Ethnics*. New York: Macmillan.

Ogbu, John U. 1974. *The Next Generation: An Ethnography of Education in an Urban Neighborhood*. New York: Academic Press.

————. 1988. "Human Intelligence Testing: A Cultural-Ecological Perspective." *National Forum* 68(2):23–29.

Ortner, Sherry B. 1974. "Is Female to Male as Nature Is to Culture?" In M. Z. Rosaldo and L. Lamphere, eds., *Woman, Culture and Society*. Stanford, Calif.: Stanford University Press, pp. 67–87.

Orwell, George. 1946. *Animal Farm*. New York: Harcourt Brace Jovanovich.

Pagels, Elaine. 1988. *Adam, Eve and the Serpent*. New York: Random House.

Parker, Sue Taylor, Robert W. Mitchell, and Maria L. Boccia, eds., 1994. *Self-Awareness in Animals and Humans: Developmental Perspectives*. New York: Cambridge University Press.

Patten, Bernard C., and Iven E. Jørgensen, eds. 1995. *Complex Ecology: The Part-Whole Relations in Ecosystems*. Englewood Cliffs, N.J.: Prentice-Hall.

Pfeiffer, John E. 1972. *The Emergence of Man*. New York: Harper & Row.

Phillips, Kevin. 1990. *The Politics of Rich and Poor: Wealth and the American Electorate in the Reagan Aftermath*. New York: Random House.

Pittsburgh Courier. 1947. "Courier Newsboys." Aug. 16:14. Microfilmed, Hillman Library, University of Pittsburgh.

————. 1954. "Courier Distributor." Sept. 4, sec. 1:3. Microfilmed, Hillman Library, University of Pittsburgh.

Piven, F. F., and R. A. Cloward. 1971. *Regulating the Poor: The Functions of Public Welfare*. New York: Vintage.

Powdermaker, H. 1939. *After Freedom: A Cultural Study of the Deep South*. New York: Viking.

Rainwater, Lee. 1974. *Behind Ghetto Walls: Black Family Life in a Federal Slum*. Chicago: Aldine.

Rappaport, Roy A. 1971. "Nature, Culture and Ecological Anthropology." In H. L. Shapiro, ed., *Man, Culture and Society*. New York: Oxford University Press, pp. 237–67.

———. 1975. "Commentary." In S. H. Katy, ed., *Biological Anthropology: Readings from Scientific American*. San Francisco: W. H. Freeman, pp. 384–87.

———. 1994. "Humanity's Evolution and Anthropology's Future." In R. Borosky, ed., *Assessing Cultural Anthropology*. New York: McGraw-Hill, pp. 153–67.

Raymond, Chris. 1991. "Increasing Use of Film by Visually Oriented Anthropologists Stirs Debate Over Ways Scholars Describe Other Cultures." *Chronicle of Higher Education* 37(28):A5 (March 27).

Rifkin, Jeremy. 1992. *Beyond Beef*. New York: Dutton.

Rigby, Peter. 1997. *African Images: Racism and the End of Anthropology*. New York: Berg Publishers.

Roberts, J. M., M. D. Williams, and G. C. Poole. 1982. "Used Car Domain: An Ethnographic Application of Clustering and Multidimensional Scaling." In H. C. Hudson, ed., *Classifying Social Data*. San Francisco: Jossey-Bass, pp. 13–38.

Robertson, Roland. 1992. *Globalization: Social Theory and Global Culture*. Newbury Park, Calif.: Sage.

Rodseth, Lars, et al. 1991. "The Human Community as a Primate Society." *Current Anthropology* 32(3):221–54.

Rogers, Alan R. 1988. "Does Biology Constrain Culture?" *American Anthropologist* 90:819–31.

Rose, Dan. 1990. *Living the Ethnographic Life*. Newbury Park, Calif.: Sage.

Rose, Deborah Bird. 1992. *Dingo Makes Us Human*. New York: Cambridge University Press.

Rosenberg, M., C. Schooler, C. Schoenbach, and F. Rosenberg. 1995. "Global Self-Esteem and Specific Self-Esteem: Different Concepts, Different Outcomes." *American Sociological Review* 60 (Feb.):141–56.

Rothschild, J. 1981. *Ethnopolitics: A Conceptual Framework*. New York: Columbia University Press.

Roy, Beth. 1995. *Some Trouble with Cows: Making Sense of Social Conflict*. Berkeley: University of California Press.

Rozin, Paul. 1992. "Learning and Memory in Human Food Selection." In L. R. Squire, ed., *Encyclopedia of Learning and Memory*. New York: Macmillan, pp. 171–73.

Ryan, William. 1971. *Blaming the Victim*. New York: Vintage Books.

Rydell, Robert W. 1993. "Human Curiosity: A Review of *Ota* by P. V. Bradford and H. Blume." *Science* 29:108.

Sacks, Karen B. 1989. "Toward a Unified Theory of Class, Race and Gender." *American Ethnologist* 16(3):534–50.

Sahlins, Marshall D. 1960. "The Origin of Society." *Scientific American* 204(Sept.):76–87.

Said, Edward. 1978. *Orientalism*. New York: Pantheon.

Sanday, Peggy R. 1973. "Toward a Theory of the Status of Women." *American Anthropologist* 75:1682–1700.

———. 1981. *Female Power and Male Dominance: On the Origins of Sexual Inequality*. Cambridge: Cambridge University Press.

————. 1990. *Fraternity Gang Rape: Sex, Brotherhood and Privilege on Campus.* New York: New York University Press.

Sapir, Edward. 1949 (orig. 1921). "Review of W. H. R. Rivers' *Instinct and the Unconscious*: A Contribution to a Biological Theory of Psycho-Neurosis." In D. G. Mandelbaum, ed., *Selected Writings of Edward Sapir.* Berkeley: University of California Press, pp. 528–29.

Schael, Ann Wilson. 1981. *Women's Reality: An Emerging Female System in a White Male Society.* Minneapolis: Winston.

Scheffel, David. 1991. *In the Shadow of Antichrist: The Old Believers of Alberta.* Lewiston, N.Y.: Broadview.

Scheler, Max. 1961. *Ressentiment.* New York: Free Press.

Scheper-Hughes, Nancy. 1994. "Embodied Knowledge: Thinking with the Body in Critical Medical Anthropology." In R. Boropky, ed., *Assuming Cultural Anthropology.* New York: McGraw-Hill, pp. 229–42.

Schermerhorn, R. A. 1978 [1970]. *Comparative Ethnic Relations.* Chicago: University of Chicago Press.

Schultz, Emily, and Robert H. Lavenda. 1995. *Cultural Anthropology: A Perspective on the Human Condition.* Toronto: Mayfield Publishing Co.

Schuman, H., C. Steeh, and L. Bobo. 1985. *Racial Attitudes in America: Trends and Interpretations.* Cambridge. Mass.: Harvard University Press.

Schweitzer, Albert. 1923. *Civilization and Ethics.* vol. 2. London: A. & C. Black.

See, K. O., and W. J. Wilson. 1988. "Race and Ethnicity." In Neil J. Smelser, ed., *Handbook of Sociology.* Newbury Park, Calif.: Sage, pp. 223–42.

Sennett, Richard. 1993. *Flesh and Stone: A History of the Body and the City in Western Civilization.* New York: W. W. Norton.

Sennet, Richard, and Jonathan Cobb. 1973. *The Hidden Inquiries of Class.* New York: Vintage Books.

Shanklin, Eugenia. 1994. *Anthropology and Race.* Belmont, Calif.: Wadsworth.

Sheets-Johnstone, Maxine, ed. 1992. *Giving the Body Its Due.* Albany: SUNY Press.

Shepard, P. 1995. *The Others: How Animals Made Us Human.* Covelo, Calif.: Shearwater Books.

Shilling, Chris. 1993. *The Body and Social Theory.* Thousand Oaks, Calif.: Sage.

Shipman, Pat. 1994. *The Evolution of Racism: Human Differences and the Use and Misuse of Science.* New York: Simon & Schuster.

Shweder, Richard, et. al. 1996. *Ethnography and Human Development.* Chicago: University of Chicago Press.

Simon, W., and J. H. Gagnon. 1976. "The Anomie of Affluence: A Post-Mertonian Conception." *American Journal of Sociology* 82:356–78.

Singer, Peter. 1977. *Animal Liberation.* New York: Avon.

————. 1981. *The Expanding Circle: Ethics and Sociobiology.* New York: Farrar, Straus & Giroux.

————. 1989. "Unkind to Animals." *New York Review of Books* 36(1):36–38 (Feb. 2).

Skinner, Barrhus Frederic. 1971. *Beyond Freedom and Dignity.* New York: Knopf.

Smedley, Audrey. 1993. *Race in North America: Origin and Evolution of a Worldview.* Boulder, Colo.: Westview.

Smith, A. D. 1986. *The Ethnic Origin of Nations.* New York: Basil Blackwell.

Smith, A.W. 1985. "Social Class and Racial Cleavages on Major Social Indicators." *Research in Race and Ethnic Relations* 4:33–65.

Smith, Darrell A. 1988. *Black Americana.* Minneapolis: Star Press.

Smith, Neil, and Peter Williams, eds. 1986. *Gentrification of the City*. Boston: Allen and Unwin.

Smuts, Barbara B. 1985. *Sex and Friendship in Baboons*. New York: Aldine.

Sontag, Susan. 1966. "The Anthropologist as Hero." In Susan Sontag, *Against Interpretation*. New York: Dell, pp. 69–81.

Sorokin, Pitirim A. 1964. "Anthropo-Racial, Selectionist and Hereditarist School." In Pitirim A. Sorokin, *Contemporary Sociological Theories: Through the First Quarter of the Twentieth Century*. New York: Harper Torchbooks, pp. 219–308.

Sowerby, Robin, 1986. *Dryden's Aeneid: A Selection with Commentary*. Bristal, Great Britain: Bristal Classical Press, p. 169.

Sperling, Susan. 1988. *Animal Liberators: Research and Morality*. Berkeley: University of California Press.

Spindler, L., and G. Spindler. 1990. *The American Cultural Dialogue and Its Transmission*. New York: Falmer Press.

Spretnak, Charlene. 1997. *The Resurgance of the Real: Body, Nature, and Place*. Wellesley, Mass.: Addison-Reading.

Spurlack, J., and C. B. Robinowitz, eds. 1990. *Women's Progress: Promises and Problems*. New York: Plenum.

Stanfield, J. H., II. 1985. "Theoretical and Ideological Barriers to the Study of Race-Making." In *Research in Race and Ethnic Relations: A Research Annual* 4:161–73. Greenwich, Conn.: JAI.

———. 1988. "Not Quite in the Club." *American Sociologist* 19:291–300.

———. 1991. Racism in America and Other Race-Centered Societies. *International Journal of Comparative Sociology* 32:243–60.

Stannard, David E. 1993. *American Holocaust: The Conquest of the New World*. New York: Oxford University Press.

Stewart, Herbert Leslie. 1915. *Nietzsche and the Ideals of Modern Germany*. London: E. Arnold.

Stewart, W. A. 1965. "Urban Negro Speech: Sociolinguistic Factors Affecting English Teaching." In R. W. Shuy, ed., *Social Dialects and Language Learning*. Champaign, Ill.: National Council of Teachers of English.

———. 1966."Observations on the Problems of Defining Negro Dialect." In *Conference on the language components in the training of teachers of English and reading: views and problems*. Washington, D.C.: Center for Applied Linguistics and the National Council of Teachers of English.

Strathern, Andrew, and Melvin D. Williams. 1991. "Healing the Patient and Not the Disease: Prayer Rituals in Two Cultures." *The Griot* 10:(2)1–8.

Suttles, Gerald D. 1972. *The Social Construction of Communities*. Chicago: University of Chicago Press.

Szwed, J. F. 1972. "An American Anthropological Dilemma: The Politics of Afro-American Cultures." In D. Hymes, ed., *Reinventing Anthropology*. New York: Pantheon, pp. 152–81.

Tabb, William K. 1971. "Race Relations Models and Social Change." *Social Problems* 18 (Spring):431–44.

Taeuber, Karl E., and Alma F. Taeuber. 1965. *Negroes in Cities*. Chicago: Aldine.

Tambiah, Stanley J. 1985. "Animals Are Good to Think and Good to Prohibit." In Stanley J. Tambiah, *Culture, Thought and Social Action*. Cambridge, Mass.: Harvard University Press.

Taylor, Branch. 1988. *Parting the Waters*. New York: Simon & Schuster.

Temple, Norman J., and Denis P. Burkitt, eds. 1994. *Western Diseases: Their Dietary Prevention and Reversibility.* Totowa, N.J.: Humana.

Terman, L. M. 1916. *Human Nature and the Social Order.* New York: Macmillan.

Terry, Don. 1990. "In Harlem, Death Is an Old and Busy Neighbor." *New York Times* 139(No. 48,227):1 (May 6).

Thomas, Keith. 1983. *Man and the Natural World.* New York: Pantheon.

Thompson, Laura M. 1979. "Endorsing the Unity of Anthropology." *Anthropology Newsletter* 20(3):2 (March).

Thorndike, E. L. 1940. *Human Nature and the Social Order.* New York: Macmillan.

Tiger, Lionel. 1969. *Men in Groups.* New York: Random House.

———. 1979a. "Anthropological Concepts." *Preventive Medicine* 8:600–607.

———. 1979b. *Optimism: The Biology of Hope.* New York: Simon & Schuster.

Tiger, Lionel, and Robin Fox. 1971. *The Imperial Animal.* New York: Holt, Rinehart and Winston.

Time. 1977. "The American Underclass: Destitute and Desperate in the Land of Plenty." 110(9)(Aug.29):14–27.

———. 1989. "Planet of the Year: Endangered Earth." 133(1)(Jan. 2):24.

Torgovnick, Marianne. 1990. *Gone Primitive: Savage Intellects, Modern Lives.* Chicago: University of Chicago Press.

Traweek, Sharon. 1988. *Beamtimes and Lifetimes: The World of High Energy Physicists.* Cambridge, Mass.: Harvard University Press.

Tuana, Nancy. 1994. *The Less Noble Sex.* Bloomington: Indiana University Press.

Tucker, H. 1908. "The Negroes of Pittsburgh." In P. U. Kellogg, ed., *Wage-Earning Pittsburgh,* vol. 6 of *Pittsburgh Survey.* New York: Russell Sage Foundation.

Turner, James. 1980. *Reckoning with the Beast.* Baltimore: Johns Hopkins University Press.

Ulrich, Roger S. 1993. "Biophilia, Biophobia, and Natural Landscapes." In S. R. Kellert and E. O. Wilson, eds., *The Biophilia Hypothesis.* Washington, D.C.: Island Press, pp. 73–137.

UMOJA. 1978. "Childhood in an Urban Black Ghetto: Two Life Histories." 2(3):169–82.

Updike, John. 1989. *Self Consciousness: Memoirs.* New York: Knopf.

Urton, Gary, ed. 1985. *Animal, Myths and Metaphors in South America.* Salt Lake City: University of Utah Press.

Van Den Berghe, P. L. 1981. *The Ethnic Phenomenon.* New York: Elsevier.

Van Dijk, Teun A. 1984. *Prejudice in Discourse.* Amsterdam: Benjamins.

———. 1987. *Communicating Racism.* Newbury Park, Calif.: Sage.

———. 1991. *Racism and the Press.* London: Routledge.

———. 1993. *Elite Discourse and Racism.* Newbury Park, Calif.: Sage.

Van Leeuwen, Mary Stewart. 1990. *Gender and Grace: Love, Work and Parenting in a Changing World.* Downers Grove, Ill.: University Press.

Veblen, Thorstein. 1915. *Imperial Germany and the Industrial Revolution.* New York: Macmillan.

———. 1987. *The Theory of the Leisure Class.* New York: Penguin.

Vidal, Gore. 1992. *Live from Golgotha.* New York: Random House.

Waldrop, M. Mitchell. 1992. *The Emerging Science at the Edge of Order and Chaos.* New York: Simon & Schuster.

Walters, S. 1994. "Algorithms and Archetypes: Evolutionary Psychology and Carl Jung's Theory of the Collective Unconscious." *Journal of Social and Evolutionary Systems* 17(3):287–306.

Warner, W. L., and Leo Shole. 1945. *The Social Systems of American Ethnic Groups*. New Haven, Conn.: Yale University Press.

Warner, W. Lloyd, et al. 1963. *Yankee City*. New Haven, Conn.: Yale University Press.

Warner, W. Lloyd, B. H. Junker, and W. A. Adams. 1941. *Color and Human Nature: Negro Personality Development in a Northern City*. Washington, D.C.: American Council on Education.

Watts, Steven. 1992. *Dreams of a Final Theory*. New York: Pantheon.

Weil, Andrew. 1995. *Spontaneous Healing: How to Discover and Enhance Your Body's Natural Ability to Maintain and Heal Itself*. New York: Knopf.

Weinberg, Steven. 1992. "Academe's Leftists Are Something of a Fraud." *Chronicle of Higher Education* 38(33):A48 (April 29).

Weisz, Paul B., ed. 1970. *The Contemporary Scene: Readings on Human Nature, Race, Behavior, Society and Environment*. New York: McGraw-Hill.

Wellman, D. T. 1977. *Portraits of White Racism*. Cambridge: Cambridge University Press.

West, James. 1945. *Plainville, USA*. New York: Columbia University Press.

Whitaker, Elizabeth D. 1997. "Ancient Bodies, Modern Customs and Our Health." In A. Podolepky and P. J. Brown, eds., *Applying Cultural Anthropology*. Calif.: Mayfield Mountian View Publishing, pp. 81–90.

White, Leslie A. 1949. *The Science of Culture*. New York: Farrar, Straus & Giroux.

———. 1973. *The Concept of Culture*. Minneapolis: Burgess.

Whyte, William F. 1943. *Street Corner Society*. Chicago: University of Chicago Press.

Williams, Brackette F. 1993. "The Impact of the Precepts of Nationalism on the Concept of Culture." *Cultural Critique* (Spring):143–91.

Williams, Melvin D. 1973a. "The Black Community." Special Hillman Issue, *The Pastoral Institute Newsletter* 1:12.

———. 1973b. "Food and Animals: Behavior Metaphors in a Black Pentecostal Church in Pittsburgh." *Urban Anthropology* 2:74.

———. 1974. *Community in a Black Pentecostal Church: An Anthropological Study*. Pittsburgh: University of Pittsburgh Press.

———. 1975a. "Children's Games and Play in Two North American Subcultures—A Poor Black Ghetto in Pittsburgh and Salish Indians of Victoria, Vancouver Island." In M. D. Williams, ed., *Selected Readings in Afro-American Anthropology*. Lexington, Mass.: Xerox Publishing Company.

———. 1975b. *Selected Readings in Afro-American Anthropology*. Lexington, Mass.: Xerox College Publishing.

———. 1978. "Childhood in an Urban Black Ghetto: Two Life Histories." *UMOJA* (University of Colorado at Boulder) 2:169–82.

———. 1979a. "Considerations of a Black Anthropologist Researching Pentecostalism." *Spirit* (Howard University) 3:20.

———. 1979b. "The Harvesting of Sluckus (*Porphyra perforate*) by the Straits Salish Indians of Vancouver Island." *Syesis* 12:63–70.

———. 1980. "Belmar: Diverse Lifestyles in a Pittsburgh Black Neighborhood." *Ethnic Groups: An International Journal of Ethnic Studies* 3:23–54.

———. 1981a. "Observations in Pittsburgh Ghetto Schools." *Anthropology and Education Quarterly* 12 (Fall):211–20.

———. 1981b. *On the Street Where I Lived*. New York: Holt, Rinehart and Winston.

———. 1983a. "The Conflict of Corporate Church and Spiritual Community: An Ethnographic Analysis," In C. S. Dudley, ed., *Building Effective Ministry: Theory and*

Practice in the Local Church. New York: Harper & Row, pp. 55–67.

———. 1983b. "Notes from a Black Ghetto in Pittsburgh." *Critical Perspective of Third World America: Race, Class, Culture in America* (Berkeley, Calif.: Ethnic Studies Student Union and Editorial Board, Council) 1:196–208.

———. 1984. Community in a Black Pentecostal Church: An Anthropological Study. Paper edition. Prospect Heights, Ill.: Waveland Press.

———. 1986. "Examining the Community through Their Congregations: Ethnography in a Small Midwestern City." *The Griot* 5:13–21.

———. 1988. "An Afro-American Anthropologist in an Urban Black 'Field': Problems, Predicaments and Dilemmas." *Western Journal of Black Studies* 12:157–66.

———. 1989a. "Children's Games and Play of the Staits Salish Indians of Vancouver Island." In R. Bolton, ed., *The Content of Culture: Constants and Variants*. New Haven, Conn.: HRAF Press, pp. 19–32.

———. 1989b. "Culture and Extinction: Man, Myth and Modernity." Ann Arbor, Mich.: Published by the author.

———. 1989c. "Education for the Disadvantaged Student." *The Griot* 8:51.

———. 1990. "The Afro-American in the Cultural Dialogue of the United States." In G. and L. Spindler, eds., *The American Cultural Dialogue and Its Transmission*. New York: Falmer Press, pp. 144–62.

———. 1991. "The Black Church in a Midwestern University Twin City." In R. Dennis, ed., *Research in Race and Ethnic Relations*, vol. 6. Greenwich, Conn.: JAI Press. pp. 27–47.

———. 1992a. *The Black Middle Class: The Production and Reproduction of Social Inferiority*. Ann Arbor, Mich.: Author's edition.

———. 1992b. *The Human Dilemma*. New York: Harcourt Brace Jovanovich.

———. 1993a. *The Academic Village: The Ethnography of an Anthropology Department*. Ann Arbor, Mich.: Author's edition.

———. 1993b. "Urban Ethnography: Another Look." In J. H. Stanfield and R. M. Dennis, eds., *Race and Ethnicity in Research Methods*. Newbury Park, Calif.: Sage 135–56.

———. 1996a. "Biophobia and the Human Body: Another Approach in Medical Anthropology." *Journal of Social and Evolutionary Systems* 19(1):55–80.

———. 1996b. "Biophobia, Social Boundaries, and Racism." *Journal of Social and Evolutionary Systems* 19(2):171–86.

———. 1997. "Supremacy Narratives and Performances." *Journal of Social and Evolutionary Systems* 19(4):313–19.

Willie, Charles V., et al., eds. 1973 and 1995. *Mental Health, Racism and Sexism*. Pittsburgh: University of Pittsburgh Press.

Willis, William S., Jr. 1974. "Skeletons in the Anthropological Closet." In Dell Hymes, ed., *Reinventing Anthropology*. New York: Vintage Books.

Wilson, C.C., and F. Gutierrez. 1985. *Minorities and the Media*. Beverly Hills, Calif.: Sage.

Wilson, Peter J. 1988. *The Domestication of the Human Species*. New Haven, Conn.: Yale University Press.

Wilson, William J. 1973. *Power, Racism and Privilege: Race Relations in Theoretical and Sociohistorical Perspective*. New York: Macmillan.

———. 1978. *The Declining Significance of Race: Blacks and Changing American Institutions*. Chicago: University of Chicago Press.

———. 1987. *The Truly Disadvantaged: The Inner City, the Underclass and Public Policy.* Chicago: University of Chicago Press.

Windell, P. 1975. *Homewood South: The Redevelopment of an Urban Subarea.* Pittsburgh: University Center for Urban Research, University of Pittsburgh.

Windisch, U. 1978. *Xénophobie? Logique de la pensée populaire* [Xenophobia? Logic of Popular Thought]. Lausanne: L'Age d'homme.

Wolf, E. 1982. *Europe and the People without History.* Berkeley: University of California Press.

Wolman, A. 1976. "Ecologic Dilemmas." *Science* 193:740.

Wright, R. 1995. *The Moral Animal: Evolutionary Psychology and Everyday Life.* New York: Vintage Books.

Wrong, Dennis. 1961. "The Oversocialized Conception of Man in Modern Sociology." *American Sociological Review* 26:183–93.

Young, Lawrence W. 1989. "Isn't She Pretty? . . . " *Black Issues of Higher Education* 5(21):124 (Jan. 19).

Zorbaugh, Harvey W. 1929. *The Gold Coast and the Slum.* Chicago: University of Chicago Press.

Index

About the Author

MELVIN D. WILLIAMS is Professor of Anthropology at the University of Michigan, Ann Arbor.